SLAVE NARRATIVES

VOLUME XVI
TEXAS NARRATIVES
PART 2

By
United States.
Work Projects Administration

Copyright © 2024 by BLACKLEGACYPRESS.ORG

All rights reserved. No part of this publication may be reproduced or transmitted in any form or by any means electronic or mechanical, including information storage and retrieval systems without permission in writing from the publisher, except for student research using the appropriate citations.

ISBN: 978-1-63652-209-8

SLAVE NARRATIVES

A Folk History of Slavery in the United States.
From Interviews with Former Slaves

**UNITED STATES.
WORK PROJECTS ADMINISTRATION**

TYPEWRITTEN RECORDS PREPARED BY
THE FEDERAL WRITERS' PROJECT
1936-1938
ASSEMBLED BY
THE LIBRARY OF CONGRESS PROJECT
WORK PROJECTS ADMINISTRATION
FOR THE DISTRICT OF COLUMBIA
SPONSORED BY THE LIBRARY OF
CONGRESS

WASHINGTON 1941

VOLUME XVI
TEXAS NARRATIVES
PART 2

Prepared by
The Federal Writers' Project of
The Works Progress Administration
For the State of Texas

CONTENTS

Willis Easter 1
Anderson And Minerva Edwards 7
Ann J. Edwards 15
Mary Kincheon Edwards 23
Lucinda Elder 27
John Ellis 33
Lorenza Ezell 37
Betty Farrow 49
John Finnely 53
Sarah Ford 61
Millie Forward 69
Louis Fowler 73
Chris Franklin 81
Orelia Alexie Franks 87
Rosanna Frazier 91
Priscilla Gibson 95
Gabriel Gilbert 99
Mattie Gilmore 103
Andrew Goodman 107
Austin Grant 115

James Green	123
O.w. Green And Granddaughter	127
Rosa Green	133
William Green	137
Pauline Grice	141
Mandy Hadnot	147
William Hamilton	153
Pierce Harper	157
Molly Harrell	165
Ann Hawthorne	169
James Hayes	177
Felix Haywood	183
Phoebe Henderson	191
Albert Hill	195
Rosina Hoard	201
Tom Holland	205
Eliza Holman	211
Larnce Holt	217
Bill Homer	221
Scott Hooper	227
Alice Houston	231
Josephine Howard	235

Lizzie Hughes	239
Moses Hursey	243
Charley Hurt	249
Wash Ingram	257
Carter J. Jackson	261
James Jackson	265
Maggie Jackson	269
Martin Jackson	271
Nancy Jackson	279
Richard Jackson	283
John James	287
Thomas Johns	293
Auntie Thomas Johns	299
Gus Johnson	303
Harry Johnson	309
James D. Johnson	315
Mary Johnson	319
Mary Ellen Johnson	325
Pauline Johnson And Felice Boudreaux	329
Spence Johnson	335
Harriet Jones	339
Lewis Jones	349

Liza Jones 355
Lizzie Jones 363
Toby Jones 367
Aunt Pinkie Kelly 373
Sam Kilgore 377
Ben Kinchlow 385
Mary Kindred 405
Nancy King 409
Silvia King 413

WILLIS EASTER

WILLIS EASTER, 85, was born near Nacogdoches, Texas. He does not know the name of his first master. Frank Sparks brought Willis to Bosqueville, Texas, when he was two years old. Willis believes firmly in "conjuremen" and ghosts, and wears several charms for protection against the former. He lives in Waco, Texas.

"I's birthed below Nacogdoches, and dey tells me it am on March 19th, in 1852. My mammy had some kind of paper what say dat. But I don't know my master, 'cause when I's two he done give me to Marse Frank Sparks and he brung me to Bosqueville. Dat sizeable place dem days. My mammy come 'bout a month after, 'cause Marse Frank, he say I's too much trouble without my mammy.

"Mammy de bes' cook in de county and a master hand at spinnin' and weavin'. She made her own dye. Walnut and elm makes red dye and walnut brown color, and shumake makes black color. When you wants yallow color, git cedar moss out de brake.

"All de lint was picked by hand on our place. It a slow job to git dat lint out de cotton and I's gone to sleep many a night, settin' by de fire, pickin' lint. In bad weather us sot by de fire and pick lint and patch harness and shoes, or whittle out something, dishes and bowls and troughs and traps and spoons.

"All us chillen weared lowel white duckin', homemake, jes' one garment. It was de long shirt. You couldn't tell gals from boys on de yard.

"I's twelve when us am freed and for awhile us lived on Marse Bob Wortham's place, on Chalk Bluff, on Horseshoe Bend. After de freedom war, dat old Brazos River done change its course up 'bove de bend, and move to de west.

"I marries Nancy Clark in 1879, but no chilluns. Dere plenty deer and bears and wild turkeys and antelopes here den. Dey's sho' fine eatin' and wish I could stick a tooth in one now. I's seed fifty antelope at a waterin' hole.

"Dere plenty Indians, too. De Rangers had de time keepin' dem back. Dey come in bright of de moon and steals and kills de stock. Dere a ferry 'cross de Brazos and Capt. Ross run it. He sho' fit dem Indians.

"Dem days everybody went hossback and de roads was jes' trails and bridges was poles 'cross de creeks. One day us went to a weddin'. Dey sot de dinner table out in de yard under a big tree and de table was a big slab of a tree on legs. Dey had pewter plates and spoons and chiny bowls and wooden dishes. Some de knives and forks was make out of bone. Dey had beef and pork and turkey and some antelope.

"I knows 'bout ghostes. First, I tells you a funny story. A old man named Josh, he purty old and notionate. Every evenin' he squat down under a oak tree. Marse Smith, he slip up and hear Josh prayin, 'Oh, Gawd, please take pore old Josh home with you.' Next day, Marse Smith wrop heself in a sheet and git in de oak tree. Old Josh come 'long and pray, 'Oh, Gawd, please come take pore old Josh home with you.' Marse say from top de tree, 'Poor Josh, I's come to take you home with me.' Old Josh, he riz up and seed dat white shape in de tree, and he yell, 'Oh, Lawd, not right now, I hasn't git forgive for all my sins.' Old Josh, he jes' shakin' and he dusts out dere faster den a wink. Dat broke up he prayin' under dat tree.

"I never studied cunjurin', but I knows dat scorripins and things dey cunjures with am powerful medicine. Dey uses hair and fingernails and tacks and dry insects and worms and bat wings and sech. Mammy allus tie a leather string round de babies' necks when dey teethin', to make dem have easy time. She used a dry frog or piece nutmeg, too.

"Mammy allus tell me to keep from bein' cunjure, I sing:

"'Keep 'way from me, hoodoo and witch,
Lend my path from de porehouse gate;
I pines for golden harps and sich,
Lawd, I'll jes' set down and wait.
Old Satan am a liar and cunjurer, too—
If you don't watch out, he'll cunjure you.'

"Dem cunjuremen sho' bad. Dey make you have pneumony and boils and bad luck. I carries me a jack all de time. It em de charm wrop in red flannel. Don't know what am in it. A bossman, he fix it for me.

"I sho' can find water for de well. I got a li'l tree limb what am like a V. I driv de nail in de end of each branch and in de crotch. I takes hold of each branch and iffen I walks over water in de ground, dat limb gwine turn over in my hand till it points to de ground. Iffen money am buried, you can find it de same way.

"Iffen you fills a shoe with salt and burns it, dat call luck to you. I wears a dime on a string round de neck and one round de ankle. Dat to keep any conjureman from sottin' de trick on ma. Dat dime be bright iffen my friends am true. It sho' gwine git dark iffen dey does me wrong.

"For to make a jack dat am sho' good, git snakeroot and sassafras and a li'l lodestone and brimstone and asafoetida and resin and bluestone and gum arabic and a pod or two red pepper. Put dis in de red flannel bag, at midnight on de dark of de moon, and it sho' do de work.

"I knowed a ghost house, I sho' did. Everybody knowed it, a red brick house in Waco, on Thirteenth and Washington St. Dey calls it de Bell house. It sho' a fine, big house, but folks couldn't use it. De white folks what owns it, dey gits one nigger and 'nother to stay round and look after things. De white folks wants me to stay dere. I goes. Every

Friday night dere am a rustlin' sound, like murmur of treetops, all through dat house. De shutters rattles—only dere ain't no shutters on dem windows. Jes' plain as anything, I hears a chair, rockin', rockin'. Footsteps, soft as de breath, you could hear dem plain. But I stays and hunts and can't find nobody nor nothin' none of dem Friday nights.

"Den come de Friday night on de las' quarter de moon. Long 'bout midnight, something lift me out de cot. I heared a li'l child sobbin', and dat rocker git started, and de shutters dey rattle softlike, and dat rustlin', mournin' sound all through dat house. I takes de lantern and out in de hall I goes. Right by de foot de stairs I seed a woman, big as life, but she was thin and I seed right through her. She jes' walk on down dat hall and pay me no mind. She make de sound like de beatin' of wings. I jes' froze. I couldn't move.

"Dat woman jes' melted out de window at de end of de hall, and I left dat place!

United States. Work Projects Administration

ANDERSON AND MINERVA EDWARDS

ANDERSON AND MINERVA EDWARDS, a Negro Baptist preacher and his wife, were slaves on adjoining plantations in Rusk County, Texas. Anderson was born March 12, 1844, a slave of Major Matt Gaud, and Minerva was born February 2, 1850, a slave of Major Flannigan. As a boy Andrew would get a pass to visit his father, who belonged to Major Flannigan, and there he met Minerva. They worked for their masters until three years after the war, then moved to Harrison County, married and reared sixteen children. Andrew and Minerva live in a small but comfortable farmhouse two miles north of Marshall. Minerva's memory is poor, and she added little to Anderson's story.

"My father was Sandy Flannigan and he had run off from his first master in Maryland, on the east shore, and come to Texas, and here a slave buyer picked him up and sold chances on him. If they could find his Maryland master he'd have to go back to him and if they couldn't the chances was good. Wash Edwards in Panola County bought the chance on him, but he run off from him, too, and come to Major Flannigan's in Rusk County. Fin'ly Major Flannigan had to pay a good lot to get clear title to him.

"My mammy was named Minerva and her master was Major Gaud, and I was born there on his plantation in 1866. You can ask that tax man at Marshall 'bout my age, 'cause he's fix my 'xemption papers since I'm sixty. I had seven brothers and two sisters. There was Frank, Joe, Sandy and Gene, Preston and William and Sarah and Delilah, and they all lived to be old folks and the younges' jus' died last year. Folks was more healthy when I growed up and I'm 93 now and ain't dead; fact is, I feels right pert mos' the time.

"My missy named Mary and she and Massa Matt lived in a hewed log house what am still standin' out there near Henderson. Our quarters was 'cross the road and set all in a row. Massa own three fam'lies of slaves and lots of hosses and sheep and cows and my father herded for him till he was freed. The government run a big tan yard there on Major Gaud's place and one my uncles was shoemaker. Jus' 'bout time of war, I was piddlin' 'round the tannery and a government man say to me, 'Boy, I'll give you $1,000 for a drink of water,' and he did, but it was 'federate money that got kilt, so it done me no good.

"Mammy was a weaver and made all the clothes and massa give us plenty to eat; fact, he treated us kind-a like he own boys. Course he whipped us when we had to have it, but not like I seed darkies whipped on other place. The other niggers called us Major Gaud's free niggers and we could hear 'em moanin' and cryin' round 'bout, when they was puttin' it on 'em.

"I worked in the field from one year end to t'other and when we come in at dusk we had to eat and be in bed by nine. Massa give us mos' anything he had to eat, 'cept biscuits. That ash cake wasn't sich bad eatin' and it was cooked by puttin' cornmeal batter in shucks and bakin' in the ashes.

"We didn't work in the field Sunday but they have so much stock to tend it kep' us busy. Missy was 'ligious and allus took us to church when she could. When we prayed by ourse'ves we daren't let the white folks know it and we turned a wash pot down to the ground to cotch the voice. We prayed a lot to be free and the Lord done heered us. We didn't have no song books and the Lord done give us our songs and when we sing them at night it jus' whispering to nobody hear us. One went like this:

> "'My knee bones am aching,
> My body's rackin' with pain,
> I 'lieve I'm a chile of God,
> And this ain't my home,
> 'Cause Heaven's my aim.'

"Massa Gaud give big corn shuckin's and cotton pickin's and the women cook up big dinners and massa give us some whiskey, and lots of times we shucked all night. On Saturday nights we'd sing and dance and we made our own instruments, which was gourd fiddles and quill flutes. Gen'rally Christmas was like any other day, but I got Santa Claus twict in slavery, 'cause massa give me a sack of molasses candy once and some biscuits once and that was a whole lot to me then.

"The Vinsons and Frys what lived next to massa sold slaves and I seed 'em sold and chained together and druv off in herds by a white man on a hoss. They'd sell babies 'way from the mammy and the Lord never did 'tend sich as that.

"I 'lieve in that hant business yet. I seed one when I was a boy, right after mammy die. I woke up and seed it come in the door, and it had a body and legs and tail and a face like a man and it walked to the fireplace and lifted the lid off a skillet of 'taters what sot there and came to my bed and raised up the cover and crawled in and I hollers so loud it wakes everybody. I tell 'em I seed a ghost and they say I crazy, but I guess I knows a hant when I sees one. Minerva there can tell you 'bout that haunted house we lived in near Marshall jus' after we's married." (Minerva says, 'Deed, I can,' and here is her story:)

"The nex' year after Anderson and me marries we moves to a place that had 'longed to white folks and the man was real mean and choked his wife to death and he lef' the country and we moved in. We heered peculiar noises by night and the niggers 'round there done told us it was hanted but I didn't 'lieve 'em, but I do now. One night we seed the woman what died come all 'round with a light in the hand and the neighbors said that candle light the house all over and it look like it on fire. She come ev'ry night and we left our crop and moved 'way from there and ain't gone back yit to gather that crop. 'Fore we moved in that place been empty since the woman die, 'cause nobody live there. One night Charlie Williams, what lives in Marshall, and runs a store out by the T. & P. Hospital git drunk and goes out there to sleep and while he sleepin' that same woman come in and nigh choked him to death. Ain't nobody ever live in that house since we is there."

Anderson then resumed his story: "I 'member when war starts and massa's boy, George it was, saddles up ole Bob, his pony, and lef'. He stays six months and when he rid up massa say, 'How's the war, George?' and massa George say, 'It's Hell. Me and Bob has been runnin' Yankees ever since us lef'.' 'Fore war massa didn't never say much 'bout slavery but when he heered us free he cusses and say, 'Gawd never did 'tend to free niggers,' and he cussed till he died. But he didn't tell us we's free till a whole year after we was, but one day a bunch of Yankee soldiers come ridin' up and massa and missy hid out. The soldiers walked into the kitchen and mammy was churnin' and one of them kicks the churn over and say, 'Git out, you's jus' as free as I is.' Then they ramsacked the place and breaks out all the window lights and when they leaves it look like a storm done hit that house. Massa come back from hidin' and that when he starts on a cussin' spree what lasts as long as he lives.

"'bout four year after that war pappy took me to Harrison County and I've lived here ever, since and Minerva's pappy moves from the Flannigan place to a jinin' farm 'bout that time and sev'ral years later we was married. It was at her house and she had a blue serge suit and I wore a cutaway Prince Albert suit and they was 'bout 200 folks at our weddin'. The nex' day they give us an infair and a big dinner. We raises sixteen chillen to be growed and six of the boys is still livin' and workin' in Marshall.

"I been preachin' the Gospel and farmin' since slavery time. I jined the church mos' 83 year ago when I was Major Gaud's slave and they baptises me in the spring branch clost to where I finds the Lord. When I starts preachin' I couldn't read or write and had to preach what massa told me and he say tell them niggers iffen they obeys the massa they goes to Heaven but I knowed there's something better for them, but daren't tell them 'cept on the sly. That I done lots. I tells 'em iffen they keeps prayin' the Lord will set 'em free. But since them days I's done studied some and I preached all over Panola and Harrison County and I started the Edward's Chapel over there in Marshall and pastored it till a few year ago. It's named for me.

"I don't preach much now, 'cause I can't hold out to walk far and I got no other way to go. We has a $14.00 pension and lives on that and what we can raise on the farm.

United States. Work Projects Administration

ANN J. EDWARDS

ANN J. EDWARDS, 81, was born a slave of John Cook, of Arlington County, Virginia. He manumitted his slaves in 1857. Four years later Ann was adopted by Richard H. Cain, a colored preacher. He was elected to the 45th Congress in 1876, and remained in Washington, D.C., until his death, in 1887. Ann married Jas. E. Edwards, graduate of Howard College, a preacher. She now lives with her granddaughter, Mary Foster, at 804 E. 4th St., Fort Worth, Texas.

"I shall gladly relate the story of my life. I was born a slave on January 27th, 1856, and my master's name was John J. Cook, who was a resident of Arlington County, Virginia. He moved to Washington, D.C., when I was nearly two years old and immediately gave my parents their freedom. They separated within a year after that, and my mother earned our living, working as a hairdresser until her death in 1861. I was then adopted by Richard H. Cain, a minister of the Gospel in the African Methodist Church.

"I remember the beginning of the war well. The conditions made a deep impression on my mind, and the atmosphere of Washington was charged with excitement and expectations. There existed considerable need for assistance to the Negroes who had escaped after the war began, and Rev. Cain took a leading part in rendering aid to them. They came into the city without clothes or money and no idea of how to secure employment. A large number were placed on farms, some given employment as domestics and still others mustered into the Federal Army.

"The city was one procession of men in blue and the air was full of martial music. The fife and drum could be heard almost all the time, so you may imagine what emotions a colored person of my age would experience, especially as father's church was a center for congregating the Negroes and advising them. That was a difficult task, because a large majority were illiterate and ignorant.

"The year father was called to Charleston, South Carolina, to take charge of a church, we became the center of considerable trouble. It was right after the close of the war. In addition to his ministerial duties, father managed a newspaper and became interested in politics. He was elected a delegate to the Constitutional Convention of South Carolina in 1868. He was also elected a Republican member of the State Senate and served from 1868 to 1872. Then he became the Republican candidate for the United States Representative of the Charleston district, was elected and served in the 45th Congress from March 4, 1877 to March 3, 1879.

"You can imagine the bitter conflict his candidacy brought on. A Negro running for public office against a white person in a Southern state that was strong for slavery does not seem the sensible thing for a man to do, but he did and was, of course, successful. From the moment he became delegate to the Constitutional Convention a guard was necessary night and day to watch our home. He was compelled to have a bodyguard wherever he went. We, his family, lived in constant fear at all times. Many times mother pleaded with him to cease his activities, but her pleadings were of no avail.

"In the beginning the resentment was not so pronounced. The white people were shocked and dejected over the outcome of the war, but gradually recovered. As they did, determination to establish order and prosperity developed, and they resented the Negro taking part in public affairs. On the other side of the cause was the excess and obstinate actions of some ignorant Negroes, acting under ill advice. Father was trying to prevent excesses being done by either side. He realized that the slaves were unfit, at that time, to take their place as dependable citizens, for the want of experience and wisdom, and that there would have to be mental development and wisdom learned by his race, and that such would only come by a gradual process.

"He entered the contest in the interest of his own race, primarily, but as a whole, to do justice to all. No one could change his course. He often stated, 'It is by the Divine will that I am in this battle.'

"The climax of the resentment against him took place when he was chosen Republican candidate to the House of Representatives. He had to maintain an armed guard at all times. Several times, despite these guards, attempts were made to either burn the house or injure some member of the family. If it had not been for the fact that the officials of the city and county were afraid of the federal government, which gave aid in protecting him, the mob would have succeeded in harming him.

"A day or two before election a mob gathered suddenly in front of the house, and we all thought the end had come. Father sent us all upstairs, and said he would, if necessary, give himself up to the mob and let them satisfy their vengeance on him, to save the rest of us.

"While he was talking, mother noticed another body of men in the alley. They were certainly sinister looking. Father told us to prepare for the worst, saying, 'What they plan to do is for those in front to engage the attention of ourselves and the guard, then those in the rear will fire the place and force us out.' He was calm throughout it all, but mother was greatly agitated and I was crying.

"The chief of the guard called father for a parley. The mob leader demanded that father come out for a talk. Then the sheriff and deputies appeared and he addressed the crowd of men, and told them if harm came to us the city would be placed under martial law. The men then dispersed, after some discussion among themselves.

"Father moved to Washington, took the oath of office and served until March 4th, 1879. He then received the appointment of Bishop of the African Methodist Church and served until his death in Washington, on Jan. 18th, 1887.

"I began my schooling in Charleston and continued in Washington, where I entered Howard College, but did not continue until graduation. I met James E. Edwards, another student, who graduated in 1881, and my heart overruled my desire for an education. We married and he entered the ministry and was called to Dallas, Texas. He remained two years, then we were called to Los Angeles. The Negroes there were privileged to enter public eating establishments, but a cafe owner we patronized told us the following:

"'After a time, I was compelled to refuse service to Negroes because they abused the privilege. They came in in a boisterous manner and crowded and shoved other patrons. It was due to a lack of wisdom and education.'

"That was true. The white people tried to give the Negro his rights and he abused the privilege because he was ignorant, a condition he could not then help.

"My husband and I were called to Kansas City in 1896 and from there to many other towns. Finally we came to Waco, and he had charge of a church there when he died, in 1927. We had a pleasant married life and I tried to do my duty as a pastor's wife and help elevate my race. We were blessed with three children, and the only one now living is in Boston, Massachusetts.

"I now reside with my granddaughter, Mary Foster, and this shack is the best her husband can afford. In fact, we are living in destitute circumstances. It is depressing to me, after having lived a life in a comfortable home. It is the Lord's will and I must accept what is provided. There is a purpose for all things. I shall soon go to meet my Maker, with the satisfaction of having done my duty—first, to my race, second, to mankind.

Note: The biography of Richard H. Cain is published in the Biographical Directory of the American Congress.

United States. Work Projects Administration

MARY KINCHEON EDWARDS

MARY KINCHEON EDWARDS says she was born on July 8, 1810, but she has nothing to substantiate this claim. However, she is evidently very old. Her memory is poor, but she knows she was reared by the Kincheons, in Baton Rouge, Louisiana, and that she spoke French when a child. The Kincheons gave her to Felix Vaughn, who brought her to Texas before the Civil War. Mary lives with Beatrice Watters, near Austin, Texas.

"When I's a li'l gal my name Mary Anne Kincheon and I's born on the eighth of July, in 1810. I lives with de Kincheon family over in Louisiana. Baton Rouge am de name of dat place. Dem Kincheons have plenty chillen. O, dey have so many chillen!

"I don't 'member much 'bout dem days. I's done forgot so many things, but I 'members how de stars fell and how scared us was. Dem stars got to fallin' and was out 'fore dey hits de ground. I don't knew when dat was, but I's good size den.

"I get give to Massa Felix Vaughn and he brung me to Texas. Dat long 'fore de war for freedom, but I don't know de year. De most work I done for de Vaughns was wet nuss de baby son, what name Elijah. His mammy jes' didn't have 'nough milk for him.

"Den I knit de socks and wash de clothes and sometimes I work in de fields. I he'ped make de baskets for de cotton. De man git white-oak wood and we lets it stay in de water for de night and de nex' mornin' and it soft and us split it in strips for makin' of de baskets. Everybody try see who could make de bes' basket.

"Us pick 'bout 100 pound cotton in one basket. I didn't mind pickin' cotton, 'cause I never did have de backache. I pick two and three hunnert pounds a day and one day I picked 400. Sometime de prize give by massa to de slave what pick de most. De prize am a big cake or some clothes. Pickin' cotton not so bad, 'cause us used to it and have de fine time of it. I gits a dress one day and a pair shoes 'nother day for pickin' most. I so fast I take two rows at de time.

"De women brung oil cloths to de fields, so dey make shady place for de chillen to sleep, but dem what big 'nough has to pick. Sometime dey sing

"'O—ho, I's gwine home,
And cuss de old overseer.'

"Us have ash-hopper and uses drip-lye for make barrels soap and hominy. De way us test de lye am drap de egg in it and if de egg float de lye ready to put in de grease for makin' de soap. Us throwed greasy bones in de lye and dat make de bes' soap. De lye eat de bones.

"Us boil wild sage and make tea and it smell good. It good for de fever and chills. Us git slippery elm out de bottom and chew it. Some chew it for bad feelin's and some jes' to be chewin'.

"Sometimes us go to dances and missy let me wear some her jewl'ry. I out dances dem all and folks didn't know dat not my jewl'ry. After freedom I stays with de Vaughns and marries, but I forgit he name. Dat 'fore freedom. After freedom I marries Osburn Edwards and has five chillen. Dey all dead now. I can still git 'round with dis old gnarly cane. Jes' you git me good and scared and see how fast I can git 'round!"

LUCINDA ELDER

LUCINDA ELDER, 86, was born a slave of the Cardwell family, near Concord Deport, Virginia. She came to Texas with Will Jones and his wife, Miss Susie, in 1860, and was their nurse-girl until she married Will Elder, in 1875. Lucinda lives at 1007 Edwards St., Houston, Texas.

"You chilluns all go 'way now, while I talks to dis gen'man. I 'clares to goodness, chilluns nowadays ain't got no manners 'tall. 'Tain't like when I was li'l, dey larnt you manners and you larnt to mind, too. Nowadays you tell 'em to do somethin' and you is jes' wastin' you breath, 'less you has a stick right handy. Dey is my great grandchilluns, and dey sho' is spoilt. Maybe I ain't got no patience no more, like I use to have, 'cause dey ain't so bad.

"Well, suh, you all wants me to tell you 'bout slave times, and I'll tell you first dat I had mighty good white folks, and I hope dey is gone up to Heaven. My mama 'long to Marse John Cardwell, what I hear was de riches' man and had de bigges' plantation round Concord Depot. Dat am in Campbell County, in Virginny. I don't 'member old missy's name, but she mighty good to de slaves, jes' like Marse John was.

"Mama's name was Isabella and she was de cook and born right on de plantation. Papa's name was Gibson, his first name was Jim, and he 'long to Marse Gibson what had a plantation next to Marse John, and I knows papa come to see mama on Wednesday and Sat'day nights.

"Lemme see, now, dere was six of us chilluns. My mem'ry ain't so good no more, but Charley was oldes', den come Dolly and Jennie and Susie and me and Laura. Law me, I guess old Dr. Bass, what was doctor for Marse John, use to be right busy with us 'bout once a year for quite a spell.

"Dem times dey don't marry by no license. Dey takes a slave man and woman from de same plantation and puts 'em together, or sometime a man from 'nother plantation, like my papa and mama. Mamma say Marse John give 'em a big supper in de big house and read out de Bible 'bout obeyin' and workin' and den dey am married. Course, de nigger jes' a slave and have to do what de white folks say, so dat way of marryin' 'bout good as any.

"But Marse John sho' was de good marse and we had plenty to eat and wear and no one ever got whipped. Marse John say iffen he have a nigger what oughta be whipped, he'd git rid of him quick, 'cause a bad nigger jes' like a rotten 'tater in a sack of good ones—it spoil de others.

"Back dere in Virginny it sho' git cold in winter, but come September de wood gang git busy cuttin' wood and haulin' it to de yard. Dey makes two piles, one for de big house and de bigges' pile for de slaves. When dey git it all hauled it look like a big woodyard. While dey is haulin', de women make quilts and dey is wool quilts. Course, dey ain't made out of shearin' wool, but jes' as good. Marse John have lots of sheep and when dey go through de briar patch de wool cotch on dem briars and in de fall de women folks goes out and picks de wool off de briars jes' like you picks cotton. Law me, I don't know nothin' 'bout makin' quilts out of cotton till I comes to Texas.

"Course I never done no work, 'cause Marse John won't work no one till dey is fifteen years old. Den dey works three hours a day and dat all. Dey don't work full time till dey's eighteen. We was jes' same as free niggers on our place. He gives each slave a piece of ground to make de crop on and buys de stuff hisself. We growed snap beans and corn and plant on a light moon, or turnips and onions we plant on de dark moon.

"When I gits old 'nough Marse John lets me take he daughter, Nancy Lee, to school. It am twelve miles and de yard man hitches up old Bess to de buggy and we gits in and no one in dat county no prouder dan what I was.

"Marse John lets us go visit other plantations and no pass, neither. Iffen de patterroller stop us, we jes' say we 'long to Marse John and dey don't bother us none. Iffen dey comes to our cabin from other plantations, dey has to show de patterroller de pass, and iffen dey slipped off and ain't got none, de patterroller sho' give a whippin' den. But dey waits till dey off our place, 'cause Marse John won't 'low no whippin' on our place by no one.

"Well, things was jes' 'bout de same all de time till jes' 'fore freedom. Course, I hears some talk 'bout bluebellies, what dey call de Yanks, fightin' our folks, but dey wasn't fightin' round us. Den one dey mamma took sick and she had hear talk and call me to de bed and say, 'Lucinda, we all gwine be free soon and not work 'less we git paid for it.' She sho' was right, 'cause Marse John calls all us to de cookhouse and reads de freedom papers to us and tells us we is all free, but iffen we wants to stay he'll give us land to make a crop and he'll feed us. Now I tells you de truth, dey wasn't no one leaves, 'cause we all loves Marse John.

"Den, jus' three weeks after freedom mama dies and dat how come me to leave Marse John. You see, Marse Gibson what owns papa 'fore freedom, was a good marse and when papa was sot free Marse Gibson gives him some land to farm. 'Course, papa was gwine have us all with him, but when mamma dies, Marse Gibson tell him Mr. Will Jones and Miss Susie, he wife, want a nurse girl for de chilluns, so papa hires me out to 'em and I want to say right now, dey jes' as good white folks as Marse John and Old Missy, and sho' treated me good.

"Law me, I never won't forgit one day. Mr. Will say, 'Lucinda, we is gwine drive you over to Appomatox and take de chilluns and you can come, too.' Course, I was tickled mos' to pieces but he didn't tell what he gwine for. You know what? To see a nigger hung. I gettin' long mighty old now, but I won't never forgit dat. He had kilt a man, and I never saw so many people 'fore, what dere to see him hang. I jes' shut my eyes.

"Den Mr. Will he take me to de big tree what have all de bark strip off it and de branches strip off, and say, 'Lucinda, dis de tree where Gen. Lee surrendered.' I has put dese two hands right on dat tree, yes, suh, I sho' has.

"Miss Susie say one day, 'Lucinda, how you like to go with us to Texas?' Law me, I didn't know where Texas was at, or nothin', but I loved Mr. Will and Miss Susie and de chilluns was all wrop up in me, so I say I'll go. And dat how come I'm here, and I ain't never been back, and I ain't see my own sisters and brother and papa since.

"We come to New Orleans on de train and takes de boat on de Gulf to Galveston and den de train to Hempstead. Mr. Will farm at first and den he and Miss Susie run de hotel, and I stays with dem till I gets married to Will Elder in '75, and I lives with him till de good Lawd takes him home.

"I has five chilluns but all dead now, 'ceptin' two. I done served de Lawd now for 64 years and soon he's gwine call old Lucinda, but I'm ready and I know I'll be better off when I die and go to Heaven, 'cause I'm old and no 'count now.

JOHN ELLIS

JOHN ELLIS, was born June 26, 1852, a slave of the Ellis family in Johnson County near Cleburne, Texas. He remained with his white folks and was paid by the month for his labor for one year after freedom, when his master died and his mistress returned to Mississippi. He worked as a laborer for many years around Cleburne, coming to San Angelo, Texas in 1928. He now lives alone and is very active for his age.

John relates:

"My father and mother, John and Fannie Ellis, were sold in Springfield, Missouri, to my marster, Parson Ellis, and taken away from all their people and brought to Johnson County, Texas.

"My marster, he was a preacher and a good man. None of de slaves ever have better white folks den we did.

"We had good beds and good food and dey teaches us to read and write too. De buffalo and de antelope and de deer was mos' as thick as de cattle now, and we was sent out after dem, so we would always have plenty of fresh meat. We had hogs and cattle too. Any of dem what was not marked was just as much ours as iffen we had raised dem, 'cause de range was all free.

"Some of de fish we would catch out of dat Brazos River would be so big dey would pull us in but finally we would manage to gits dem out. De rabbits and de 'possum was plentiful too and wid de big garden what our marster had for us all, we sho' had good to eat.

"I's done all kinds of work what it takes to run a fa'm. My boss he had only fourteen slaves and what was called a small fa'm, compared wid de big plantations. After our days work was done we would set up at night and pick de seed out of de cotton so dey could spin it into thread. Den we goes out and gits different kinds of bark and boils it to git dye for de thread 'fore it was spinned into cloth. De chillun jes' have long shirts and slips made out of dis home spun and we makes our shoes out of rawhide, and Lawdy! Dey was so hard we would have to warm dem by de fire and grease dem wid tallow to ever wear dem 'tall.

"We had good log huts and our boss had a bigger log house. We never did work long into de night and long 'fore day like I hear tell some did. We didn' have none of dem drivers and when we done anything very bad old marster he whoop us a little but we never got hurt.

"I didn' see no slaves sold. Dat was done, I hear, but not so much in Texas. I never did see no jails nor chains nor nothin' like dat either, but I hears 'bout dem.

"We never worked Sat'days and de colored went to church wid de whites and jine de church too, but dey never baptized dem so far as I knows.

"We had lots to eat and big times on Christmas, mos' as big as when de white folks gits married. Umph, um! One of de gi'ls got married once and she had such a long train on dat weddin' gown 'til me and my sister, we have to walks along behind her and carry dat thing, all of us a-walkin' on a strip of nice cloth from de carriage to de church. We sho' have de cakes and all dem good eats at dem weddin' suppers.

"I nev'r hear tell of many colored weddin's. We jes' jumps over de broom an' de bride she has to jump over it backwards and iffen she couldn' jump it backwards she couldn't git married. Dat was sho' funny, seein' dem colored gi'ls a tryin' to jump dat broom.

"Our boss, he tells us 'bout bein' free and he say he hire us by de month and we stays dere a year and he dies, den ole miss she go back to Mississippi and we jes' scatter 'round, some a workin' here and some a workin' yonder, mos' times for our victuals and clothes. I couldn' tell much difference myself 'cause I had good people to live wid and when it was dat way de whites and de colored was better off de way I sees it den dey is now, some of dem.

"I seem jes' punyin' away, de doctors don' know jes' what's wrong wid me but I never was use to doctors anyway, jes' some red root tea or sage weed and sheep waste tea for de measles am all de doctoring we gits when we was slaves and dat done jes' as well.

"My wife she been dead all dese years an' I jes' lives here alone.

"Chillun? No mam, I never had no chillun 'fore I was married an' I only had twelve after I was married; yes mam, jes' nine boys and three girls, but I prefers to live here by myself, 'cause I gits along alright."

LORENZA EZELL

LORENZA EZELL, Beaumont, Texas, Negro, was born in 1850 on the plantation of Ned Lipscomb, in Spartanburg County, South Carolina. Lorenza is above the average in intelligence and remembers many incidents of slavery and Reconstruction days. He came to Brenham, Texas, in 1882, and several years later moved to Beaumont, where he lives in a little shack almost hidden by vines and trees.

"Us plantation was jes' east from Pacolet Station on Thicketty Creek, in Spartanburg County, in South Carolina. Dat near Little and Big Pacolet Rivers on de route to Limestone Springs, and it jes' a ordinary plantation with de main crops cotton and wheat.

"I 'long to de Lipscombs and my mama, Maria Ezell, she 'long to 'em, too. Old Ned Lipscomb was 'mongst de oldest citizens of dat county. I's born dere on July 29th, in 1850 and I be 87 year old dis year. Levi Ezell, he my daddy, and he 'long to Landrum Ezell, a Baptist preacher. Dat young massa and de old massa, John Ezell, was de first Baptist preacher I ever heered of. He have three sons, Landrum and Judson and Bryson. Bryson have gif' for business and was right smart of a orator.

"Dey's fourteen niggers on de Lipscomb place. Dey's seven of us chillen, my mamma, three uncle and three aunt and one man what wasn't no kin to us. I was oldest of de chillen, and dey called Sallie and Carrie and Alice and Jabus and Coy and LaFate and Rufus and Nelson.

"Old Ned Lipscomb was one de best massa in de whole county. You know dem old patterrollers, dey call us 'Old Ned's free niggers,' and sho' hate us. Dey cruel to us, 'cause dey think us have too good a massa. One time dey cotch my uncle and beat him most to death.

"Us go to work at daylight, but us wasn't 'bused. Other massas used to blow de horn or ring de bell, but massa, he never use de horn or de whip. All de man folks was 'lowed raise a garden patch with tobaccy or cotton for to sell in de market. Wasn't many massas what 'lowed dere niggers have patches and some didn't even feed 'em enough. Dat's why dey have to git out and hustle at night to git food for dem to eat.

"De old massa, he 'sisted us go to church. De Baptist church have a shed built behind de pulpit for cullud folks, with de dirt floor and split log seat for de women folks, but most de men folks stands or kneels on de floor. Dey used to call dat de coop. De white preacher back to us, but iffen he want to he turn 'round and talk to us awhile. Us mess up songs, 'cause us couldn't read or write. I 'member dis one:

> 'De rough, rocky road what Moses done travel,
> I's bound to carry my soul to de Lawd;
> It's a mighty rocky road but I mos' done travel,
> And I's bound to carry my soul to de Lawd.'

"Us sing 'Sweet Chariot,' but us didn't sing it like dese days. Us sing:

> 'Swing low, sweet chariot,
> Freely let me into rest,
> I don't want to stay here no longer;
> Swing low, sweet chariot,
> When Gabriel make he las' alarm
> I wants to be rollin' in Jesus arm,

'Cause I don't want to stay here no longer.'

Us sing 'nother song what de Yankees take dat tune and make a hymm out of it. Sherman army sung it, too. We have it like dis:

> 'Our bodies bound to morter and decay,
> Our bodies bound to morter and decay,
> Our bodies bound to morter and decay,
> But us souls go marchin' home.'

"Befo' de war I jes' big 'nough to drap corn and tote water. When de little white chillen go to school 'bout half mile, I wait till noon and run all de way up to de school to run base when dey play at noon. Dey sev'ral young Lipscombs, dere Smith and Bill and John and Nathan, and de oldest son, Elias.

"In dem days cullud people jes' like mules and hosses. Dey didn't have no last name. My mamma call me after my daddy's massa, Ezell. Mamma was de good woman and I 'member her more dan once rockin' de little cradle and singin' to de baby. Dis what she sing:

> "Milk in de dairy nine days old,
> Sing-song Kitty, can't you ki-me-o?
> Frogs and skeeters gittin' mighty bol!
> Sing-song, Kitty, can't you ki-me-o?
>
> (Chorus)

Keemo, kimo, darro, wharro,
With me hi, me ho;
In come Sally singin'
Sometime penny winkle,
Lingtum nip cat,
Sing-song, Kitty, can't you ki-me-o?

Dere a frog live in a pool,
Sing-song, Kitty, can't you ki-me-o?
Sure he was de bigges' fool,
Sing-song Kitty, can't you ki-me-o?

For he could dance and he could sing
Sing-song, Kitty, can't you ki-me-o?
And make de woods aroun' him ring
Sing-song, Kitty, can't you ki-me-o?'

"Old massa didn't hold with de way some mean massas treat dey niggers. Dere a place on our plantation what us call 'De old meadow.' It was common for runaway niggers to have place 'long de way to hide and res' when dey run off from mean massa. Massa used to give 'em somethin' to eat when dey hide dere. I saw dat place operated, though it wasn't knowed by dat den, but long time after I finds out dey call it part of de 'Underground railroad.' Dey was stops like dat all de way up to de north.

"We have went down to Columbia when I 'bout 11 year old and dat where de first gun fired. Us rush back home, but I could say I heered de first guns of de war shot, at Fort Sumter.

"When Gen'ral Sherman come 'cross de Savannah River in South Carolina, some of he sojers come right 'cross us plantation. All de neighbors have brung dey cotton and stack it in de thicket on de Lipscomb place. Sherman men find it and sot it on fire. Dat cotton stack was big as a little courthouse and it took two months' burnin'.

"My old massa run off and stay in de woods a whole week when Sherman men come through. He didn't need to worry, 'cause us took care of everythin'. Dey a funny song us make up 'bout him runnin' off in de woods. I know it was make up, 'cause my uncle have a hand in it. It went like dis:

> 'White folks, have you seed old massa
> Up de road, with he mustache on?
> He pick up he hat and he leave real sudden
> And I 'lieve he's up and gone.
>
> (Chorus)
>
> 'Old massa run away
> And us darkies stay at home.
> It mus' be now dat Kingdom's comin'
> And de year of Jubilee.
>
> 'He look up de river and he seed dat smoke
> Where de Lincoln gunboats lay.

He big 'nuff and he old 'nuff and he orter know better,
But he gone and run away.

'Now dat overseer want to give trouble
And trot us 'round a spell,
But we lock him up in de smokehouse cellar,
With de key done throwed in de well.'

"Right after dat I start to be boy what run mail from camp to camp for de sojers. One time I capture by a bunch of deserters what was hidin' in de woods 'long Pacolet River. Dey didn't hurt me, though, but dey mos' scare me to death. Dey parole me and turn me loose.

"All four my young massas go to de war, all but Elias. He too old. Smith, he kilt at Manassas Junction. Nathan he git he finger shot at de first round at Fort Sumter. But when Billy was wounded at Howard Gap in North Carolina and dey brung him home with he jaw split open, I so mad I could have kilt all de Yankees. I say I be happy iffen I could kill me jes' one Yankee. I hated dem 'cause dey hurt my white people. Billy was disfigure awful when he jaw split and he teeth all shine through he cheek.

"After war was over, old massa call us up and told us we free but he 'vise not leave de place till de crop was through. Us all stay. Den us select us homes and move to it. Us folks move to Sam Littlejohn's, north of Thickettty Creek, where us stay two year. Den us move back to Billy Lipscomb, de young massa, and stay dere two more year. I's right smart good banjo picker in dem day. I kin 'member one dem songs jes' as good today as when I pick it. Dat was:

> 'Early in de mornin'
> Don't you hear de dogs a-barkin'?
> Bow, wow, wow!

> (Chorus)

> 'Hush, hush, boys
> Don't make a noise,
> Massa's fast a-sleepin'.
> Run to de barnyard
> Wake up de boys
> Let's have banjo pickin.'.

> 'Early in de mornin'
> Don't you hear dem roosters crowin'?
> Cock-a-doodle-do.

"I come in contac' with de Klu Klux. Us lef' de plantation in '65 or '66 and by '68 us was havin' sich a awful time with de Klu Klux. First time dey come to my mamma's house at midnight and claim dey sojers done come back from de dead. Dey all dress up in sheets and make up like spirit. Dey groan 'round and say dey been kilt wrongly and come back for justice. One man, he look jus' like ordinary man, but he spring up 'bout eighteen feet high all of a sudden.

Another say he so thirsty he ain't have no water since he been kilt at Manassas Junction. He ask for water and he jes' kept pourin' it in. Us think he sho' must be a spirit to drink dat much water. Course he not drinkin' it, he pourin' it in a bag under he sheet. My mama never did take up no truck with spirits so she knowed it jes' a man. Dey tell us what dey gwine do iffen we don't all go back to us massas and us all 'grees and den dey all dis'pear.

"Den us move to New Prospect on de Pacolet River, on de Perry Clemmons' place. Dat in de upper edge of de county and dat where de second swarm of de Klu Klux come out. Dey claim dey gwine kill everybody what am Repub'can. My daddy charge with bein' a leader 'mongst de niggers. He make speech and 'struct de niggers how to vote for Grant's first 'lection. De Klu Klux want to whip him and he have to sleep in a holler log every night.

"Dey's a old man name Uncle Bart what live 'bout half mile from us. De Klu Klux come to us house one night, but my daddy done hid. Den I hear dem say dey gwine go kill old man Bart. I jump out de window and cut short cut through dem wood and warn him. He git out de house in time and I save he life. De funny thing, I knowed all dem Klu Klux. Spite dey sheets and things, I knowed dey voices and dey saddle hosses.

"Dey one white man name Irving Ramsey. Us play fiddle together lots of time. When de white boys dance dey allus wants me to go to play for dey party. One day I say to dat boy, 'I done knowed you last night.' He say, 'What you mean?' I say, 'You one dem Klu Klux.' He want to know how I know. I say, 'Member when you go under de chestnut tree and say, "Whoa, Sont, whoa, Sont, to your hoss?" He say, 'Yes,' and I laugh and say, 'Well, I's right up in dat tree.' Dey all knowed I knowed dem den, but I never told on dem. When dey seed I ain't gwineter tell, dey never try whip my daddy or kill Uncle Bart no more.

"I ain't never been to school but I jes' picked up readin'. With some my first money I ever earn I buy me a old blue-back Webster. I carry dat book wherever I goes. When I plows down a row I stop at de end to rest and den I overlook de lesson. I 'member one de very first lessons was, 'Evil communications 'rupts good morals.' I knowed de words 'evil' and 'good' and a white man 'splain de others. I been done use dat lesson all my life.

"After us left de Pacolet River us stay in Atlanta a little while and den I go on to Louisiana. I done lef' Spartanburg completely in '76 but I didn't git into Texas till 1882. I fin'lly git to Brenham, Texas and marry Rachel Pinchbeck two year after. Us was marry in church and have seven chillen. Den us sep'rate. I been batching 'bout 20 year and I done los' track mos' dem chillen. My gal, Lula, live in Beaumont, and Will, he in Chicago.

"Every time I tells dese niggers I's from South Carolina dey all say, 'O, he bound to make a heap.' I could be a conjure doctor and make plenty money, but dat ain't good. In slavery time dey's men like dat 'garded as bein' dangerous. Dey make charms and put bad mouth on you. De old folks wears de rabbit foot or coon foot and sometime a silver dime on a fishin' string to keep off de witches. Some dem old conjure people make lots of money for charm 'gainst ruin or cripplin' or dry up de blood. But I don't take up no truck with things like dat.

BETTY FARROW

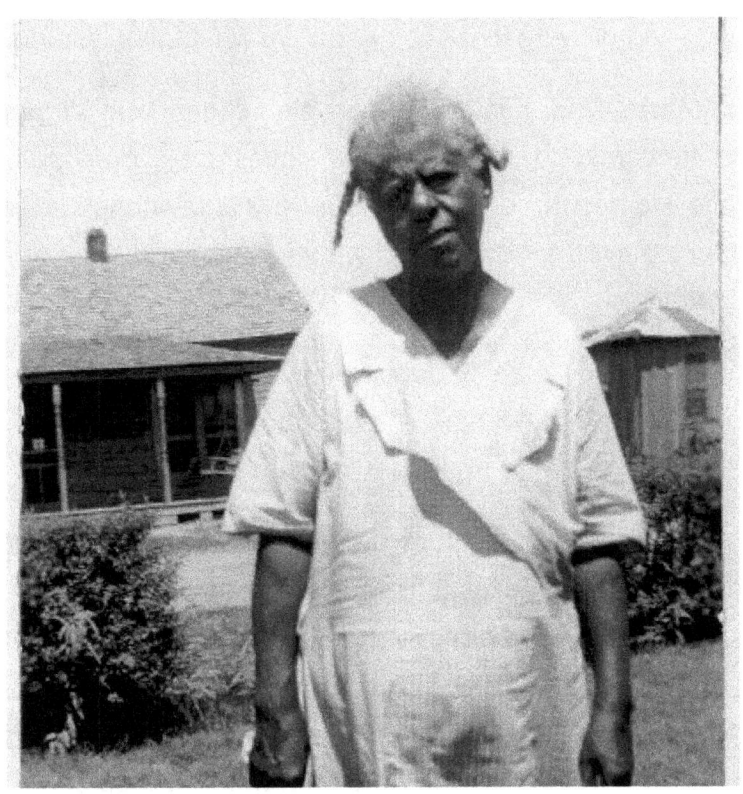

BETTY FARROW, 90, now living with a son on a farm in Moser Valley, a Negro settlement ten miles northeast of Fort Worth on Texas Highway No. 15, was born a slave to Mr. Alex Clark, plantation owner in Patrick Co., Virginia.

"I's glad to tell what I knows, but yous have to 'scuse me, 'cause my 'collection am bad. I jus' don' 'member much, but

I's bo'n on Masta Alex Clark's plantation in Patrick County, Virginny, on June 28th, 1847. Dat's what my mammy tol' me. You see, we cullud folks have no schoolin' dem days and I can't read or write. I has to depen' on what folks tells me.

"Masta Clark has right smart plantation in ole Virginny and he owns 'bout twenty other slaves dat wo'ked de big place. He had three girls and four boys and when I's a chile we'uns played togedder and we'uns 'tached to each other all our lives.

"In mammy's family dere was five boys and four girls. I don' 'member my pappy. When I's 'bout ten, I's set to work, peddalin' 'round de house.

"'bout three years 'fore de war marster sol' his plantation for to go to Texas. I 'members de day we'uns started in three covered wagons, all loaded. 'Twas celebration day for us chillun. We travels from daylight to dark, 'cept to feed and res' de mules at noon. I don' rec'lec' how long we was on de way, but 'twas long time and 'twarn't no celebration towards de las'. After while we comes to Sherman, in Texas, to our new farm.

"When we was dere 'bout a year, dere am heaps of trouble. Dere was a neighbor, Shields, he's drivin' wood to town and goes n'cross masta's yard and dey have arg'ments. One day we chillen playin' and masta settin' on de front porch and Shields come up de road. Masta stops him when he starts to cross de yard and de fust thing we knows, we hears 'bang' and dat Shields shoot de masta and we sees him fall. Dey sen's young Alex for de doctor and he makes dat mule run like he never run 'fore. De doctor comes in de house and looks at de masta, and listens to his heart and says, 'He am dead.' Dere was powerful sorrow in dat home.

"After dat, Masta Alex takes charge, and in 'bout one year, he says, 'We'uns goin' to Fort Worth.' So we goes, and if I rec'lec's right, dat year de war started. After dat, dere was times dere wasn' enough to make de clothes, but we'uns allus had plenty to eat, and we gives lots of feed to de army mans.

"I don' 'member bein' tol' I's free. We'uns stayed right dere on de farm 'cause it was de only home we knew and no reason to go. I stays dere till I's twenty-seven years ole, den I marries and my husban' rents land. We'uns has ten chillun and sometimes we has to skimp, but we gets on. When my husban' dies fifteen years ago, I comes here. I's allus been too busy tendin' to my 'sponsibilities for to git in de debilmen' and now I's happy, tendin' to my great gran'chile.

United States. Work Projects Administration

JOHN FINNELY

JOHN FINNELY, 86, was born a slave to Martin Finnely, in Jackson Co., Alabama. During the Civil War ten slaves escaped from the Finnely plantation. Their success led John to escape. He joined the Federal Army. John farmed from 1865 until 1917, then moved to Fort Worth, Tex., and worked in packing plants until 1930. He now lives at 2812 Cliff St., Fort Worth, his sole support a $17.00 monthly pension.

"Alabama am de state where I's born and dat 86 year ago, in Jackson County, on Massa Martin Finnely's plantation, and him owns 'bout 75 other slaves 'sides mammy and me. My pappy am on dat plantation but I don't know him, 'cause mammy never talks 'bout him 'cept to say, 'He am here.'

"Massa run de cotton plantation but raises stock and feed and corn and cane and rations for de humans sich as us. It am diff'rent when I's a young'un dan now. Den, it am needful for to raise everything yous need, 'cause dey couldn't 'pend on factory made goods. Dey could buy shoes and clothes and sich, but we'uns could make dem so much cheaper.

"What we'uns make? 'Low me to 'collect a li'l. Let's see, we'uns make shoes, and leather and clothes and cloth and grinds de meal. And we'uns cures de meat, preserves de fruit and make 'lassas and brown sugar. All de harness for de mules and de hosses is make and de carts for haulin'. Am dat all? Oh, yes, massa make peach brandy and him have he own still.

"De work am 'vided 'twixt de cullud folks and us allus have certain duties to do. I's am de field hand and befo' I's old 'nough for to do dat, dey has me help with de chores and errands.

"Us have de cabins of logs with one room and one door and one window hole and bunks for sleepin'. But no cookin' am done dere. It am done in de cookhouse by de cooks for all us niggers and we'uns eats in de eatin' shed. De rations am good, plain victuals and dere plenty of it and 'bout twict a week dere somethin' for treat. Massa sho' am 'ticular 'bout feedin', 'specially for de young'uns in de nursery. You see, dere am de nursery for sich what needs care while dere mammies am a-workin'.

"Massa feed plenty and him 'mand plenty work. Dat cause heap of trouble on dat plantation, 'cause whippin's am given and hard ones, too. Lots of times at de end of de day I's so tired I's couldn't speak for to stop de mule, I jus' have to lean back on de lines.

"Dis nigger never gits whupped 'cept for dis, befo' I's a field hand. Massa use me for huntin' and use me for de gun rest. When him have de long shot I bends over and puts de hands on de knees and massa puts his gun on my back for to git de good aim. What him kills I runs and fotches and carries de game for him. I turns de squirrels for him and dat disaway: de squirrel allus go to udder side from de hunter and I walks 'round de tree and de squirrel see me and go to massa's side de tree and he gits de shot.

"All dat not so bad, but when he shoots de duck in de water and I has to fotch it out, dat give me de worryment. De fust time he tells me to go in de pond I's skeert, powe'ful skeert. I takes off de shirt and pants but there I stands. I steps in de water, den back 'gain, and 'gain. Massa am gittin' mad. He say, 'Swim in dere and git dat duck.' 'Yes, sar, massa,' I says, but I won't go in dat water till massa hit me some licks. I couldn't never git use to bein' de water dog for de ducks.

"De worst whuppin' I seed was give to Clarinda. She hits massa with de hoe 'cause he try 'fere with her and she try stop him. She am put on de log and give 500 lashes. She am over dat log all day and when dey takes her off, she am limp and act deadlike. For a week she am in de bunk. Dat whuppin' cause plenty trouble and dere lots of arg'ments 'mong de white folks 'round dere.

"We has some joyments on de plantation, no parties or dancin' but we has de corn huskin' and de nigger fights. For de corn huskin' everybody come to one place and dey gives de prize for findin' de red ear. On massa's place de prize am brandy or you am 'lowed to kiss de gal you calls for. While us huskin' us sing lots. No, no, I's not gwine sing any dem songs, 'cause I's forgit and my voice sound like de bray of de mule.

"De nigger fights am more for de white folks' joyment but de slaves am 'lowed to see it. De massas of plantations match dere niggers 'cording to size and bet on dem. Massa Finnely have one nigger what weighs 'bout 150 pounds and him powerful good fighter and he like to fight. None lasts long with him. Den a new niggers comes to fight him.

"Dat fight am held at night by de pine torch light. A ring am made by de folks standin' 'round in de circle. Deys 'lowed to do anything with dey hands and head and teeth. Nothin' barred 'cept de knife and de club. Dem two niggers gits in de ring and Tom he starts quick, and dat new nigger he starts jus' as quick. Dat 'sprise Tom and when dey comes togedder it like two bulls—kersmash—it sounds like dat. Den it am hit and kick and bite and butt anywhere and any place for to best de udder. De one on de bottom bites knees or anything him can do. Dat's de way it go for half de hour.

"Fin'ly dat new nigger gits Tom in de stomach with he knee and a lick side de jaw at de same time and down go Tom and de udder nigger jumps on him with both feets, den straddle him and hits with right, left, right, left, right, side Tom's head. Dere Tom lay, makin' no 'sistance. Everybody am saysin', 'Tom have met he match, him am done.' Both am bleedin' and am awful sight. Well, dat new nigger 'laxes for to git he wind and den Tom, quick like de flash, flips him off and jump to he feet and befo' dat new nigger could git to he feet, Tom kicks him in de stomach, 'gain and 'gain. Dat nigger's body start to quaver and he massa say, 'Dat 'nough.' Dat de closest Tom ever come to gittin' whupped what I's know of.

"I becomes a runaway nigger short time after dat fight. De war am started den for 'bout a year, or somethin' like dat, and de Fed'rals am north of us. I hears de niggers talk 'bout it, and 'bout runnin' 'way to freedom. I thinks and thinks 'bout gittin' freedom, and I's gwine run off. Den I thinks of de patter rollers and what happen if dey cotches me off de place without de pass. Den I thinks of some joyment sich as de corn huskin' and de fights and de singin' and I don't know what to do. I tells you one singin' but I can't sing it:

> "'De moonlight, a shinin' star,
> De big owl hootin' in de tree;
> O, bye, my baby, ain't you gwineter sleep,
> A-rockin' on my knee?

"'Bye, my honey baby,
A-rockin' on my knee,
Baby done gone to sleep,
Owl hush hootin' in de tree.

"'She gone to sleep, honey baby sleep,
A-rockin' on my, a-rockin' on my knee.'

"Now, back to de freedom. One night 'bout ten niggers run away. De next day we'uns hears nothin', so I says to myself, 'De patters don't cotch dem.' Den I makes up my mind to go and I leaves with de chunk of meat and cornbread and am on my way, half skeert to death. I sho' has de eyes open and de ears forward, watchin' for de patters. I steps off de road in de night, at sight of anything, and in de day I takes to de woods. It takes me two days to make dat trip and jus' once de patters pass me by. I am in de thicket watchin' dem and I's sho' dey gwine search dat thicket, 'cause dey stops and am a-talkin' and lookin' my way. Dey stands dere for a li'l bit and den one comes my way. Lawd A-mighty! Dat sho' look like de end, but dat man stop and den look and look. Den he pick up somethin' and goes back. It am a bottle and dey all takes de drink and rides on. I's sho' in de sweat and I don't tarry dere long.

"De Yanks am camped nere Bellfound and dere's where I gits to. 'Magine my 'sprise when I finds all de ten runaway niggers am dere, too. Dat am on a Sunday and on de Monday, de Yanks puts us on de freight train and we goes to Stevenson, in Alabama. Dere, us put to work buildin' breastworks. But after de few days, I gits sent to de headquarters at Nashville, in Tennessee.

"I's water toter dere for de army and dere am no fightin' at first but 'fore long dey starts de battle. Dat battle am a 'sperience for me. De noise am awful, jus' one steady roar of de guns and de cannons. De window glass in Nashville am all shoke out from de shakement of de cannons. Dere am dead mens all over de ground and lots of wounded and some cussin' and some prayin'. Some am moanin' and dis and dat one cry for de water and, God A-mighty, I don't want any sich 'gain. Dere am men carryin' de dead off da field, but dey can't keep up with de cannons. I helps bury de dead and den I gits sent to Murphysboro and dere it am jus' de same.

"You knows when Abe Lincoln am shot? Well, I's in Nashville den and it am near de end of de war and I am standin' on Broadway Street talkin' with de sergeant when up walk a man and him shakes hands with me and says, 'I's proud to meet a brave, young fellow like you.' Dat man am Andrew Johnson and him come to be president after Abe's dead.

"I stays in Nashville when de war am over and I marries Tennessee House in 1875 and she died July 10th, 1936. Dat make 61 year dat we'uns am togedder. Her old missy am now livin' in Arlington Heights, right here in Fort Worth and her name am Mallard and she come from Tennessee, too.

"I comes here from Tennessee 51 year ago and at fust I farms and den I works for de packin' plants till dey lets me out, 'cause I's too old for to do 'nough work for dem.

"I has eight boys and three girls, dat make eleven chillen, and dey makin' scatterment all over de country so I's alone in my old age. I has dat $17.00 de month pension what I gits from de State.

"Dat am de end of de road.

SARAH FORD

SARAH FORD, whose age is problematical, but who says, "I's been here for a long time," lives in a small cottage at 3151 Clay St., Houston, Texas. Born on the Kit Patton plantation near West Columbia, Texas, Aunt Sarah was probably about fifteen years old when emancipated. She had eleven children, the first born during the storm of 1875, at East Columbia, in which Sarah's mother and father both perished.

"Law me, you wants me to talk 'bout slave times, and you is cotched me 'fore I's had my coffee dis mornin', but when you gits old as I is, talk is 'bout all you can do, so 'scuse me whilst I puts de coffee pot on de fire and tell you what I can.

"Now, what I tells you is de truth, 'cause I only told one little lie in my whole life and I got cotched in it and got whipped both ways. Oh, Lawd, I sho' never won't forget dat, mama sho' was mad. Mama sends me over to Sally Ann, the cow woman, to get some milk and onions. I never did like to borrow, so I comes back with the milk and tell mama Sally Ann say she ain't got no onions for no Africans. Dat make mamma mad and she goes tell dat Sally Ann Somethin'. She brung back de onions and say, 'You, Sarah, I'll larn you not to tell no lie.' She sho' give me a hidin'.

"Now, I tells you 'bout de plantation what I's born on. You all knows where West Columbia is at? Well, dat's right where I's born, on Massa Kit Patton's Plantation, dey calls it de Hogg place now." (Owned by children of Gov. Will Hogg.)

"Mamma and papa belongs to Massa Kit and mama born there, too. Folks called her 'Little Jane,' 'cause she's no bigger'n nothing.

"Papa's name was Mike and he's a tanner and he come from Tennessee and sold to Massa Kit by a nigger trader. He wasn't all black, he was part Indian. I heared him say what tribe, but I can't 'lect now. When I's growed mama tells me lots of things. She say de white folks don't let de slaves what works in de field marry none, dey jus' puts a man and breedin' woman together like mules. Iffen the women don't like the man it don't make no diff'rence, she better go or dey gives her a hidin'.

"Massa Kit has two brothers, Massa Charles and Massa Matt, what lives at West Columbia. Massa Kit on one side Varney's Creek and Massa Charles on de other side. Massa Kit have a African woman from Kentucky for he wife, and dat's de truth. I ain't sayin' iffen she a real wife or not, but all de slaves has to call her 'Miss Rachel.' But iffen a bird fly up in de sky it mus' come down sometime, and Rachel jus' like dat bird, 'cause Massa Kit go crazy and die and Massa Charles take over de plantation and he takes Rachel and puts her to work in de field. But she don't stay in de field long, 'cause Massa Charles puts her in a house by herself and she don't work no more.

"If us gits sick us call Mammy Judy. She de cook and iffen you puts a sugar barrel 'long side her and puts a face on dat barrel, you sho' can't tell it from her, she so round and fat. Iffen us git real sick dey calls de doctor, but iffen it a misery in de stomach or jus' de flux, Mammy Judy fix up some burr vine tea or horsemint tea. Dey de male burr vine and de female burr vine and does a woman or gal git de misery, dey gives 'em de female tea, and does a man, or boy chile git it, dey gives him de male vine tea.

"Scuse me while I pours me some coffee. It sho' do fortify me. You know what us drink for coffee in slave times? Parched meal, and it purty good iffen you know's how.

"Us don't have much singin' on our place, 'cepting at church on Sunday. Law me, de folks what works in de fields feels more like cryin' at night. Us chillen used to sing dis:

> "'Where you goin', buzzard,
> Where you gwine to go?
> I's goin' down to new ground,
> For to hunt Jim Crow.'

"I guess Massa Charles, what taken us when Massa Kit die, was 'bout de same as all white folks what owned slaves, some good and some bad. We has plenty to eat—more'n I has now—and plenty clothes and shoes. But de overseer was Uncle Big Jake, what's black like de rest of us, but he so mean I 'spect de devil done make him overseer down below long time ago. Dat de bad part of Massa Charles, 'cause he lets Uncle Jake whip de slaves so much dat some like my papa what had spirit was all de time runnin' 'way. And even does your stomach be full, and does you have plenty clothes, dat bullwhip on your bare hide make you forgit de good part, and dat's de truth.

"Uncle Big Jake sho' work de slaves from early mornin' till night. When you is in de field you better not lag none. When its fallin' weather de hands is put to work fixin' dis and dat. De woman what has li'l chillen don't have to work so hard. Dey works 'round de sugar house and come 11 o'clock dey quits and cares for de babies till 1 o'clock, and den works till 3 o'clock and quits.

"Massa Charles have a arbor and dat's where we has preachin'. One day old Uncle Law preachin' and he say, 'De Lawd make everyone to come in unity and on de level, both white and black.' When Massa Charles hears 'bout it, he don't like it none, and de next mornin' old Uncle Jake git Uncle Law and put him out in de field with de rest.

"Massa Charles run dat plantation jus' like a factory. Uncle Cip was sugar man, my papa tanner and Uncle John Austin, what have a wooden leg, am shoemaker and make de shoes with de brass toes. Law me, dey heaps of things go on in slave time what won't go on no more, 'cause de bright light come and it ain't dark no more for us black folks. Iffen a nigger run away and dey cotch him, or does he come back 'cause he hongry, I seed Uncle Jake stretch him out on de ground and tie he hands and feet to posts so he can't move none. Den he git de piece of iron what he call de 'slut' and what is like a block of wood with little holes in it, and fill de holes up with tallow and put dat iron in de fire till de grease sizzlin' hot and hold it over de pore nigger's back and let dat hot grease drap on he hide. Den he take de bullwhip and whip up and down, and after all dat throw de pore nigger in de stockhouse and chain him up a couple days with nothin' to eat. My papa carry de grease scars on he back till he die.

"Massa Charles and Uncle Jake don't like papa, 'cause he ain't so black, and he had spirit, 'cause he part Indian. Do somethin' go wrong and Uncle Big Jake say he gwine to give papa de whippin', he runs off. One time he gone a whole year and he sho' look like a monkey when he gits back, with de hair standin' straight on he head and he face. Papa was mighty good to mama and me and dat de only reason he ever come back from runnin' 'way, to see us. He knowed he'd git a whippin' but he come anyway. Dey never could cotch papa when he run 'way, 'cause he part Indian. Massa Charles even gits old Nigger Kelly what lives over to Sandy Point to track papa with he dogs, but papa wade in water and dey can't track him.

"Dey knows papa is de best tanner 'round dat part de country, so dey doesn't sell him off de place. I 'lect papa sayin' dere one place special where he hide, some German folks, de name Ebbling, I think. While he hides dere, he tans hides on de sly like and dey feeds him, and lots of mornin's when us open de cabin door on a shelf jus' 'bove is food for mama and me, and sometime store clothes. No one ain't see papa, but dere it is. One time he brung us dresses, and Uncle Big Jake heered 'bout it and he sho' mad 'cause he can't cotch papa, and he say to mama he gwine to whip her 'less she tell him where papa is. Mama say, 'Fore God, Uncle Jake, I don't know, 'cause I ain't seed him since he run 'way,' and jus' den papa come 'round de corner of de house. He save mama from de whippin' but papa got de hot grease drapped on him like I told you Uncle Big Jake did, and got put in de stockhouse with shackles on him, and kep' dere three days, and while he in dere mama has de goin' down pains and my sister, Rachel, is born.

"When freedom come, I didn't know what dat was. I 'lect Uncle Charley Burns what drive de buggy for Massa Charles, come runnin' out in de yard and holler, 'Everybody free, everybody free,' and purty soon sojers comes and de captain reads a 'mation. And, Law me, dat one time Massa Charley can't open he mouth, 'cause de captain tell him to shut up, dat he'd do de talkin'. Den de captain say, 'I come to tell you de slaves is free and you don't have to call nobody master no more.' Well, us jus' mill 'round like cattle do. Massa Charley say iffen us wants to stay he'll pay us, all 'cepting my papa. He say, 'You can't stay here, 'cause you is a bad 'fluence.'

"Papa left but come back with a wagon and mules what he borrows and loads mama and my sister and me in and us go to East Columbia on de Brazos river and settles down. Dey hires me out and us have our own patch, too, and dat de fust time I ever seed any money. Papa builds a cabin and a corn crib and us sho' happy, 'cause de bright light done come and dey no more whippin's.

"One night us jus' finish eatin supper and someone holler 'Hello.' You know who it was holler? Old Uncle Big Jake. De black folks all hated him so dey wouldn't have no truck with him and he ask my papa could he stay. Papa didn't like him none, 'cause he done treat papa so bad, but de old devil jus' beg so hard papa takes him out to de corn crib and fix a place for him and he stay most a month till he taken sick and died.

"I stays with papa and mama till I marries Wes Ford and I shows you how de Lawd done give and take away. Wes and I has a cabin by ourselves near papa's and I is jus' 'bout to have my first baby. De wind start blowin' and it git harder and harder and right when its de worst de baby comes. Dat in '75 and whilst I havin' my baby, de wind tear de cabin where mama and papa is to pieces and kilt 'em. My sister Rachel was with me so she wasn't kilt.

"Well, I can't complain, 'cause de Lawd sho' been good to me. Wes and all 'cept four my chillen is dead now. I has six boys and five gals. But de ones what is alive is pore like dey mammy. But I praises de Lawd 'cause de bright light am turned on.

MILLIE FORWARD

MILLIE FORWARD, about 95 years old, was born a slave of Jason Forward, in Jasper, Texas. She has spent her entire life in that vicinity, and now lives in Jasper with her son, Joe McRay. Millie has been totally blind for fifteen years and is very deaf.

"Us used to live 'bout four mile east of Jasper, on de Newton Highway. I reckon I's 'bout 95 year old and I thank de Lawd I's been spared dis long. Some my old friends say I's 100, and maybe I is. I feels like it.

"I's born in Alabama and mammy have jus' got up when de white folks brung us out west. Pappy's name Jim Forward and mammy name Mary. Dey lef' pappy in Alabama, 'cause he 'long to 'nother massa.

"My massa name Jason Forward and he own a lot of slaves. I work as housegirl and wait on de white women. Missus name am Sarah Ann Forward. Massa Jason he own de fust drugstore in Jasper. I have de sister, Susan, and de brudder, Tom. Massa and missus, dey treats us jes' like dey us pappy and mammy.

"Us have more to eat den dan us do now. Us never was knowed to be without meat, 'cause massa raise plenty pigs. Us have fish and possum and coon and deer and everything. Us have biscuits and cake, too, but us drink bran meal coffee. Massa and missus has no chillen and dey give us feast and have biscuits and cake. Befo' Christmas massa go to town and buy all kinds candy and toys and say, 'Millie, you go out on de gallery and holler and tell Santy not forgit fill your stockin' tonight.' I holler loud as I can and nex' mornin' my stockin' chock full.

"After freedom come, us stays right on with massa and missus. Massa teach school for us at night. Us learn A B C and how spell cat and dog and nigger. Den one day he git cross and scold us and us didn't go back to school no more. Us didn't have sense 'nough to know he tryin' do us good.

"Den missus git sick, but she dat good, dat when one cullud man git drown in de 'river she sit up in bed and make he shroud and massa feed de whole crowd de two days dey findin' de body. After him bury, missus git worse and say, 'Jason, pull down de blind, de light am so bright it hurt my eyes.' Den a big, white crane come light on de chimney and us chillen throw rocks at him, but he jes' shake he head and ruffle he feathers and still sit dere. I tells you dat de light of Heaven shinin' on missus and iffen ever a woman went dere, she did. She de bes' white woman I ever see. De day she die, I cry all day.

"When de sojers go to de war, every man take a slave to wait on him and take care he camp and cook. After de end of war, when de sojers gwine home, don't know how many Yankees pass through Jasper, but it sound like de roar of a storm comin'. Every officer have he wife ridin' right by he side. Dey wives come to go home with dem. Dey thousands bluecoats, ridin' two abreas'.

"When I young lady, dey have tourn'ments at Adrian Ryall place west of Jasper and de one what cotch de hoss bridle de most times, git crown queen. I gits to be queen every time. I looks like a queen now, doesn't I?

"After us git free a long time, me and Susan and Tom us work hard and buy us de black land farm. But de deed git' burnt up and us didn't know how to git 'nother deed, and a young nigger call McRay, he come foolin' 'round me and makin' love to me. He find out us don't have no deed no more and he claim dat farm and take it 'way from us and leave me with li'l baby boy what I names Joe Millie McRay. But never 'gain. I never marries.

"Us done work in de cotton field and wash many a long day to pay for dat farm. But dat boy growed to be a good man and I live with him and he wife now. And he boy, Bob, am better still. He jes' work so hard and he buy fine li'l home in Jasper and marry de bes' gal, mos' white. Dey have nice fur'ture and gas and lights and everything.

"Dey treat us purty good in slavery days but I'd rather be free, but it purty hard to be blind so long and most deaf, too, but I thank de Lawd I's not sufferin'. I gits de pension of 'leven dollars a month. I's so old I can't 'member much, only sometime, things comes to me I thought I forgot long time ago. I's had it purty hard to pay for de farm and den have it stoled from me when I's old and blind, but de good Lawd, he know all 'bout it and we all got to stand 'fore de jedgment some day soon.

LOUIS FOWLER

LOUIS FOWLER, 84, was born a slave to Robert Beaver, in Macon Co., Georgia. Fowler did not take his father's name, but that of his stepfather, J. Fowler. After he was freed, Louis farmed for several years, then worked in packing plants in Fort Worth, Tex. He lives at 2706 Holland St., Fort Worth.

"Dis cullud person am 84 years old and I's born on de plantation of Massa Robert Beaver, in old Georgia. He owned my mammy and 'bout 50 slaves. Now, 'bout my pappy, I lets you judge. Look at my hair. De color am red, ain't it? My beard am red and my eyes is brown and my skin am light yellow. Now, who does you think my pappy was? You don't know, of course, but I knows, 'cause on dat plantation am a man dat am over six feet tall and his hair as red as a brick.

"My mammy am married to a man named Fowler and he am owned by Massa Jack Fowler, on de place next to ours. Our place am middlin' big and fixed first class. He has first-class quarter for us cullud folks. De cabins am two and some three rooms and dey all built of logs and chinked with a piece of wood and daubed with dirt to fill de cracks. De way we'uns fix dat dirt am take de clay or gumbo which am sticky when it am wet. Dat dirt am soaked with water till it stick together and den hay or straw am mixed with it. When sich mud am daubed in de cracks it stay and dem cabins am sho' windproof and warm.

"De treatment am good and Massa Beaver have de choice name 'mong he neighbors for bein' good to he niggers. No work on Sunday, no work on Saturday evenin's. Dem times was for de cullud folks to do for demselves. Massa Beaver have it fixed disaway, he 'low each family a piece of groun' and dey can raise what dey likes.

"De rations am measure out and de massa allus 'low plenty of meat and we has wheat flour. Mos' de niggers don't have wheat flour, but massa raises de wheat and we gits it. We kin have 'lasses and brown sugar but one thing we'uns has to watch am de waste, 'cause massa won't stand for dat.

"De meat am cured with de hick'ry wood smoke and if you could git jus' one taste dat ham and bacon you'd never eat none of this nowadays meat. It sho' have a dif'rent taste.

"We makes de cloth and de wool and I could card and spin and weave 'fore I's big 'nough to work in de field. My mammy larned me to help her. We makes dye from de bark of walnut and de cherry and red oak trees, and some from berries but what dey is I forgit. Iffen we'uns wants clay red, we buries de cloth in red clay for a week and it takes on de color. Den we soaks de cloth in cold salt water and it stays colored.

"Massa builded a log church house for we'uns cullud folks for to go to God. Dat nigger named Allen Beaver am de preacherman and de leader in all de parties, 'cause him can play de fiddle. No, Allen am not educated, but can he preach a pow'ful sermon. O, Lawd! He am inspire from de Lawd and he preached from his heartfelt.

"Dere am only one time dat a nigger gits whupped on dat plantation and dat am not given by massa but by dem patterrollers. Massa don't gin'rally 'low dem patterrollers whup on his place, and all de niggers from round dere allus run from de patterrollers onto massa's land and den dey safe. But in dis 'ticlar case, massa make de 'ception.

"'Twas nigger Jack what dey chases home and he gits under de cabin and 'fused to come out. Massa say, 'In dis case I gwine make 'ception, 'cause dat Jack he am too unreas'able. He allus chasin' after some nigger wench and not satisfied with de pass I give. Give him 25 lashes but don't draw de blood or leave de marks.'

"Well, sar, it am de great sight to see Jack git dat whuppin'. Him am skeert, but dey ain't hurtin' him bad. Massa make him come out and dey tie him to a post and he starts to bawl and beller befo' a lick am struck. Say! Him beg like a good fellow. It am, 'Oh, massa, massa, Oh, massa, have mercy, don't let 'em whup me. Massa, I won't go off any more.' De patterrollers gives him a lick and Jack lets out a yell dat sounds like a mule bray and twice as loud.

"Dere used to be a patterroller song what sent like dis:

> "Up 'de hill and down de holler
> White man cotch nigger by de collar
> Dat nigger run and dat nigger flew,
> Dat nigger tore he shirt in two.'

"Well, while dey's whuppin' dat nigger, Jack, he couldn't run and he couldn't tear he shirt in two, but he holler till he tear he mouth in two. Jack say he never go off without de pass 'gain and he kept he word, too.

"De big doin's am on Christmas Day and de massa have present for each cullud person. Dey am little things and I laughs when I thinks of them, but de cullud folks sho' 'joy dem and it show massa's heart am right. For de chillen it am candy and for de women, a pin or sich, and for de men, a knife or sich. On dat day, preacherman Allen sho' have de full heart, and he preach and preach.

"But de war starts and it not so happy on massa's place and 'fore long he two sons goes to dat war. De massa show worryment 'cause dey fightin' here and dere and den come de day when dey fight right nex' to de massa's place. It am in de field next to we'uns and de two boys, young Charley and he brother, Bob, am in de fight. It am for sev'ral days de army am a-marchin' to de field and gittin' ready for de battle. Durin' dat time, de two boys comes home for a spell every day. Early one mornin' de shootin' starts and it am not much at first but it ain't long till it am a steady thunder and it keep up all day.

"De missy am walkin' in de yard and den go in de house and out 'gain. She am a-twistin' her hands and cryin'. She keeps sayin', 'Dey sho' gits kilt, my poor babies.' De massa talk to her to quiet her. Dat help me, too, 'cause I sho' skeert. Nobody do much work dat day, but stand round with quiverments and when dey talk, dey voice quiver. Why, even de buildin's quivered. Every once in de while, dere am an extry roar. Dat de cannon and every time I heered it, I jumps. I's sent to git de eggs and have 'bout five dozen in de basket, holdin' it in front of me with my two hands. All a sudden, one of dem extry shoots comes and down dis nigger kid go and my head hits into de basket. Dere I is, eggs oozin' all round me and I so skeert and fussed up I jus' lays and kicks. I wants to scream but I can't for de eggs in my mouth. To dis day I thinks of dat battle every time I eats eggs.

"De nex' day after de battle am over, mos' us cullud folks goes to de field. Some of 'em buries de dead, and I hears 'em tell how in de low places de blood stand like water and de bodies all shoot to pieces.

"Massa's sons not kilt and am de missy glad! She have allus colored folks come to de house and make us kneel down and she thank de Lawd for savin' her sons. Dey even go to other places and fights, but dey comes home after de war am over.

"Surrender come and massa tells us we can stay or go and if we stay he pay us wages or we works on shares. Some go and some stay. Mammy and me goes to de Fowler place with my stepfather and we share crops for three year.

"I stays with dem till I's 18 and den I gits married. Dat in 1871 and my wife died in 1928 and we'uns have four chillen. All dat time I's farmed till 'bout 30 year ago when I works in de packin' plant here in Fort Worth. I works dere 20 years and den dey say I's too old and since den I works at de odd jobs till 'bout five years ago.

"Since I's quit work at de packin' plant it am hard for dis cullud person. I soon uses up my savin's and den I's gone hongry plenty times. My chillen am old and dey havin' de hard time, too. My friends helps me a little and I gits de pension, but it am only $3.00 a month and, course, dat ain't 'nough.

"After all dese years I's worked and 'haved, I never thinks I comes to where I couldn't git 'nough to eat. I's am wishful for de Lawd to call me to jedgment.

United States. Work Projects Administration

80

CHRIS FRANKLIN

CHRIS FRANKLIN, 82, was born a slave of Judge Robert J. Looney, in Bossier Parish, Louisiana. Chris now lives in Beaumont, Texas, and supports himself by gardening and yard work. He is thrifty and owns his own home.

"Yes, suh, dis is Chris Franklin. I signs my name C.C. Franklin, dat for Christopher Columbus Franklin. I's born in Bossier Parish, up in Louisiana, jes' twenty-five miles de other side of Shreveport. I's born dere in 1855, on Christmas Day, but I's raise up in Caddo Parish. Old massa move over dere when I 'bout a year old.

"Old massa name Robert J. Looney and he a jedge and lawyer. He have a boy name R.J., Jr., but I's talkin' 'bout de old head, de old 'riginal. De missy, her name Lettie Looney. He weren't no farmer, jes' truck farm to raise de livin' for he household and slaves. He didn't have over a half dozen growed up slaves. Course, dey rears a lot of young'uns.

"My pappy's name Solomon Lawson. He 'long to Jedge Lawson, what live near us. When freedom come, he done take de name Sol Franklin, what he say am he pappy's name.

"Jedge Looney have de ord'nary frame house. Dey 'bout six, seven rooms in it, all under one roof. De dinin' room and cook room wasn't built off to deyself, like mos' big houses. It was a raise house, raise up on high pillars and dey could drive a hoss and buggy under it. He live on de Fairview Road.

"Us slaves all live in one big slave cabin, built out of plank. It built sort-a like de 'partment house. Dey four rooms and each fam'ly have one room. Dey have a lamp and a candle for our comfort. It jes' a li'l, ord'nary brass lamp. Dey used to make 'em out of wax and tallow. Dey raise dere own bees and when dey rob de bee gums dey strain de honey and melt de wax with tallow to make it firmer. Dey tie one end de wick on de stick 'cross de mold and put in de melted wax and tallow.

"Dey have a table and benches, too. But a chair de rare thing in a cabin. Dey make some with de split hick'ry or rawhide bottom. Dey have hay mattress. De tickin' am rice sacks. Us have mud chimney. Dey fix sticks like de ladder and mix mud and moss and grass in what dey calls 'cats'. Dey have rock backs, and, man, us have a sho' 'nough fire in 'em. Put a stick long as me and big as a porch post in dat fireplace. In cold weather dat last all day and all night.

"When de parents workin' in de field, somebody look after de chillen. De nannies come in and nuss dem when time come. De white folks never put on 'strictions on de chillen till dey twelve, fourteen years old. Dey all wear de straight-cut slip. Dey give de li'l gals de slip dress and li'l panties. In wintertime dey give de boy's de li'l coat and pants and shoes, but no drawers or unnerwear. Dey give dem hard russet shoes in wintertime. Dey have brass toes. Dey plenty dur'ble. In summertime us didn't see no shoe.

"Massa Looney jes' as fine de man as ever make tracks. Christmas time come, he give 'em a few dollars and say go to the store and buy what us want. He give all de li'l nigger chillen gif's, jes' like he own. He git de jug of whiskey and plenty eggs and make de big eggnog for everybody. He treat us cullud folks jes' like he treat he own fam'ly. He never take no liquor 'cept at Christmas. He give us lots to eat at Christmas, too.

"Sometime old missy come out and call all de li'l niggers in de house to play with her chillen. When us eat us have de tin plate and cup. Dey give us plenty milk and butter and 'taters and sich. Us all set on de floor and make 'way with dem rations.

"Dey had a li'l church house for de niggers and preachin' in de afternoon, and on into de night lots of times. Dey have de cullud preacher. He couldn't read. He jes' preach from nat'ral wit and what he larn from white folks. De whole outfit profess to be Baptis'.

"De marryin' business go through by what massa say. De fellow git de massa's consen'. Massa mos'ly say yes without waitin', 'cause marryin' mean more niggers for him comin' on. He git de jedge or preacher to marry dem. Iffen de man live on one plantation and de gal on 'nother, he have to git de pass to go see her. Dat so de patterrollers not git him.

"De slaves used to have balls and frolics in dey cabins. But iffen dey go to de frolic on 'nother plantation dey git de pass. Dat so dey can cotch runaway niggers. I never heared of stealin' niggers, 'cept dis-a-way. Sometime de runaway nigger git fifty or hundred miles away and show up dere as de stray slave. Dat massa where he show up take care of him so long, den lay claim to him. Dat call harborin' de nigger.

"Dey lots of places where de young massas has heirs by nigger gals. Dey sell dem jes' like other slaves. Dat purty common. It seem like de white women don't mind. Dey didn't 'ject, 'cause dat mean more slaves.

"Sometimes de white folks has de big deer drive. Dem and de niggers go down in de bottoms to drive deers up. Dey rid big, fine hosses and start de deers runnin'. Dey raise dere own dogs. Massa sho' careful 'bout he hounds. He train dem good and treat dem good, too. He have somethin' cook reg'lar for dem. Dey hunts foxes and wolves and plenty dem kinds varmints.

"I seen sojers' by de thousands. When 'mancipation come out massa come to de back door with de paper and say, 'Yous free.' He furnish dem with all dey needs and give dem part de crop. He 'vide up de pig litters and such 'mongst dem. He give dem de start. Den after two, three year he commence takin' out for dere food and boots and clothes and sich.

"De night de pusson die dey has de wake and sing and pray all night long. Dey all very 'ligious in dere profession. Dey knock off all work so de slaves can go to de buryin'.

"De white folks 'low dem to have de frolic with de fiddle or banjo or windjammer. Dey dances out on de grass, forty or fifty niggers, and dem big gals nineteen year old git out dere barefoot as de goose. It jes' de habit of de times, 'cause dey all have shoes. Sometimes dey call de jig dance and some of dem sho' dance it, too. De prompter call, 'All git ready.' Den he holler, 'All balance,' and den he sing out, 'Swing you pardner,' and dey does it. Den he say, 'First man head off to de right,' and dere dey goes. Or he say, 'All promenade,' and dey goes in de circle. One thing dey calls, 'Bird in de Cage.' Three joins hands round de gal in de middle, and dance round her, and den she git out and her pardner git in de center and dey dance dat way awhile.

"After freedom dey have de log cabin schoolhouse. De first teacher was de cullud women name Mary Chapman. I near wore out dat old blueblack speller tryin' to larn A B C's.

"I leaves Caddo Parish in 1877 for Galveston, and leaves dere on de four mast schooner for Leesburg and up de Calcasieu River. Den I goes to de Cameron Parish and in 1879 I comes to Beaumont. I marries Mandy Watson in 1882 and she died in 1932. Us never have no chillen but 'dopts two. Us marry in de hotel dinin'-room, 'cause I's workin' for de hotel man, J.B. Goodhue. De Rev. Elder Venable, what am da old cullud preacher, marries us. I didn't git marry like in slavery time, I's got a great big marriage certif'cate hangin' on de wall of my house.

"I 'longs to several lodges, de Knights of Labor and de Knights of Honor and de Pilgrims. I never hold no office. I's jes' de bench member. I's a member of de Live Lake Missionary Baptist Church.

"I's got de big house of my own, on de corner of Roberts Avenue and San Antonio street. After my wife die, I gits de man to come and live dere with me. Dat's all I knows.

ORELIA ALEXIE FRANKS

ORELIA ALEXIE FRANKS was born on the plantation of Valerian Martin, near Opelousas, Louisiana. She does not know her age, but thinks she is near ninety. Her voice has the musical accent of the French Negro. She has lived in Beaumont, Texas, many years.

"I's born on Mr. George Washington's birthday', the twenty-second of February but I don't know what year. My old massa was Valerian Martin and he come from foreign country. He come from Canada and he Canada French. He wife name Malite Guidry. Old massa a good Catholic and he taken all the li'l slave chillen to be christen. Oh, he's a Christian massa and I used to be a Catholic but now I's a Apostolic, but I's christen in St. Johns Catholic Church, what am close to Lafayette, where I's born.

"My pa name Alexis Franks and he was American and Creole. My ma name Fanire Martin and I's raise where everybody talk French. I talks American but I talks French goodest.

"Old massa he big cane and cotton farmer and have big plantation and raise everything, and us all well treat. Dey feed us right, too. Raise big hawg in de pen and raise lots of beef. All jes' for to feed he cullud folks.

"Us quarters out behind de big house and old massa come round through de quarters every mornin' and see how us niggers is. If us sick he call nuss. She old slavery woman. She come look at 'em. If dey bad sick dey send for de doctor. Us house all log house. Dey all dab with dirt 'tween de logs. Dey have dirt chimney make out of sticks and dab with mud. Dey [Transcriber's Note: unfinished sentence at end of page] "Lots of time we eat coosh-coosh. Dat make out of meal and water. You bile de water and salt it, den put in de cornmeal and stir it and bile it. Den you puts milk or clabber or syrup on it and eat it.

"Old massa have de graveyard a purpose to bury de cullud folks in. Dey have cullud preacher. Dey have funeral in de graveyard. Dat nigger preacher he a Mef'dist.

"Old massa son-in-law, he overseer. He 'low nobody to beat de slaves. Us li'l ones git spank when we bad. Dey put us 'cross de knee and spank us where dey allus spank chillen.

"Christmas time dey give big dinner. Dey give all de old men whiskey. Everybody have big time.

"Dey make lots of sugar. After dey finish cookin' de sugar dey draw off what left from de pots and give it to us chillen. Us have candy pullin'.

"Dey weave dey own cloth. Us have good clothes. Dey weave de cloth for make mattress and stuff 'em with moss. Massa sho' believe to serve he niggers good. I see old massa when he die. Us see old folks cry and us cry, too. Dey have de priest and burn de candles. Us sho' miss old massa.

"I see lots of sojers. Dey so many like hair on your head. Dey Yankees. Dey call 'em bluejackets. Dey a fight up near massa's house. Us climb in tree for to see. Us hear bullets go 'zoom' through de air 'round dat tree but us didn't know it was bullets. A man rid up on a hoss and tell massa to git us pickaninnies out dat tree or dey git kilt. De Yankees have dat battle and den sot us niggers free.

"Old massa, he de kind man what let de niggers have dey prayer-meetin'. He give 'em a big cabin for dat. Shout? Yes, Lawd! Sing like dis:

>"'Mourner, fare you well,
>Gawd 'Mighty bless you,
>Till we meets again.'

>"Us sings 'nother song:
>"'Sinner blind,
>Johnnie, can't you ride no more?
>Sinner blind.
>Your feets may be slippin'
>Your soul git lost.
>Johnnie, can't you ride no more?
>Yes, Lawd,
>Day by day you can't see,
>Johnnie, can't you ride no more?
>Yes, Lawd.'"

ROSANNA FRAZIER

ROSANNA FRAZIER was born a slave on the Frazier plantation in Mississippi. She does not remember her masters given name, nor does she know her age, although from her memories of various events during the Civil War, she believes she is close to ninety, at least. Rosanna is blind and bedridden, and is cared for by friends in a little house in Pear Orchard Negro Settlement, in Beaumont, Texas.

"My mammy was a freeborn woman named Viny Frazier and she come from a free country. She was on her way to school when dey stoled her, when she de young gal. De spec'lator gang stoled her and brung her and sold her in Red River, in Mississippi. Missy Mary, she buy her. Missy Mary married den to one man named Pool and she have two boys call Josh and Bill. After dat man die, she marry Marse Frazier.

"My daddy name Jerry Durden and after I's born they brings us all to Texas, but my daddy belong to de Neylands, so we loses him. My white folks moves to a big plantation close to Woodville, in Tyler County, and Marse Frazier have de store and plenty of stock. He come first from Georgia.

"All us little chillen, black and white, play togedder and Marse Frazier, he raise us. His chillen call Sis and Texana and Robert and John. Marse Frazier he treat us nice and de other white folks calls us 'free niggers', and wouldn't 'low us on dere places. Dey 'fraid dere niggers git dissatisfy with dey own treatment. Sho's you born, iffen one of us git round dem plantations, dey jus' cut us to pieces with de whip. Some of dem white folks sho' was mean, and dey work de niggers all day in de sun and cut dem with de whip, and sho' done 'em up bad. Dat on other places, not on ours.

"Marse Frazier, he didn't work us too hard and give Saturday and Sunday off. He's all right and give good food. People sho' would rare off from him, 'cause he too good. He was de Methodist preacher and furnish us church. Sometimes he has camp meeting and dey cook out doors with de skillicks. Sometimes he has corn shucking time and we has hawg meat and meal bread and whiskey and eggnog and chicken.

"De books he brung us didn't do us no good, 'cause us wouldn't larn nothin'. Us too busy playin' and huntin' good berries in de wood, de huckleberry and grape and muscadine and chinquapins. All dis time de war was fixin' and I seed two, three soldiers round spyin'. When peace 'clared missy's two boys come back from de war. We stays with Marse Frazier two year and den I goes and gits married to de man call Baker.

"I done been blind like dis over 40 year. One Sunday I stay all night with a man and he wife and I was workin' as woodchopper on de Santa Fe route up Beaumont to Tyler County. After us git up and I starts 'way, I ain't gone but 15, 16 yard when I hear somethin' say, 'Rose, you done somethin' you ain't ought.' I say, 'No, Lawd, no.' Den de voice say, 'Somethin' gwine happen to you,' and de next mornin' I's blind as de bat and I ain't never seed since.

"Some try tell me snow or sweat or smoke de reason. Dat ain't de reason. Dey a old, old, slowfooted somethin' from Louisiana and dey say he de conjure man, one dem old hoodoo niggers. He git mad at me de last plum-ripenin' time and he make up powdered rattlesnake dust and pass dat through my hair and I sho' ain't seed no more.

"Dat not de onliest thing dem old conjure men do. Dey powder up de rattle offen de snake and tie it up in de little old rag bag and dey do devilment with it. Day git old scorpion and make bad medicine. Dey git dirt out de graveyard and dat dirt, after dey speak on it, would make you go crazy.

"When dey wants conjure you, dey sneak round and git de hair combin' or de finger or toenail, or anything natural 'bout your body, and works de hoodoo on it.

"Dey make de straw man or de clay man and dey puts de pin in he leg and you leg gwineter git hurt or sore jus' where dey puts de pin. Iffen dey puts de pin through de heart you gwineter die and ain't nothin' kin save you.

"Dey make de charm to wear round de neck or de ankle and dey make de love powder, too, out de love vine, what grow in de woods. Dey biles de leaves and powders 'em. Dey sho' works, I done try 'em.

PRISCILLA GIBSON

PRISCILLA GIBSON is not sure of her age, but thinks she was born about 1856, in Smith County, Mississippi, to Mary Puckett and her Indian husband. They belonged to Jesse Puckett, who owned a plantation on the Strong River. Priscilla now lives in Jasper, Texas.

"Priscilla Gibson is my name, and I's bo'n in Smith County, way over in Mis'ippi, sometime befo' de War. I figger it was 'bout 1856, 'cause I's old enough to climb de fence and watch dem musterin' in de troops when de war began. Dey tol' me I's nine year ole when de War close, but dey ain' sure of dat, even. My neighbor, Uncle Bud Adams, he 83, and I's clippin' close at he heels.

"Mammy's name was Mary Puckett, but I never seed my father as I knows of. Don' know if he was a whole Injun or part white man. Never seed but one brother and his name was Jake. Dey took him to de War with de white boys, to cook and min' de camp and he took pneumony and die.

"Massa's name was Jesse Puckett, and Missus' name Mis' Katie. Dey hab big fam'ly and dey live in a big wooden-beam house with a big up-stair'. De house was right on de highway from Raleigh to Brandon, with de Strong River jis' below us. Dey took in and 'commadated travelers 'cause dey warn' hotels den.

"Massa have hunner's of acres. You could walk all day and you never git offen his lan'. An' he have gran' furniture and other things in de house. I kin remember dem, 'cause I use' to he'p 'round de house, run errands and fan Mis' Katie and sich. I 'members chairs with silk coverin's on 'em and dere was de gran' lights, big lamps with de roses on de shades. And eve'ywhere de floors with rugs and de rugs was pretty, dey wasn' like dese thin rugs you sees nowadays. No, ma'am, dey has big flowers on 'em and de feets sinks in 'em. I useter lie down on one of dem rugs in Mis' Katie's room when she's asleep and I kin stop fannin.'

"Massa Puckett was tol'able good to de slaves. We has clothes made of homespun what de nigger women weaved, and de little boys wo' long-tail shirts, with no pants till they's grown. Massa raised sheep and dey make us wool clothes for winter, but we has no shoes.

"De white folks didn' larn us read and write but dey was good to us 'cep' when some niggers try to run away and den dey whips 'em hard. We has plenty to eat and has prayer meetin's with singin' and shoutin', and we chilluns played marbles and jump de rope.

"After freedom come all lef' but me 'cause Missus say she have me boun' to her till I git my age. But I's res'less one night and my sister, Georgy Ann, come see me, and I run off with her, but dey never comes after me. I was scart dey would, 'cause I 'membered 'bout our neighbor, ole Means, and his slave, Sylvia, and she run away and was in de woods, and he'd git on de hoss, take de dogs and set 'em on her, and let dem bite her and tear her clothes.

GABRIEL GILBERT

GABRIEL GILBERT was born in slavery on the plantation of Belizare Brassard, in New Iberia Parish, Louisiana. He does not know his age, but appears to be about eighty. He has lived in Beaumont, Texas, for sixteen years.

"My old massa was Belizare Broussard. He was my mom's massa. He had a big log house what he live in. De places 'tween de logs was fill with dirt. De quarters de slaves live in was make out of dirt. Dey put up posties in de ground and bore holes in de posts and put in pickets 'cross from one post to the other. Den dey build up de sides with mud. De floor and everything was dirt. Dey had a schoolhouse built for de white chillen de same way. De cullud chillen didn't have no school.

"Dem was warm healthy houses us grew up in. Dey used to raise better men den in dem houses dan now. My pa name was Joseph Gilbert. He old massa was Belleau Prince.

"I didn't know what a store was when I was growin' up. Us didn't have store things like now. Us had wooden pan and spoon dem times. I never see no iron plow dem days. Nothin' was iron on de plow 'cept de share. I tell dese youngsters, 'You in hebben now from de time I come up.' When a man die dem days, dey use de ox cart to carry de corpse.

"Massa have 'bout four hundred acres and lots of slaves. He raise sugar cane. He have a mill and make brown sugar. He raise cotton and corn, too. He have plenty stock on de place. He give us plenty to eat. He was a nice man. He wasn't brutish. He treat he slaves like hisself. I never 'member see him whip nobody. He didn't 'low no ill treatment. All de folks round he place say he niggers ruint and spoiled.

"De li'l white folks and nigger folks jus' play round like brudder and sister and us all eat at de white table. I slep' in de white folks house, too. My godfather and godmother was rich white folks. I still Cath'lic.

"I seed sojers but I too li'l to know nothin' 'bout dem. Dey didn't worry me a-tall. I didn't git close to de battle.

"My mammy weave cloth out cotton and wool. I 'member de loom. It go 'boom-boom-boom.' Dat de shuttle goin' cross. My daddy, he de smart man. I'll never be like him long as I live in dis world. He make shoes. He build house. He do anything. He and my mammy neither one ever been brutalize'.

"De first work I done was raisin' cotton and sugar cane and sweet and Irish 'taters. I used to cook sugar.

"I marry on twenty-second of February. My wife was Medora Labor. She been dead thirty-five year now. I never marry no second woman. I love my wife so much I never want nobody else. Us had six chillen. Two am livin'.

"Goin' back when I a slave, massa have a store. When de priest come dey hold church in dat store. Old massa have sev'ral boys. Dey went after some de slave gals. Dey have chillen by dem. Dem gals have dere cabins and dere chillen, what am half white.

"After while dem boys marry. But dey allus treat dey chillen by de slave womens good. Dey white wife treat dem good, too, most like dey dere own chillen.

"Old massa have plenty money. Land am only two bits de acre. Some places it cost nothing. Dey did haulin' in ox-carts. A man what had mules had something extra.

"Us have plenty wild game, wild geese and ducks. Fishin' am mighty good. Dey was 'gaters, too. I seed dem bite a man's arm off.

"If a slave feelin' bad dey wouldn't make him work. My uncle and my mammy dey never work nothing to speak of. Dey allus have some kind complaint. Ain't no tellin' what it gwine be, but you could 'low something ailin' dem!

"I 'member dey a white man. He had a gif'. I don't care what kind of animal, a dog or a hoss, dat man he work on it and it never leave you or you house. If anybody have toothache or earache he take a brand new nail what ain't never work befo' and work dat round you tooth or ear. Dat break up de toothache or earache right away. He have li'l prayer he say. I don't know what it was.

"I's seed ghosties. I talk with dem, too. Sometimes dey like people. Sometimes dey like animal, maybe white dog. I allus feel chilly when dey come round me. I talk with my wife after she dead. She tell me, 'Don't you forgit to pray.' She say dis world corrupt and you got to fight it out."

MATTIE GILMORE

MATTIE GILMORE lives in a little cabin on E. Fifth Avenue, in Corsicana, Texas. A smile came to her lips, as she recalled days when she was a slave in Mobile, Alabama. She has no idea how old she is. Her master, Thomas Barrow, brought his slaves to Athens, Texas, during the Civil War, and Mattie had two children at that time, so she is probably about ninety.

"I's born in Mobile, Alabama, and I don't have no idea when. My white folks never did tell me how old I was. My own dear mammy died 'fore I can remember and my stepma didn't take no time to tell me nothin'. Her name was Mary Barrow and papa's name was Allison Barrow, and I had sisters, Rachel and Lou and Charity, and a brother, Allison.

"My master sold Rachel when she was jus' a girl. I sho' did cry. They put her on a block and sold her off. I heared they got a thousand dollars for her, but I never seed her no more till after freedom. A man named Dick Burdon, from Kaufman County, bought her. After freedom I heared she's sick and brung her home, but she was too far gone.

"We lived in a log house with dirt floors, warm in winter but sho' hot in summer, no screens or nothin', jus' homemade doors. We had homemade beds out of planks they picked up around. Mattresses nothin', we had shuck beds. But, anyway, you takes it, we was better off den dan now.

"I worked in the fields till Rachel was sold, den tooken her place, doin' kitchen work and fannin' flies off de table with a great, long limb. I liked dat. I got plenty to eat and not so hot. We had jus' food to make you stand up and work. It wasn't none the good foolish things we has now. We had cornbread and blackeyed peas and beans and sorghum 'lasses. Old master give us our rations and iffen dat didn't fill us up, we jus' went lank. Sometimes we had possum and rabbits and fish, iffen we cotched dem on Sunday. I seed Old Missy parch coffee in a skittle, and it good coffee, too. We couldn't go to the store and buy things, 'cause they warn't no stores hardly.

"When dey's hoein' cotton or corn, everybody has to keep up with de driver, not hurry so fast, but workin' steady. Some de women what had suckin' babies left dem in de shade while dey worked, and one time a big, bald eagle flew down by one dem babies and picked it up and flew away with it. De mama couldn't git it and we never heared of dat baby 'gain.

"I 'member when we come from Mobile to Texas. By time we heared de Yankees was comin' dey got all dere gold together and Miss Jane called me and give me a whole sack of pure gold and silver, and say bury it in de orchard. I sho' was scart, but I done what she said. Dey was more gold in a big desk, and de Yanks pulled de top of dat desk and got de gold. Miss Jane had a purty gold ring on her finger and de captain yanked it off. I said, 'Miss Jane, is dey gwine give you ring back?' All she said was, 'Shet you mouth,' and dat's what I did.

"Dat night dey digs up de buried gold and we left out. We jus' traveled at night and rested in daytime. We was scart to make a fire. Dat was awful times. All on de way to de Mississip', we seed dead men layin' everywhere, black and white.

"While we's waitin' to go cross de Mississip' a white man come up and asks Marse Barrow how many niggers he has, and counts us all. While we's waitin' de guns 'gins to go boom, boom, and you could hear all dat noise, it so close. When we gits on de boat it flops dis way and dat scart me. I sho' don't want to see no more days like dat one, with war and boats.

"We fixes up a purty good house and quarters and gits settled up round Athens. And it ain't so long 'fore a paper come make us free. Some de slaves laughin' and some cryin' and it a funny place to be. Marse Barrow asks my stepma to stay cook and he'd pay her some money for it. We stayed four or five years. Marse Barrow give each he slaves somethin' when dey's freed. Lots of master put dem out without a thing. But de trouble with most niggers, dey never done no managin' and didn't know how. De niggers suffered from de war, iffen dey did git freedom from it.

"I's already married de slave way in Mobile and had three chillen. My husband died 'fore war am over and I marries Las Gilmore and never has no more chillen. I has no livin' kinfolks I knows of. When we come here Las done any work he could git and bought this li'l house, but I can't pay taxes on it, but, sho', de white folks won't put me out. I done git my leg cut off in a train wreck, so I can't work, and I's too old, noways. I don't has no idea how old I is.

ANDREW GOODMAN

ANDREW GOODMAN, 97, was born a slave of the Goodman family, near Birmingham, Alabama. His master moved to Smith County, Texas, when Andrew was three years old. Andrew is a frail, kindly old man, who lives in his memories. He lives at 2607 Canton St., Dallas, Texas.

"I was born in slavery and I think them days was better for the niggers than the days we see now. One thing was, I never was cold and hongry when my old master lived, and I has been plenty hongry and cold a lot of times since he is gone. But sometimes I think Marse Goodman was the bestes' man Gawd made in a long time.

"My mother, Martha Goodman, 'longed to Marse Bob Goodman when she was born, but my paw come from Tennessee and Marse Bob heired him from some of his kinfolks what died over there. The Goodmans must have been fine folks all-a-way round, 'cause my paw said them that raised him was good to they niggers.

"Old Marse never 'lowed none of his nigger families separated. He 'lowed he thought it right and fittin' that folks stay together, though I heard tell of some that didn't think so.

"My Missus was just as good as Marse Bob. My maw was a puny little woman that wasn't able to do work in the fields, and she puttered round the house for the Missus, doin' little odd jobs. I played round with little Miss Sallie and little Mr. Bob, and I ate with them and slept with them. I used to sweep off the steps and do things, and she'd brag on me and many is the time I'd git to noddin' and go to sleep, and she'd pick me up and put me in bed with her chillun.

"Marse Bob didn't put his little niggers in the fields till they's big 'nough to work, and the mammies was give time off from the fields to come back to the nursin' home to suck the babies. He didn't never put the niggers out in bad weather. He give us something to do, in out of the weather, like shellin' corn and the women could spin and knit. They made us plenty of good clothes. In summer we wore long shirts, split up the sides, made out of lowerings—that's same as cotton sacks was made out of. In winter we had good jeans and knitted sweaters and knitted socks.

"My paw was a shoemaker. He'd take a calfhide and make shoes with the hairy sides turned in, and they was warm and kept your feet dry. My maw spent a lot of time cardin' and spinnin' wool, and I allus had plenty things.

"Life was purty fine with Marse Bob. He was a man of plenty. He had a lot of land and he built him a big log house when he come to Texas. He had sev'ral hundred head of cattle and more than that many hawgs. We raised cotton and grain and chickens and vegetables, and most anything anybody could ask for. Some places the masters give out a peck of meal and so many pounds of meat to a family for them a week's rations, and if they et it up that was all they got. But Marse Bob allus give out plenty, and said, 'If you need more you can have it, 'cause ain't any going to suffer on my place.'

"He built us a church, and a old man, Kenneth Lyons, who was a slave of the Lyon's family nearby, used to git a pass every Sunday mornin' and come preach to us. He was a man of good learnin' and the best preacher I ever heard. He baptised in a little old mudhole down back of our place. Nearly all the boys and gals gits converted when they's 'bout twelve or fifteen year old. Then on Sunday afternoon, Marse Bob larned us to read and write. He told us we oughta git all the learnin' we could.

"Once a week the slaves could have any night they want for a dance or frolic. Mance McQueen was a slave 'longing on the Dewberry place, what could play a fiddle, and his master give him a pass to come play for us. Marse Bob give us chickens or kilt a fresh beef or let us make 'lasses candy. We could choose any night, 'cept in the fall of the year. Then we worked awful hard and didn't have the time. We had a gin run by horsepower and after sundown, when we left the fields, we used to gin a bale of cotton every night. Marse allus give us from Christmas Eve through New Year's Day off, to make up for the hard work in the fall.

"Christmas time everybody got a present and Marse Bob give a big hawg to every four families. We had money to buy whiskey with. In spare time we'd make cornshuck horse collars and all kinds of baskets, and Marse bought them off us. What he couldn't use, he sold for us. We'd take post oak and split it thin with drawin' knives and let it git tough in the sun, and then weave it into cotton baskets and fish baskets and little fancy baskets. The men spent they money on whiskey, 'cause everything else was furnished.

We raised our own tobacco and hung it in the barn to season, and a'body could go git it when they wanted it.

"We allus got Saturday afternoons off to fish and hunt. We used to have fish fries and plenty game in them days.

"Course, we used to hear 'bout other places where they had nigger drivers and beat the slaves. But I never did see or hear tell of one of master's slaves gittin' a beatin'. We had a overseer, but didn't know what a nigger driver was. Marse Bob had some nigger dogs like other places, and used to train them for fun. He'd git some the boys to run for a hour or so and then put the dogs on the trail. He'd say, 'If you hear them gittin' near, take to a tree.' But Marse Bob never had no niggers to run off.

"Old man Briscoll, who had a place next to ours, was vicious cruel. He was mean to his own blood, beatin' his chillen. His slaves was afeared all the time and hated him. Old Charlie, a good, old man who 'longed to him, run away and stayed six months in the woods 'fore Briscoll cotched him. The niggers used to help feed him, but one day a nigger 'trayed him, and Briscoe put the dogs on him and cotched him. He made to Charlie like he wasn't goin' to hurt him none, and got him to come peaceful. When he took him home, he tied him and beat him for a turrible long time. Then he took a big, pine torch and let burnin' pitch drop in spots all over him. Old Charlie was sick 'bout four months and then he died.

"Marse Bob knowed me better'n most the slaves, 'cause I was round the house more. One day he called all the slaves to the yard. He only had sixty-six then, 'cause he had 'vided with his son and daughter when they married. He made a little speech. He said, 'I'm going to a war, but I don't think I'll be gone long, and I'm turnin' the overseer off and leavin' Andrew in charge of the place, and I wants everything to go on, just like I was here. Now, you all mind what Andrew says, 'cause if you don't, I'll make it rough on you when I come back home.' He was jokin', though, 'cause he wouldn't have done nothing to them.

"Then he said to me, 'Andrew, you is old 'nough to be a man and look after things. Take care of Missus and see that none the niggers wants, and try to keep the place going.'

"We didn't know what the war was 'bout, but master was gone four years. When Old Missus heard from him, she'd call all the slaves and tell us the news and read us his letters. Little parts of it she wouldn't read. We never heard of him gittin' hurt none, but if he had, Old Missus wouldn't tell us, 'cause the niggers used to cry and pray over him all the time. We never heard tell what the war was 'bout.

"When Marse Bob come home, he sent for all the slaves. He was sittin' in a yard chair, all tuckered out, and shuck hands all round, and said he's glad to see us. Then he said, 'I got something to tell you. You is jus' as free as I is. You don't 'long to nobody but you'selves. We went to the war and fought, but the Yankees done whup us, and they say the niggers is free. You can go where you wants to go, or you can stay here, jus' as you likes.' He couldn't help but cry.

"The niggers cry and don't know much what Marse Bob means. They is sorry 'bout the freedom, 'cause they don't know where to go, and they's allus 'pend on Old Marse to look after them. Three families went to get farms for they-selves, but the rest just stay on for hands on the old place.

"The Federals has been comin' by, even 'fore Old Marse come home. They all come by, carryin' they little budgets, and if they was walkin' they'd look in the stables for a horse or mule, and they jus' took what they wanted of corn or livestock. They done the same after Marse Bob come home. He jus' said, 'Let them go they way, 'cause that's what they're going to do, anyway.' We was scareder of them than we was of the debbil. But they spoke right kindly to us cullud folks. They said, 'If you got a good master and want to stay, well, you can do that, but now you can go where you want to, 'cause ain't nobody going to stop you.'

"The niggers can't hardly git used to the idea. When they wants to leave the place, they still go up to the big house for a pass. They jus' can't understand 'bout the freedom. Old Marse orMissus say, 'You don't need no pass. All you got to do is jus' take you foot in you hand and go.'

"It seem like the war jus' plumb broke Old Marse up. It wasn't long till he moved into Tyler and left my paw runnin' the farm on a halfance with him and the niggers workers. He didn't live long, but I forgits jus' how long. But when Mr. Bob heired the old place, he 'lowed we'd jus' go 'long the way his paw has made the trade with my paw.

"Young Mr. Bob 'parently done the first rascality I ever heard of a Goodman doin'. The first year we worked for him we raised lots of grain and other things and fifty-seven bales of cotton. Cotton was fifty-two cents a pound and he shipped it all away, but all he ever gave us was a box of candy and a sack of store tobacco and a sack of sugar. He said the 'signment done got lost. Paw said to let it go, 'cause we had allus lived by what the Goodman had said.

"I got married and lived on the old place till I was in my late fifties. I had seven chillun, but if I got any livin' now, I don't know where they is now. My paw and maw got to own a little piece of land not far from the old place, and paw lived to be 102 and maw 106. I'm the last one of any of my folks.

"For twenty years my health ain't been so good, and I can't work even now, though my health is better'n in the past. I had hemorraghes. All my folks died on me, and it's purty rough on a old man like me. My white folks is all dead or I wouldn't be 'lowed to go hongry and cold like I do, or have to pay rent.

AUSTIN GRANT

AUSTIN GRANT came to Texas from Mississippi with his grandfather, father, mother and brother. George Harper owned the family. He raised cotton on Peach Creek, near Gonzales. Austin was hired out by his master and after the war his father hired him out to the Riley Ranch on Seco Creek, above D'hanis. He then bought a farm in the slave settlement north of Hondo. He is 89 or 90 years old.

"I'm mixed up on my age, I'm 'fraid, for the Bible got burned up that the master's wife had our ages in. She told me my age, which would make me 89, but I believe I come nearer bein' 91, accordin' to the way my mother figured it out.

"I belonged to George Harper, he was Judge Harper. The' was my father, mother and two boys. He brought us from Mississippi, but I don' 'member what part they come from. We settled down here at Gonzeles, on Peach Creek, and he farmed one year there. Then he moved out here to Medina County, right here on Hondo Creek. I dont 'member how many acres he had, but he had a big farm. He had at least eight whole slave families. He sold 'em when he wanted money.

"My mother's name was Mary Harper and my father's name was Ike Harper, and they belonged to the Harpers, too. You know, after they was turned loose they had to name themselves. My father named himself Grant and his brother named himself Glover, and my grandfather was Filmore. They had some kin' of law you had to git away from your boss' name so they named themselves.

"Our house we had to live in, I tell you we had a tough affair, a picket concern, you might say no house a-tall. The beds was one of your own make; if you knowed how to make one, you had one, but of course the chillen slept on the floor, patched up some way.

"We went barefooted in the summer and winter, too. You had to prepare that for yourself, and if you didn' have head enough to prepare for yourself, you went without. I don' see how they done as well as they done, 'cause some winters was awful cold, but I always said the Lawd was with 'em.

[Handwritten Note: 'used']

"We didn' have no little garden, we never had no time to work no garden. When you could see to work, you was workin' for him. Ho! You didn' know what money was. He never paid you anything, you never got to see none. Some of the Germans would give the old ones a little piece of money, but the chillen, pshaw! They never got to see nothin.'

"He was a pretty good boss. You didn' have to work Sunday and part of Saturday and in the evenin', you had that. He fed us good. Sometimes, if you was crowded, you had to work all day Saturday. But usually he give you that, so you could wash and weave cloth or such. He had cullud women there he kep' all the time to weave and spin. They kep' cloth made.

"On Saturday nights, we jes' knocked 'round the place. Christmas? I don' know as I was ever home Christmas. My boss kep' me hired out. The slaves never had no Christmas presents I know of. And big dinners, I never was at nary one. They didn' give us nothin, I tell you, but a grubbin' hoe and axe and the whip. They had co'n shuckin's in them days and co'n shellin's, too. We would shuck so many days and so many days to shell it up.

"We would shoot marbles when we was little. It was all the game the niggers ever knowed, was shootin' marbles.

"After work at nights there wasn't much settin' 'round; you'd fall into bed and go to sleep. On Saturday night they didn' git together, they would jes' sing at their own houses. Oh, yes'm, I 'member 'em singin' 'Run, nigger, run,' but it's too far back for me to 'member those other songs. They would raise up a song when they was pickin' cotton, but I don' 'member much about those songs.

"My old boss, I'm boun' to give him praise, he treated his niggers right. He made 'em work, though, and he whipped 'em, too. But he fed good, too. We had rabbits and possums once in awhile. Hardly ever any game, but you might git a deer sometimes.

"Let 'em ketch you with a gun or a piece of paper with writin' on it and he'd whip you like everything. Some of the slaves, if they ever did git a piece of paper, they would keep it and learn a few words. But they didn' want you to know nothin', that's what, nothin' but work. You would think they was goin' to kill you, he would whip you so if he caught you with a piece of paper. You couldn' have nothin' but a pick and axe and grubbin' hoe.

"We never got to play none. Our boss hired us out lots of times. I don' know what he got for us. We farmed, cut wood, grubbed, anything. I herded sheep and I picked cotton.

"We got up early, you betcha. You would be out there by time you could see and you quit when it was dark. They tasked us. They would give us 200 or 300 pounds of cotton to bring in and you would git it, and if you didn' git it, you better, or you would git it tomorrow, or your back would git it. Or you'd git it from someone else, maybe steal it from their sacks.

"My grandfather, he would tell us things, to keep the whip off our backs. He would say, 'Chillen, work, work and work hard. You know how you hate to be whipped, so work hard!' And of course we chillen tried, but of course we would git careless sometimes.

"The master had a 'black snake'—some called it a 'bull whip,' and he knew how to use it. He whipped, but I don' 'member now whether he brought any blood on me, but he cut the blood outta the grown ones. He didn' tie 'em, he always had a whippin' block or log to make 'em lay down on. They called 500 licks a 'light breshin,' and right on your naked back, too. They said your clothes wouldn' grow but your hide would. From what I heered say, if you run away, then was when they give you a whippin,' prob'bly 1500 or 2000 licks. They'd shore tie you down then, 'cause you couldn' stan' it. Then you'd have to work on top of all that, with your shirt stickin' to your back.

"The overseer woke us up. Sometimes he had a kin' of horn to blow, and when you heered that horn, you'd better git up. He would give you a good whippin' iffen he had to come and wake you up. He was the meanest one on the place, worse'n the boss man.

"The boss man had a nice rock house, and the women didn' work at all.

"I never did see any slaves auctioned off, but I heered of it. My boss he would take 'em there and sell 'em.

"They had a church this side of New Fountain and the boss man 'lowed us to go on Sunday. If any of the slaves did join, they didn' baptize them, as I know of.

"When one of the slaves would die, they would bury 'em on the land there. Reg'lar little cemetery there. Oh, yes, they would have doctors for 'em. If anybody died, they would tell some of the other slaves to dig the grave and take 'em out there and bury 'em. They jes' put 'em in a box, no preachin' or nothin.' But, of course, if it was Sunday the slaves would follow out there and sing. No, if they didn' die on Sunday, you couldn' go; you went to that field.

"If you wanted to go to any other plantation you had to git a pass to go over there, and if you didn' and got caught, you got one of the worst whippins'. If things happened and they wanted to tell 'em on other plantations, they would slip out at night and tell 'em.

"We never heered much about the fightin' or how it was goin.' When the war finally was over, our old boss called us all up and had us to stand in abreast, and he stood on the gallery and he read the verdict to 'em, and said, 'Now, you can jes' work on if you want to, and I'll treat you jes' like I always did.' I guess when he said that they knew what he meant. The' wasn't but one family left with 'im. They stayed about two years. But the rest was just like birds, they jes' flew.

"I went with my father and he hired me out for two years, to a man named Riley, over on the Seco. I did most everythin', worked the field and was house rustler, too. But I had a good time there. After I left 'im, I came to D'Hanis. I worked on a church house they was buildin'. Then I went back to my father and worked for him a long time, freightin' cotton to Eagle Pass. I used horses and mules and hauled cotton and flour and whiskey and things like that.

"I met my wife down on Black Creek, and I freighted two years after we was married. We got married so long ago, but in them days anything would do. You see, these days they are so proud, but we was glad to have anything. I had a black suit to be married in, and a pretty long shirt, and I wore boots. She wore a white dress, but in them days they didn' have black shoes. Yes'm, they had a dance, down here on Black Creek. Danced half the night at her house and two men played the fiddle. Eat? We had everythin' to eat, a barbecued calf and a hog, too, and all kinds of cakes and pies. Drink? Why, the men had whiskey to drink and the women drank coffee. We married about 7 or 8 in the evenin' at her house. My wife's name was Sarah Ann Brackins.

"Did I see a ghost? Well, over yonder on the creek was a ghost. It was a moonlight night and it passed right by me and it never had no head on it a-tall. It almost breshed me. It kep' walkin' right by side of me. I shore saw it and I run like a good fellow. Lots of 'em could see wonnurful sights then and I heered lots of noises, but that's the only ghost I ever seen.

"No, I never knowed nothing 'bout charms. I've seen 'em have a rabbit heel or coon heel for good luck. I seen a woman one time that was tricked, or what I'd call poisoned. A place on her let, it was jes' the shape of these little old striped lizards. It was somethin' they called 'trickin it,' and a person that knowed to trick you would put it there to make you suffer the balance of your days. It would go 'round your leg clear to the hip and be between the skin and the flesh. They called it the devil's work."

JAMES GREEN

JAMES GREEN is half American Indian and half Negro. He was born a slave to John Williams, of Petersburg, Va., became a "free boy", then was kidnapped and sold in a Virginia slave market to a Texas ranchman. He now lives at 323 N. Olive St., San Antonio, Texas.

"I never knowed my age till after de war, when I's set free de second time, and then marster gits out a big book and it shows I's 25 year old. It shows I's 12 when I is bought and $800 is paid for me. That $800 was stolen money, 'cause I was kidnapped and dis is how it come:

"My mammy was owned by John Williams in Petersburg, in Virginia, and I come born to her on dat plantation. Den my father set 'bout to git me free, 'cause he a full-blooded Indian and done some big favor for a big man high up in de courts, and he gits me set free, and den Marster Williams laughs and calls me 'free boy.'

"Then, one day along come a Friday and that a unlucky star day and I playin' round de house and Marster Williams come up and say, 'Delia, will you 'low Jim walk down de street with me?' My mammy say, 'All right, Jim, you be a good boy,' and dat de las' time I ever heared her speak, or ever see her. We walks down whar de houses grows close together and pretty soon comes to de slave market. I ain't seed it 'fore, but when Marster Williams says, 'Git up on de block,' I got a funny feelin', and I knows what has happened. I's sold to Marster John Pinchback and he had de St. Vitus dance and he likes to make he niggers suffer to make up for his squirmin' and twistin' and he the bigges' debbil on earth.

"We leaves right away for Texas and goes to marster's ranch in Columbus. It was owned by him and a man call Wright, and when we gits there I's put to work without nothin' to eat. Dat night I makes up my mind to run away but de nex' day dey takes me and de other niggers to look at de dogs and chooses me to train de dogs with. I's told I had to play I runnin' away and to run five mile in any way and then climb a tree. One of de niggers tells me kind of nice to climb as high in dat tree as I could if I didn't want my body tore off my legs. So I runs a good five miles and climbs up in de tree whar de branches is gettin' small.

"I sits dere a long time and den sees de dogs comin'. When dey gits under de tree dey sees me and starts barkin'. After dat I never got thinkin' of runnin' away.

"Time goes on and de war come along, but everything goes on like it did. Some niggers dies, but more was born, 'cause old Pinchback sees to dat. He breeds niggers as quick as he can, 'cause dat money for him. No one had no say who he have for wife. But de nigger husbands wasn't de only ones dat keeps up havin' chillen, 'cause de marsters and de drivers takes all de nigger gals dey wants. Den de chillen was brown and I seed one clear white one, but dey slaves jus' de same.

"De end of dat war comes and old Pinchback says, 'You niggers all come to de big house in de mornin'. He tells us we is free and he opens his book and gives us all a name and tells us whar we comes from and how old we is, and says he pay us 40 cents a day to stay with him. I stays 'bout a year and dere's no big change. De same houses and some got whipped but nobody got nailed to a tree by de ears, like dey used to. Finally old Pinchback dies and when he buried de lightnin' come and split de grave and de coffin wide open.

"Well, time goes on some more and den Lizzie and me, we gits together and we marries reg'lar with a real weddin'. We's been together a long time and we is happy.

"I 'members a old song like dis:
"'Old marster eats beef and sucks on de bone,
And give us de gristle—
To make, to make, to make, to make,
To make de nigger whistle.'

"Dat all de song I 'member from dose old days, 'ceptin' one more:
"'I goes to church in early morn,
De birds just a-sittin' on de tree—
Sometimes my clothes gits very much worn—
'Cause I wears 'em out at de knee.

"'I sings and shouts with all my might,
To drive away de cold—
And de bells keep ringin' in gospel light,
Till de story of de Lamb am told.'"

O.W. GREEN AND GRANDDAUGHTER

O.W. Green, son of Frank and of Mary Ann Marks, was born in slavery at Bradly Co., Arkansas, June 26, 1859. His owners, the Mobley family, owned a large plantation and two or three thousand slaves. Jack Mobley, Green's young master, was killed in the Civil War, and Green became one of the "orphan chillen." When the Ku Klux Klan became active, the "orphan chillen" were taken to Little Rock, Ark. Later on, Green moved to Del Rio, Texas, where he now lives.

"I was bo'ned in Arkansas. Frank Marks was my father and Mary Ann Marks my mother. She was bo'n on the plantation. I had two brothers.

"I don' 'member de quarters, but dey mus' of had plenty, 'cause dey was two, three thousand slaves on de plantation. All my kin people belonged to Massa Mobley. My grandfather was a millman and dey had one de bigges' grist mills in de country.

"Our Massa was good and we had plenty for to eat. Dere was no jail for slaves on our place but not far from dere was a jail.

"De Ku Klux Klan made everything pretty squally, so dey taken de orphan chillen to Little Rock and kep' 'em two, three years. Dere was lots of slaves in dat country 'round Rob Roy and Free Nigger Bend. Old Churchill, who used to be governor, had a plantation in dere.

"When I was nine years ol' dey had de Bruce and Baxter revolution. 'Twas more runnin' dan fightin'. Bruce was 'lected for governor but Baxter said he'd be governor if he had to run Brooks into de sea.

"My young Massa, Jack Mobley, was killed in de war, is how I come to be one of de orphan chillen.

"While us orphan chillen was at Little Rock dere come a terrible soreness of de eyes. I heard tell 'twas caused from de cholera. Every little child had to take turns about sittin' by de babies or totin' them. I was so blind, my eyes was so sore, I couldn't see. The doctor's wife was working with us. She was tryin' to figure up a cure for our sore eyes, first using one remedy and den another. An old herb doctor told her about a herb he had used on de plantations to cure de slaves' sore eyes. Dey boiled de herb and put hit on our eyes, on a white cloth. De doctor's wife had a little boy about my age. He would play with me, and thought I was about hit. He would lead me around, then he would run off and leave me and see if I could see. One day between 'leven and twelve o'clock—I never will fergit hit—he taken me down to de mess room. De lady was not quite ready to dress my eyes. She told me to go on and come back in a little while. When I got outside I tore dat old rag off of my eyes and throwed hit down. I told the little boy, 'O, I can see you!' He grabbed me by de arm and ran yellin' to his mammy, 'Mama, he can see! Mama, Owen can see!' I neva will fo'git dat word. Dey were all in so a rejoicin', excitable way. I was de first one had his eyes cured. Dey sent de lady to New York and she made plenty of money from her remedy.

"Things sure was turrible durin' de war. Dey just driv us in front of de soldiers. Dere was lots of cholera. We was just bedded together lak hogs. The Ku Klux Klan come behind de soldiers, killin' and robbin'.

"After two or three years in de camp with de orphans, my kin found me and took me home.

"My grandfather and uncle was in de fightin'. My grandfather was a wagon man. De las' trip he made, he come home bringin' a load of dead soldiers to be buried. My grandfather told de people all about de war. He said hit sure was terrible.

"When de war was over de people jus' shouted for joy. De men and women jus' shouted for joy. 'Twas only because of de prayers of de cullud people, dey was freed, and de Lawd worked through Lincoln.

"My old masta was a doctor and a surgeon. He trained my grandmother; she worked under him thirty-seven years as a nurse. When old masta wanted grandmother to go on a special case he would whip her so she wouldn't tell none of his secrets. Grandmother used herbs fo' medicine—black snake root, sasparilla, blackberry briar roots—and nearly all de young'uns she fooled with she save from diarrhea.

"My old masta was good, but when he found you shoutin' he burnt your hand. My grandmother said he burnt her hand several times. Masta wouldn't let de cullud folks have meetin', but dey would go out in de woods in secret to pray and preach and shout.

"I jist picked up enough readin' to read my bible and scratch my name. I went to school one mo'ning and didn't git along wid de teacher so I didn't go no mo'.

"I 'member my folks had big times come Christmas. Dey never did work on Sundays, jist set around and rest. Dey never worked in bad weather. Dey never did go to de field till seven o'clock.

"I married in 1919. I have two step-daughters and one step-son. My step-son lives in San Antonio. I have six step-grandchillen. I was a member of de Baptist church befo' you was bo'n, lady.

ROSA GREEN

Dibble, Fred
Beaumont, Jefferson Co. Dist. #3

ROSA GREEN, 85 years old, was born at Ketchi, Louisiana, but as soon as she was old enough became a housegirl on the plantation of Major "Bob" Hollingsworth at Mansfield, Louisiana. To the best of her knowledge, she was about 13 when the "freedom papers" were read. She had had 13 children by her two husbands, both deceased, and lives with her youngest daughter in Beaumont. Their one-room, unpainted house is one of a dozen unprepossessing structures bordering an alleyway leading off Pine Street. Rosa, a spry little figure, crowned with short, snow-white pigtails extending in various directions, spends most of her time tending her small flowerbeds and vegetable garden. She is talkative and her memory seems quite active.

"When de w'ite folks read de freedom paper I was 13 year old. I jes' lean up agin de porch, 'cause I didn' know den what it was all about. I war'nt bo'n in Texas, I was bo'n in Ketchi, but I was rais' in Manfiel'. Law, yes, I 'member de fight at Manfiel'. My ol' marster tuk all he niggers and lef' at night. Lef' us little ones; say de Yankees could git us effen day wan' to, 'cause we no good no way, and I wouldn' care if dey did git us. Dey put us in a sugar hogshead and give us a spoon to scrape out de sugar. 'Bout de ol' plantation, I work a little w'ile in de fiel'. I didn' know den like I see now. Dese chillen bo'n wid mo' sense now dan we was den. Dey was 'bout ten cullud folks on de place. My ol' marster name Bob Hollingsworth, but dey call 'im Major, 'cause he was a major in de war, not de las' one, but de one way back yonder. Ol' missus work de little ones roun' de house and under de house and kep' ev'yt'ing clean as yo' han'. The ol' marster I thought was de meanes' man de Lawd ever made. Look like he cuss ev'y time he open he mouth. De neighbor w'ite folks, some good, some bad. My work was cleanin' up 'roun de house and nussin' de chillen. Only times I went to church when day tuk us long to min' de chillen. When de battle of Manfiel' was, we didn' git out much. When de Yankees was comin' to Gran' Cane, my w'ite folks dig a big pit and put der meat and flour and all in it and cover it over wid dirt and put wagon loads of pine straw over it. It was 'bout five or six mile to Manfield and 'bout 49 or 50 mile to Shreveport. My ol' marster tuk all he niggers and went off somweres, dey called it Texas, but I didn' know where. De ol'er ones farm. Dey rais' ev'yt'ing dey could put in de groun', dey did. My pa was kirrige(carriage) driver for my ol' missus. He was boss nigger fo' de cullud men when marster wan't right dere. My father jis' stay dere. See, dey free our people in July. Dat leave de whole crop stanin' dere in de fiel'. Dey had to stay dere and take care of de crop. After dat dey commence makin' contraks and bargins. I was 22 years ol' when I marry de fus' time. Both my husban's dead. I had 13 chillen in all.

"De fus' time I went to church, missus tuk me and another gal to min' de chillen. I never heared a preacher befo'. I 'member how de preacher word de hymn:

'Come, ye sinners, po' and needy. Weak and wounded, sick and so'.'

United States. Work Projects Administration

WILLIAM GREEN

WILLIAM GREEN, or "Reverend Bill", as he is call by the other Negroes, was brought to Texas from Mississippi in 1862. His master was Major John

Montgomery. William is 87 years old. He has lived in San Antonio, Texas, for 50 years.

"I is Reverend Bill, all right, but I is 'fraid dat compliment don't belong to me no more, 'cause I quit preachin' in favor of de young men.

"I kin tell you my 'speriences in savin'—mis'ry dat was, is peace dat is. I tells you dis 'spite of bein' alone in de world with no chillun.

"I is raised a slave and 'mancipated in June, but I 'members de old plantation whar I is born. Massa John Montgomery, he owned me, and he went to de war and git kilt. I knowed 'bout de war, though us slaves wasn't sposed to know nothin' 'bout it. I was livin' in Texas then, 'cause Massa John moved over here from Mis'sippi. In dat place niggers was allus wrong, no matter what, but it was better in dis place. We used to think we was lucky to git over here to Texas, and we used to sing a song 'bout it:

> "'Over yonder is de wild-goose nation,
> Whar old missus has sugar plantation—
> Sugar grows sweet but de plantation's sour,
> 'cause de nigger jump and run every hour.
>
> "'I has you all to know, you all to know,
> Dare's light on de shore,
> Says little Bill to big Bill,
> There's a li'l nigger to write and cipher.'

"I don't know what de song meant but we thought we'd git free here in Texas, and we'd git eddicated, and dat's de meanin' of de talk about writin' and cipherin'.

"Well, when I is free I isn't free, 'cause de boss wants me and another boy to stay till we's 21 year old. But old Judge Longworth, he come down dere and dere was pretty near a fight, and he 'splains to us we was free.

"'bout five year after dat I takes up preachin' and I preaches for a long time, and I works on a farm, half and half with de owner. I has a good life, but now I's too old to preach.

United States. Work Projects Administration

PAULINE GRICE

PAULINE GRICE, 81, was born a slave of John Blackshier, who owned her mother, about 150 slaves, 50 slave children, and a large plantation near Atlanta, Georgia. Pauline married Navasota Grice in 1875 and they moved to Texas in 1917. Since her husband's death in 1928 Pauline has depended on the charity of friends, with whom she lives at 2504 Ross Ave., North Fort Worth, Texas.

"White man, dis old cullud woman am not strong. 'Bout all my substance am gone now. De way you sees me layin' on dis bed am what I has to do mos' de time. My mem'randum not so good like 'twas.

"De place I am borned am right near Atlanta, in Georgia, and on dat plantation of Massa John Blackshier. A big place, with 'bout 150 growed slaves and 'bout 50 pickininnies. I doesn't work till near de surrender, 'cause I's too small. But us don't leave Massa John, us go right on workin' for him like 'fore.

"Massa John am de kind massa and don't have whuppin's. He tell de overseer, 'If you can't make dem niggers work without de whup, den you not de man I wants.' Mos' de niggers 'have theyselves and when dey don't massa put dem in de li'l house what he call de jail, with nothin' to eat till deys ready to do what he say. Onct or twict he sell de nigger what won't do right and do de work.

"Us have de cabin what am made from logs but us only sleeps dere. All us cookin' done in de big kitchen. Dere am three women what do dat, and give us de meals in de long shed with de long tables.

"To de bes' of dis nigger's mem'randum, de feed am good. Plenty of everything and corn am de mostest us have. Dere am cornbread and cornmeal mush and corn hominy and corn grits and parched corn for drink, 'stead of tea or coffee. Us have milk and 'lasses and brown sugar, and some meat. Dat all raise on de place. Stuff for to eat and wear, dat am made by us cullud folks and dat place am what dey calls se'f-s'portin'. De shoemaker make all de shoes and fix de leather, too.

"After breakfas' in de mornin' de niggers am gwine here, dere and everywhere, jus' like de big factory. Every one to he job, some a-whistlin', some a-singin'. Dey sings diff'rent songs and dis am one when deys gwine to work:

> "'Old cotton, old corn, see you every morn,
> Old cotton, old corn, see you since I's born.
> Old cotton, old corn, hoe you till dawn,
> Old cotton, old corn, what for you born?'

"Yes, suh, everybody happy on massa's place till war begin. He have two sons and Willie am 'bout 18 and Dave am 'bout 17. Dey jines de army and after 'bout a year, massa jine too, and, course, dat make de missy awful sad. She have to 'pend on de overseer and it warn't like massa keep things runnin'.

"In de old days, if de niggers wants de party, massa am de big toad in de puddle. And Christmas, it am de day for de big time. A tree am fix, and some present for everyone. De white preacher talk 'bout Christ. Us have singin' and 'joyment all day. Den at night, de big fire builded and all us sot 'round it. Dere am 'bout hundred hawg bladders save from hawg killin'. So, on Christmas night, de chillen takes dem and puts dem on de stick. Fust dey is all blowed full of air and tied tight and dry. Den de chillen holds de bladder in de fire and purty soon, 'BANG,' dey goes. Dat am de fireworks.

"Dat all changed after massa go to war. Fust de 'federate sojers come and takes some mules and hosses, den some more come for de corn. After while, de Yankee sojers comes and takes some more. When dey gits through, dey ain't much more tookin' to be done. De year 'fore surrender, us am short of rations and sometime us hongry. Us sees no battlin' but de cannon bang all day. Once, dey bang two whole days 'thout hardly stoppin'. Dat am when missy go tech in de head, 'cause massa and de boys in dat battle. She jus' walk 'round de yard and twist de hands and say, 'Dey sho' git kilt. Dey sho' dead.' Den when extra loud noise come from de cannon, she scream. Den word come Willie am kilt. She gits over it, but she am de diff'rent woman. For her, it am trouble, trouble and more trouble.

"She can't sell de cotton. Dey done took all de rations and us couldn't eat de cotton. One day she tell us, 'De war am on us. De sojers done took de rations. I can't sell de cotton, 'cause of de blockade.' I don't know what am dat blockade, but she say it. 'Now,' she say, 'All you cullud folks born and raise here and us allus been good to you. I can't help it 'cause rations am short and I'll do all I can for you.

Will yous be patient with me?' All us stay dere and holp missy all us could.

"Den massa come home and say, 'Yous gwine be free. Far as I cares, you is free now, and can stay here and tough it through or go where you wants. I thanks yous for all de way yous done while I's gone, and I'll holp you all I can.' Us all stay and it sho' am tough times. Us have most nothin' to eat and den de Ku Klux come 'round dere. Massa say not mix with dat crowd what lose de head, jus' stay to home and work. Some dem niggers on other plantations ain't keep de head and dey gits whupped and some gits kilt, but us does what massa say and has no trouble with dem Klux.

"It 'bout two year after freedom mammy gits marry and us goes and works on shares. I stays with dem till 1875 and den marries Navasota Robert Grice and us live by farmin' till he die, nine year since. 'Bout 20 year since us come here from Georgia and works de truck farm. I has two chillen but dey dead. De way I feels now, 'twon't be long 'fore I goes, too. My friends is good to me and lets me stay with dem.

United States. Work Projects Administration

MANDY HADNOT

MANDY HADNOT, small and forlorn looking, as she lies in a huge, old-fashioned wooden bed, appears very black in contrast to the clean white sheets and a thick mop of snowy wool on her head. She does not know her age, but from her appearance and the details she remembers of her years as slave in the Slade home, near Cold Springs, Texas, she must be very old. She lives in Woodville, Texas, with her husband, Josh, to whom she has been married 13 years.

"I's too small to 'member my father, 'cause he die when I jus' a baby. Dey was my mudder and me and de ole mistus and marster on de plantation. It were mo' jus' a farm, but dey raise us all we need to eat and feed de cows and hosses.

"De earlies' 'membrance I hab is when de ole marster drive into de town for supplies every two weeks. Us place was right near Col' Springs. He was a good man. He treat dis lil' darky jus' like he own chile, 'cause he never hab any chillen of his own. I know 'bout de time he comin' home when he go to town and I wait down by de big gate. Purty soon I see de big ox comin' and see de smoke from de road dust flyin'. Den I know he almos' home and I holler and wave my han' and he holler and wave he han' right back. He allus brung me somethin', jus' like I he own little gal. Sometime he brung me a whistle or some candy or doll or somethin'.

"One Easter he brung me de purties' lil' hat I ever did see. My ole mistus took me to Sunday school with her and I spruce up in dat hat.

"Every Christmas 'fore ole marster die he fix me up a tree out de woods. Dey put popco'n on it to trim it and dey give me sometime a purty dress or shoes and plenty candy and maybe a big, red apple. Dey hab a big san' pile for me to play in, but I never play with any other chillen. My mammy, Emily Budle, she cook and clean up mistus log house cabin. After de ole marster die dey both work in de fiel' and raise plenty vegetables to can and eat. My task was to shell peas and watch and stir de big cookin' pots on de fireplace.

"My mistus hav lots of company. When she come in and say, 'Mandy, shine up de knife and fork and put de polish on de pianny, I allus happy, 'cause I lub to see folks come. Us hab chicken and all kinds of good things. De preacher, he was big, jolly man, he come to de house 'bout one Sunday in every month. Sometime dey brung lil' white chillen to dinner. Den us play

>'Rabbit, rabbit.
>Jump fru' de crack.'

and
>'Kitty, kitty,
>In de corner,
>Meow, meow,
>Run, kitty, run.'

"De ole marster pick me out a lil', gentle hoss named Julie and dat was my very own hoss. It was jus' a common lil' hoss. I uster sneak sugar out de barrel to feed Julie. Dey had a big smokehouse on de farm where dey kep' all kin's of good things like sugar and sich. Dey had fruits of all kin's put up.

"Every mornin' de ole mistus took out de big Bible and hab prayer meetin' for jus' us three. Us never learn read much, tho' she try teach me some. When I's 'bout nine year ole she buy me a purty white dress and took me to jine de church. She was a little, white-hair' woman, what never los' her temper 'bout nothin'. She use' to let me bump on her pianny and didn' say nothin'. She couldn' play de pianny but she kinder hope maybe I could, but I never did learn how.

"When freedom come my mudder and me pay no 'tention to it. Us stay right on de place. Purty soon my mudder die and I jus' took up her shoes. One day I's makin' a bonfire in de yard and ketch my dress on fire. De whol side of my lef' leg mos' bu'n off. Mistus was so lil' she couldn' lif' me but she fin'ly git me to bed. Dere I stay for long, long time, and she wait on me han' and feet. She make linseed poultice and kep' de bu'n grease good. Mos' time she leave all de wo'k stan' in de middle of de floor and read de Bible and pray for me to git heal up and not suffer. She cry right 'long with me when I cry, 'cause I hurt so.

"When I's 16 year ole I want to hab courtin'. Mistus 'low me to hab de boy come right to de big house to see me. He come two mile every Sunday and us go to Lugene Baptist church. Den she hav nice Sunday dinner for both us. She let me go to ice cream supper, too. Dey didn' hab no freezer den, jus' a big pan in some ice. De boys and girls took tu'ns stirrin' de cream. It never git real ha'd but stay kinder slushy. Dey serve cake. Us hav pie supper, too. Whoever git de girl's pie eat it with her.

"My ole mistus she pay me money right 'long after freedom but I too close to spen' any. Den when I 'cide to marry Bob Thomas, she he'p me fix a hope ches'. I buys goods for sheets and table kivers and one nice Sunday set dishes.

"Us marry right in de parlor of de mistus house. De white man preacher marry us and mistus she give me 'way. Ole mistus he'p me make my weddin' dress outta white lawn. I hab purty long, black hair and a veil with a ribbon 'round de fron'. De weddin' feas' was strawberry ice cream and yaller cake. Ole mistus giv me my bedstead, one of her purtiest ones, and de set dishes and glasses us eat de weddin' dinner outta. My husban' gib me de trabblin' dress, but I never use dat dress for three weeks, though, 'cause ole mistus cry so when I hafter leave dat I stay for three weeks after I marry.

"She all 'lone in de big house and I think it break her heart. I ain' been gone to de sawmill town very long when she sen' for me. I go to see her and took a peach pie, 'cause I lub her and I know dat's what she like better'n anything. She was sick and she say, 'Mandy, dis de las' time us gwineter see each other, 'cause I ain' gwineter git well. You be a good girl and try to git through de worl' dat way.' Den she make me say de Lord Prayer for her jus' like she allus make me say it for a night prayer when I lil' gal. I never see her no mo'.

"Me and Bob Thomas and dis husban', Josh, what I marry thirteen year ago, hab 'bout 10 chillen all togedder. Us been lib here many a year. I don' care so much 'bout leavin' dis yearthly home, 'cause I knows I gwineter see de ole mistus up dere and I tell her I allus 'member what she tell me and try lib dat way all time.

WILLIAM HAMILTON

WILLIAM HAMILTON belonged to a slave trader, who left him on the Buford plantation, near Village Creek, Texas. The trader did not return, so the Buford family raised the child with their slaves. William now lives at 910 E. Weatherford St., Ft. Worth, Texas.

"Who I is, how old I is and where I is born, I don't know. But Massa Buford told me how durin' de war a slave trader name William Hamilton, come to Village Creek, where Massa Buford live. Dat trader was on his way south with my folks and a lot of other slaves, takin' 'em somewheres, to sell. He camped by Massa Buford's plantation and asks him, 'Can I leave dis li'l nigger here till I comes back?' Massa Buford say, 'Yes,' and de trader say he'll be back in 'bout three weeks, soon as he sells all the slaves. He mus' still be sellin' 'em, 'cause he never comes back so far and there I am and my folks am took on, and I is too li'l to 'member 'em, so I never knows my pappy and mammy. Massa Buford says de trader comes from Missouri, but if I is born dere I don't know.

"De only thing I 'members 'bout all dat, am dere am lots of cryin' when dey tooks me 'way from my mammy. Dat something I never forgits.

"I only 'members after de war, and most de cullud folks stays with Massa Buford after surrender and works de land on shares. Dey have good times on dat place, and don't want to leave. Day has dances and fun till de Ku Klux org'nizes and den it am lots of trouble. De Klux comes to de dance and picks out a nigger and whups him, jus' to keep de niggers scart, and it git so bad dey don't have no more dances or parties.

"I 'members seein' Faith Baldwin and Jeb Johnson and Dan Hester gittin' whupped by de Klux. Dey wasn't so bad after women. It am allus after dark when dey comes to de house and catches de man and whups him for nothin'. Dey has de power, and it am done for to show dey has de power. It gits so bad round dere, dat de menfolks allus eats supper befo' dark and takes a blanket and goes to de woods for to sleep. Alex Buford don't sleep in de house for one whole summer.

"No one knowed when de Klux comin'. All a-sudden up dey gallops on hosses, all covered with hoods, and bust right into de house. Jus' latches 'stead of locks was used dem days. Dey comes sev'ral times to Alex' house but never cotches him. I'd hear dem comin' when dey hit de lane and I'd holler, 'De Klux am comin'.' It was my job, after dark, listenin' for dem Klux, den I gits under de bed.

"Why dey comes so many times round dere, am 'cause de second time dey comes, Jane Bensom am dere. Jane am lots of woman, wide as de door and tall, and weighs 'bout three hunder pounds. I calls, 'Here comes de Klux,' and makes for under de bed. There am embers in de fireplace and she fills a pail with dem and when de Klux busts in de door she lets dem have de embers in de face, and den out de back door she goes. Two of dem am burnt purty bad. De nex' night back dey comes and asks where Jane am. She 'longs to Massa John Ditto and am so big everybody knows her, but de niggers won't tell on her. She leaves de country fin'ly, but dey comes lookin' for her every night for two months.

"Right over on Massa Ditto's place, am a killin' of a baby by dem Klux. De baby am in de mammy's arms and a bunch of Klux ridin' by takes a shot at de mammy, and it hits de baby and kills it.

"Right after de baby killin', sojers with blue coats comes dere and camps front of Massa Buford's place and pertects de cullud folks. I goes over to dey camp every day and dey gives me lots of good eats.

"De cullud folks has lots of trouble after de war, 'cause dey am ir'rant niggers and gits foolishment in de head. They gits de idea de white folks should give dem land and mules and sich. Over in de valley, Massa Moses owns lots of land and fifty nigger families, and he gives each family a deed to 'bout fifty acres. Some dem cullud folks grandchillen still on dat land, too, de Parkers and Farrows and Nelsons and some others. Den all de other niggers thinks dey should git land, too, but dey don't, and it make dem git foolishment and git in trouble.

"In 1897 I marries Effie Coleman and has no chillens, so I is alone in de world now. I can't do much and lives on de $10.00 de month pension. De white folks lets me live in dis shack for mowin' de lawn, but I worries 'bout when I can't do no more work. It am de awful way to spend you last days.

PIERCE HARPER

PIERCE HARPER, 86, was born on the Subbs plantation near Snow Hill, North Carolina. When eight years old he was sold for $1,150 [Handwritten Note: '?'] to the Harper family, who lived in Snow Hill. After the Civil War, Pierce farmed a small place near Snow Hill and saw many raids of the Klu Klux Klan. He came to Galveston, Texas, in 1877. Pierce attended a Negro school after he was grown, learned to read and write, and is interested in the betterment of his race.

"When you ask me is I Pierce Harper, you kind of 'sprised me. I reckoned everybody know old Pierce Harper. Sister Johnson say to me outside of services last Sunday night, 'Brother Harper, you is de beatines' man I ever seen. You know everybody and everybody know you.' And I said, 'Sister Johnson, dat's 'cause I keep faith with de Lawd. I love de Lawd and my neighbors and de Lawd and my neighbors love me.' Dat's what my old mother told me 'way back in slavery, before I was ever sold. But here I is talking 'bout myself when you want to hear me talk 'bout slavery. Let's see, now.

"I was born way back in 1851 in North Carolina, on Mr. Subbs' plantation, clost to Snow Hill, which was the county seat. My daddy was a field hand and my mother worked in the fields, too, right 'longside my daddy, so she could keep him lined up. The master said that Calisy, that my mother, was the best fieldhand he had, and Calvin, that my daddy, was the laziest. My mother used to say he was chilesome.

"Then when I was eight years old they sold me. The market place was in Snow Hill on the public square near the jailhouse. It was jus' a little stand built out in the open with no top on it, that the slaves stood on to get sold while the white folks auctioned 'em off. I was too little to get on the stand, so they had to hold me up and Mr. Harper bought me for $1,100. [Handwritten Note: '?'] That was cheap for a boy.

"He lived in a brick house in town and had two-three slaves 'sides me. I run errands and kept the yard clean, things a little boy could do. They didn't have no school for slaves and I never learned to read and write till after freedom. After I was sold, they let me go visit my mother once a year, on Sunday morning, and took me back at night.

"The masters couldn't whip the slaves there. The law said in black and white no master couldn't whip no slave, no matter what he done. When a slave got bad they took him to the county seat and had him whipped. One day I seen my old daddy get whipped by the county and state 'cause he wouldn't work. They had a post in the public square what they tied 'em to and a man what worked for the county whipped 'em.

"After he was whipped my daddy run away to the north. Daddy come by when I was cleanin' the yard and said, 'Pierce, go 'round side the house, where nobody can't see us.' I went and he told me goodbye, 'cause he was goin' to run away in a few days. He had to stay in the woods and travel at night and eat what he could find, berries and roots and things. They never caught him and after he crossed the Mason-Dixon line he was safe.

"There used to be a man who raised bloodhounds to hunt slaves with. I seen the dogs on the trail a whole day and still not catch 'em. Sometimes the slave made friends with the dogs and they wouldn't let on if they found him. Three dogs followed one slave the whole way up north and he sold them up there.

"I heered 'em talk about some slaves what run barefooted in cold weather and you could trail 'em by blood in the snow and ice where they hurt their feet.

"Most of the time the master gave us castor oil when we were sick. Some old folks went in the woods for herbs and made medicine. They made tea out of 'lion's tongue' for the stomach and snake root is good for pains in the stomach, too. Horse mint breaks the fever. They had a vermifuge weed.

"I seed a lot of Southern soldiers and they'd go to the big house for something to eat. Late in '63 they had a fight at a place called Kingston, only 12 miles from our place, takin' how the jacks go. We could hear the guns go off when they was fightin'. The Yankees beat and settled down there and the cullud folks flocked down on them and when they got to the Yankee lines they was safe. They went in droves of 25 or 50 to the Yankees and they put 'em to work fightin' for freedom. They fit till the war was over and a lot of 'em got kilt. My mother and sister run away to the Yankees and they paid 'em big money to wash for 'em.

"When peace come they read the 'mancipation law to the cullud people and they stayed up half the night at Mr. Harper's, singing and shouting. They spent that night singin' and shoutin'. They wasn't slaves no more. The master had to give 'em a half or third of what he made. Our master parceled out some land to 'em and told 'em to work it their selves and some done real well. They got hosses that the soldiers had turned loose to die, and fed them and took good care of 'em and they got good stock that way. Cotton was twenty and thirty cents a pound then.

"After us cullud folks was 'sidered free and turned loose, the Klu Klux broke out. Some cullud people started to farmin', like I told you, and gathered the old stock. If they got so they made good money, and had a good farm, the Klu Klux would come and murder 'em. The gov'ment builded school houses and the Klu Klux went to work and burned 'em down. They'd go to the jails and take the cullud men out and knock their brains out and break their necks and throw 'em in the river.

"There was a cullud man they taken, his name was Jim Freeman. They taken him and destroyed his stuff and him, 'cause he was making some money. Hung him on a tree in his front yard, right in front of his cabin.

"There was some cullud young men went to the schools they'd opened by the gov'ment. Some white woman said someone had stole something of hers so they put them young men in jail. The Klu Klux went to the jail and took 'em out and killed 'em. That happened the second year after the War.

"After the Klu Kluxes got so strong the cullud men got together and made the complaint before the law. The Gov'nor told the law to give 'em the old guns in the com'sary, what the Southern soldiers had used, so they issued the cullud men old muskets and said protect themselves. They got together and organized the militia and had leaders like reg'lar soldiers. They didn't meet 'cept when they heered the Klu Kluxes was coming to get some cullud folks. Then they was ready for 'em. They'd hide in the cabins and then's when they found out who a lot of them Klu Kluxes was, 'cause a lot of 'em was kilt. They wore long sheets and covered the hosses with sheets so you couldn't rec'nize 'em. Men you thought was your friend was Klu Kluxes and you'd deal with 'em in stores in the daytime and at night they'd come out to your house and kill you. I never took part in none of the fights, but I heered the others talk 'bout them, but not where them Klu Klux could hear 'em.

"One time they had 12 men in jail, 'cused of robbin' white folks. All was white in jail but one, and he was cullud. The Klu Kluxes went to the jailor's house and got the jail key and got them men out and carried 'em to the River Bridge, in the middle. Then they knocked their brains out and threw 'em in the river.

"We was 'fraid of them Klu Kluxes and come to town, to Snow Hill. We rented a little house and my mother took in washing and ironing. I went to school and learned to read and write, then worked on farms, and fin'ly went to Columbia, in South Carolina, and worked in the turpentine country. I stayed there a while and got married.

"I come to Texas in 1877 and Galveston was a little pen then, a little mess. I worked for some white people and then went to Houston and it wasn't nothing but a mudhole. So I messed 'round in South Carolina again a while and then come back to Galveston.

"The Lawd called me then and I answered and was preacher here at the Union Baptist Church, on 11th and K, 'bout 25 years.

"I knowed Wright Cuney well and he held the biggest place a cullud man ever helt in Galveston. He was congressman and the white people looked up to him just like he was white.

"Durin' the Spanish-American War I went to Washington, D.C., to see my sister and got in the soldier business. The gov'ment give me $30.00 a month for drivin' a four-mule wagon for the army. I druv all through Pennsylvania and Virginia and South Carolina for the gov'ment. I was a——what do they call a laborer in the army?

"When war was over I come back here and now I'm too old to work and the state gives me a pension and me and my granddaughter live on that. The young folks is makin' their mark now. One thing about 'em, they get educated, but there's not much for them to do when they get finished with school but walk the streets now. I been always trying to help my people to rise 'bove their station and they are rising all the time, and some day they'll be free."

during the Spanish-American War. I went to Washington, D.C. to see my sister and got in the coffin business. The government gives a $50.00 a month for drivin' a loaded wagon for the army. Drove all through Pennsylvania and Virginia and South Carolina for the government. I was a——What do they call a labor or time army?——a——"

"When war was over I come back here and now I'm too old to work and if the state gives me a pension and me and my grandchildren live on that. The young folks in town, their main idea is what? About em, they get educated but there's nothin' for them to do when they get out and with school and clothes these days, been always trying to pole the people to not move their station and if they are doing all the time than its pre-day they had."

MOLLY HARRELL

MOLLY HARRELL was born a slave on the Swanson plantation, near Palestine, Texas. She was a housegirl, but must have been too small to do much work. She does not know her age, but thinks she was about seven when she was freed. Molly lives at 3218 Ave H., Galveston, Texas.

"Don't you tell nobody dat I use to be a slave. I 'most forgot it myself till you got round me jes' den. Course, I ain't blamin' you for it, but what you done say 'bout all de plantations havin' schools was wrong, so I jes' had to tell you I been a slave myself. It jes' slip out.

"Like I jes' say, I knows what I's talkin' 'bout, 'cause I use to be a slave myself and I don't know how to read and write. Dat why I say I can't see so good. It don't do to let folks know dey's smarter'n you, 'cause den dey got you right where dey wants you. Now, Will, dat de man I's marry to, am younger'n me but he don't know it. When you git marry, you don't tell de man how old you is. He wouldn't have you if you did. 'Course, Will ain't so young heself, but he's born after de war and I's born durin' slavery, so dat make me older.

"Mr. Swanson use to own de big plantation in Palestine. Everybody in dat part de country knowed him. He use to live in a plain, wood house on de Palestine road. My mother use to cook and wait on tables. John was my father.

"Dey use to have de little whip dey use on de women. Course de field hands got it worse, but den, dey was men. Mr. Swanson was good and he was mean. He was nice one day and mean as Hades de next. You never knowed what he gwine to do. But he never punish nobody 'cept dey done somethin'. My father was a field hand, and Mr. Swanson work de fire out dem. Work, work—dat all dey know from time dey git up in de mornin' till dey went to bed at night. But he wasn't hard on dem like some masters was. If dey sick, dey didn't habe to work and he give dem de med'cine hisself. If he cotch dem tryin' play off sick, den he lay into dem, or if he cotch dem loafin'. Course, I don't blame him for dat, 'cause dere ain't anythin' lazier dan a lazy nigger. Will am 'bout de laziest one in de bunch. You ain't never find a lazier nigger dan Will.

"I was purty little den, but I done my share. I holp my mother dust and clean up de house and peel 'tatoes. Dere some old men dat too old to work so dey sot in de sun all day and holp with de light work. Dey carry grub and water to de field hands.

"Somebody run 'way all de time and hide in de woods till dere gut pinch dem and den dey have to come back and git somethin' to eat. Course, dey got beat, but dat didn't worry dem none, and it not long till dey gone 'gain.

"My mother sold into slavery in Georgia, or round dere. She tell me funny things 'bout how dey use to do up dere. A old white man think so much of he old nigger when he die he free dat nigger in he will, and lef' him a little money. He open de blacksmith shop and buy some slaves. Mother allus say dose free niggers make de hardes' masters. One in Palestine marry a nigger slave and buy her from her master. Den he tell everybody he own a slave.

"Everybody talk 'bout freedom and hope to git free 'fore dey die. I 'member de first time de Yankees pass by, my mother lift me up on de fence. Dey use to pass by with bags on de mules and fill dem with stuff from de houses. Dey go in de barn and holp deyself. Dey go in de stables and turn out de white folks' hosses and run off what dey don't take for deyself.

"Den one night I 'member jes' as well, me and my mother was settin' in de cabin gettin' ready to go to bed, when us hear somebody call my mother. We listen and de overseer whisper under de door and told my mother dat she free but not to tell nobody. I don't know why he done it. He allus like my mother, so I guess he do it for her. The master reads us de paper right after dat and say us free.

"Me and my mother lef' right off and go to Palestine. Most everybody else go with us. We all walk down de road singin' and shoutin' to beat de band. My father come nex' day and jine us. My sister born dere. Den us go to Houston and Louisiana for a spell and I hires out to cook. I works till us come to Galveston 'bout ten year ago.

ANN HAWTHORNE

Dibble, Fred, P.W., Beehler, Rheba, P.W., Beaumont, Jefferson, Dist. #3.

ANN HAWTHORNE, Beaumont, Tex., was clad in a white dress which was protected by a faded blue checked apron. On her feet she wore men's bedroom slippers much too large for her, and to prevent their falling off, were tied around the ankle by rag strings. She wore silk hose with the heels completely worn out of them. Her figure is generous in proportions, and her hair snow white, fixed in little pig tails and wrapped in black string. Ann related her story in a deep voice and a jovial manner. Although born and raised in Jasper county, she speaks boastfully about having been to Houston.

"If you's lookin' for Ann Hawthorne, dis is me. I was bo'n in slavery, and I was a right sizeable gal when freedom come. I was 'bout 10 or 12 year' ol' when freedom riz up."

"I was bo'n up here in Jasper. Ol' marster Woodruff Norsworthy and Miss Ca'lina, dey was my ol' marster and mistus. Miss Ca'lina she name' me."

"My pa was Len Norsworthy. My ma was name Ca'line after ol' mistus. Dat how come I 'member ol' mistus name so good. I got fo' brudders livin', but nary a sister. My brudders is Newton and Silas and Willie and Frank. I say dey's livin'. I mean dat de las' time I heard of 'em dey was livin'."

"Yas, I 'member de house I was raise in. It was jis' a one-room log house. Dey was a ol' Geo'gia hoss bed in it. It was up pretty high and us chillun had to git on a box to git in dat bed. De mattress was mek outer straw. Sometime dey mek 'em in co'n sacks and sometime dey put 'em in a tick what dey weave on de loom. I had a aunt what was de weaver. She weave all de time for ol' marster. She uster weave all us clo's."

"My ma she was jis' a fiel' han' but my gramma and my aunt dey hab dem for wuk 'roun' de house. I didn' do nuthin' but chu'n (churn) and clean de yard, and sweep 'roun' and go to de spring and tote de water. I l'arn how to hoe, too."

"Dat was a big plantation. Fur as I kin 'member I t'ink dey was 'bout 25 or 30 slaves on de place. You see I done git ol' and childish and I can't 'member like what I uster could. I 'member though, dat my pa uster drive a team for ol' marster. Sometime he fiel' han' on de plantation, too."

"Ol' marster he was good to his slaves. I heerd of slaves bein' whip' but I ain't never see any git whip. Dey was a overseer on de place and iffen dey was any whippin' to be did, he done it."

"Me? I never did git no lickin's when I was a li'l slave. No mam. I allus did obey jis' like I was teached to do and dey didn' hafter whip me. I 'members dat."

"We done our playin' 'roun' dat big house, but dat front gate, we dassen' go outside dat. We uster jump de rope and play ring plays and sich. You know how dey yoke dey han's togedder? Dat de way us uster do and go 'roun' and 'roun' singin' our li'l jumped up songs. Den us jis' play 'roun' lots of times anyt'ing what happen to come up in our min's."

"Dey feed us good back in slavery. Give us plenty of meat and bread and greens and t'ings. Ye, dey feed us good and us had plenty. Dey give us plenty of co'nbread. Dat's de reason I's a co'nbread eater now. I ain't no flour-bread eater. I lubs my co'nbread. Us all eat outer one big pan. Dey give each li'l nigger a big iron spoon and us sho' go to it. Dey give us milk in a sep'rate vessel, and dey give eb'ryone a slice of meat in our greens. And dey never dassent tek de other feller's piece of meat. Eb'ryt'ing better go 'long smoove wid us chillun. We better eat and shut our mouf. We dassent raise no squall."

"I tell dese chillun here dey ain't know nuffin'. Dey got dey glass. We had our li'l go'ds (gourds) pretty and clean and white. I wish I had one of dem ol' time go'ds now to drink my milk outer."

"In good wedder dey feed us under a big tree out in de yard. And us better leave eb'ryt'ing clean and no litter 'roun'. In de winter time dey fed us in de kitchen."

"Us gals wo' plain, long waisted dress. Dey was cut straight and wid long waist and dey button down de back."

"Dey was a cullud man what mek shoes for de slaves to wear in de winter time. He mek 'em outer rough red russet ledder. Dat ledder was hard and lots of times it mek blister on us feet. I uster be glad when summer time come so's I could go barefoot."

"Dey had cabins for de slaves to live in. Dere was jis' one room and one family to de cabin. Some of 'em was bigger dan others and dey put a big family in a big cabin and a li'l family in a li'l cabin."

"I never see no slaves bought and sol'. I heerd my gramma and ma say dey ol' marster wouldn' sell none of his slaves."

"I heerd 'bout dem broom-stick marriages, but I ain't never seed none. Dat was dey law in dem days."

"Dey didn' know nuffin' 'bout preachin' and Sunday School in dem times. De fus' preachin' I heerd was atter dat. I hear a white preacher preach. He uster preach to de white folks in de mornin' and de cullud folks in de afternoons. But de slaves some of 'em uster had family prayer meetings to deyselfs."

"De ol' marster he didn' work he han's on Sunday and he give 'em half de day off on Sadday, too. But he never give 'em a patch to work for deyself. Dat half a day off on Sadday was for de slaves to wash and clean up deyselfs."

"I never git marry 'till way atter freedom come. Dat was up in Jasper county where I's bred and bo'n. I marry Hyman Hawthorne. Near as you kin guess, dat was 'bout 50 year' ago. Den he die and lef' me wid eight chillun. My baby gal she ain't never see no daddy."

"Atter he dead I wash and iron and cook out and raise my chillun. I was raise up in de fiel' all my life. When I git disable' to wuk in de time of de 'pressure (depression) I git on my walkin' stick. I wag up town and I didn' fail to ax de white folks 'cause I wo' myself out wukkin' for 'em. Dey load up my sack and sometime dey bring me stuff in a car right dere to dat gate. But I's had two strokes and I ain't able to go to town no mo'."

"I tell you I never hear nuthin' 'bout chu'ch 'till way atter freedom. Sometime den us go to chu'ch. Dey was one Mef'dis' Chu'ch and one Baptis' Chu'ch in Jasper. Dere moughta been a Cabilic (Catholic) Chu'ch dere too, but I dunno 'bout dat."

"I don' 'member seein' no sojers. I t'ink some of ol' marster's boys went to de war but de ol' man didn' go. I dunno 'bout wedder dey come back or not 'cep'n' I 'member dat Crab Norsworthy he come back."

"When any of de slaves git sick ol' mistus and my gramma dey doctor 'em. De ol' mistus she a pretty good doctor. When us chillun git sick dey git yarbs or dey give us castor oil and turpentine. Iffen it git to be a ser'ous ailment dey sen' for de reg'lar doctor. Dey uster hang asafoetida 'roun' us neck in a li'l bag to keep us from ketch' de whoopin' cough and de measles."

"Dey was a gin and cotton press on de place. Ol' marster gin' and bale' he own cotton. Dat ol' press had dem long arms a-stickin' down what dey hitch hosses to and mek 'em go 'roun' and 'roun' and press de bale."

"Dey raise dey own t'bacco on de place. I didn' use snuff nor chew 'till after I growed up and marry. Back in slavery you couldn' let 'em ketch you wid a chew of t'bacco or snuff in your mouf. Iffen you did dey wouldn' let you forgit it."

"I uster like to go and play 'roun' de calfs, jis' go up and pet 'em and rub 'em. But we dassent git on 'em to ride 'em."

"Marster uster sit 'roun' and watch us chillun play. He enjoy dat. He call me his Annie 'cause I name' after my mistus. Sometime he hab a wagon load of watermilion haul' up from de fiel' and cut 'em. Eb'ry chile hab a side of watermilion. And us hab all de sugar cane and sweet 'taters us want."

"Dey had a big smokehouse. Dey hab big hog killin' time, and dey dry and salt de meat in a big long trough. Dey git oak and ash and hick'ry wood and mek a fire under it and smoke it. My gramma toted de key to dat smokehouse and ol' mistus she'd tell her what to go and git for de white folks and de cullud folks."

"When Crismus come 'roun' dey give us big eatin'. Us hab chicken and turkey and cake. I don' 'member dat dey give us no presents."

"My gramma and my ma and ol' man Norsworthy dey come from Alabama. I never hear of him breakin' up a family. But when dey was livin' in Geo'gy, my ma marry a man name' Hawthorne in Geo'gy. He wouldn' sell him to Marse Norsworthy when he come to Texas. Atter freedom marster go to Geo'gy to git him and bring him to Texas, but he done raisin' up anudder family dere and won't come. Li'l befo' she die her husban' come. When he 'bout wo' out and ready to die, den he come. Some of de ol'es' chillun 'member dey daddy and dey crazy for him to come and dey mek up de money for him. When he git here dey tek care of him 'till he die right dere at Olive. Ma tell 'em to write him he neenter (need not) come. She say he ain't no service to her. But he come and de daughter tek care of her ma and pa bofe."

"I's got 8 gran'chillun and 5 great-gran'chillun. I 'vides (divide) my time 'tween my daughter here and de one in Houston."

"You wants to tek my picture? Daughter, I don' want dat hat you got dere. Dat one of de chillun' hats. Git dat li'l bonnet. Dat becomes me better. I can't stan' much sun. Dey say I's got high blood pressue."

JAMES HAYES

JAMES HAYES, 101, was born a slave to a plantation owner whose name he does not now recall, in Shelby Co., two miles from Marshall, Texas. Mr. John Henderson bought the place, six slaves and James and his mother. James, known as Uncle Jim, seems happy, still stands erect, and is very active for his age. He lives on a green slope overlooking the Trinity river, in Moser Valley, a Negro settlement ten miles northeast of Fort Worth.

"Dis nigger have lived a long time, yas, suh! I's 101 years ole, 'cause I's bo'n Dec. 28, 1835. Dat makes me 102 come nex' December. I can' 'member my fust marster's name, 'cause when I's 'bout two years ole, me and my sis, 'bout five, and our mammy was sol' to Marster John Henderson. I don' 'member anything 'bout my pappy, but I 'member Marster Henderson jus' like 'twas las' week. I's settin' hear a thinkin' of dem ole days when I's a li'l nigger a cuttin' up on ole marster's plantation. How I did play roun' with de chilluns till I's big enough for to wo'k. After I's 'bout 13, I jus' peddles roun' de house for 'bout a year, den 'twarn't long till I hoes co'n and potatoes. Dere's six slaves on dat place and I coul' beat dem all a-hoein'.

"De marster takes good care of us and sometimes give us money, 'bout 25¢, and lets us go to town. Dat's when we was happy and celebrates. We'uns spent all de money on candy and sweet drinks. Marster never crowded us 'bout de wo'k, and never give any of us whuppin's. I's sev'ral times needed a whuppin', but de marster never gives dis nigger more'n a good scoldin'. De nearest I comes to gittin whupped, 'twas once when I stole a plate of biscuits offen de table. I warn't in need of 'em, but de devil in me caused me to do it. Marster and all de folks comes in and sets down, and he asks for de biscuits, and I's under de house and could hear 'em talk. De cook says, 'I's put de biscuits on de table.' Marster says, 'If you did, de houn' got 'em.' Cook says, 'If a houn' got 'em, 'twas a two-legged one, 'cause de plate am gone, too.' I's made de mistake of takin' de plate. Marster give me de wors' scoldin' I ever has and dat larned me a lesson.

"Not long after dat, Marster sol' my mammy to his brudder who lived in Fort Worth. When dey took her away, I's powerful grieved. 'Bout dat time de War started. De marster and his boy, Marster Ben, jined de army. De marster was a sergeant. De women folks was proud of dere men folks, but dey was powerful grieved. All de time de men's away, I could tell Missy Elline and her mamma was worried. Dey allus sen's me for de mail, and when I fotches it, dey run to meet me, anxious like, to open de letter, and was skeert to do it. One day I fotches a letter and I could feel it in my bones, dere was trouble in dat letter. Sure 'nough, dere was trouble, heaps of it. It tells dat Marster Ben am kilt and dat dey was a shippin' him home. All de ole folks, cullud and white, was cryin'. Missy Elline, she fainted. When de body comes home, dere's a powerful big funeral and after dat, dere's powerful weepin's and sadness on dat place. De women folks don' talk much and no laughin' like 'fore. I 'members once de missy asks me to make a 'lasses cake. I says, 'I's got no 'lasses.' Missy says, 'Don' say 'lasses, say molasses.' I says, 'Why say molasses when I's got no 'lasses.' Dat was de fus' time Missy laugh after de funeral.

"Durin' de War, things was 'bout de same, like always, 'cept some vittles was scarce. But we'uns had plenty to eat and us slaves didn' know what de War was 'bout. I guess we was too ign'rant. De white folks didn' talk 'bout it 'fore us. When it's over, de Marster comes home and dey holds a big celebration. I's workin' in de kitchen and dey tol' me to cook heaps of ham, chicken, pies, cakes, sweet 'taters and lots of vegetables. Lots of white folks comes and dey eats and drinks wine, dey sings and dances. We'uns cullud folks jined in and was singin' out in de back, 'Massa's in de Col', Har' Groun'. Marster asks us to come in and sing dat for de white folks, so we'uns goes in de house and sings dat for de white folks and dey jines in de chorus.

"Three days after de celebration, de marster calls all de slaves in de house and says, 'Yous is all free, free as I am.' He tol' us we'uns could go if we'uns wanted to. None of us knows what to do, dere warn't no place to go and why would we'uns wan' to go and leave good folks like de marster? His place was our home. So we'uns asked him if we could stay and he says, 'Yous kin stay as long as yous want to and I can keep yous.' We'uns all stayed till he died, 'bout a year after dat.

"When he was a-dyin', marster calls me to his bed and says, 'My dyin' reques' is dat yous be taken to your mama.' He calls his son, Zeke, in and tells him dat I should be fotched to my mamma. And 'bout in a year, Marster Zeke fotches me to my mamma, in Johnson Station, south of Arlington. She's wo'kin' for Jack Ditto and I's pleased to see her.

I's pleased to see my mammy, but after a few days I wants to go back to Marshall with Marster Zeke. Dat was my home, so I kep' pesterin' marster to fetch me back, but he slips off and leaves me. I has to stay and I's been here ever since.

"I gits my fust job with Carter Cannon, on a farm, and stays seven years. Den I goes to Fort Worth and takes a job cookin' in de Gran' Hotel for three years. Den I goes to Dallas and cooks for private families, and wo'ks for Marster James Ellison for 30 years. I stops four years ago and comes out here to wait till de good Lawd calls me home.

"Bout gittin' married, after I quits de Gran' Hotel I marries and we'uns has two chillen. My wife died three years later.

"You knows, I believes I's mo' contented as a slave. I's treated kind all de time and had no frettin' 'bout how I gwine git on. Since I's been free, I sometimes have heaps of frettin'. Course, I don' want to go back into slavery, but I's paid for my freedom.

"I's never been sick abed, but I's had mo' misery dis las' year dan all my life. It's my heart. If I live till December, I'll be 102 years old, and dis ole heart have been pumpin' and pumpin' all dem years and have missed nary a beat till dis las' year. I knows 'twon't be long till de good Lawd calls dis ole nigger to cross de Ribber Jordan and I's ready for de Lawd when he calls.

FELIX HAYWOOD

F ELIX HAYWOOD is a temperamental and whimsical old Negro of San Antonio, Texas, who still sees the sunny side of his 92 years, in spite of his total blindness. He was born and bred a slave in St. Hedwig, Bexar Co., Texas, the son of slave parents bought in Mississippi by his master, William Gudlow. Before and during the Civil

War he was a sheep herder and cowpuncher. His autobiography is a colorful contribution, showing the philosophical attitude of the slaves, as well as shedding some light upon the lives of slave owners whose support of the Confederacy was not accompanied by violent hatred of the Union.

"Yes, sir, I'm Felix Haywood, and I can answer all those things that you want to know. But, first, let me ask you this: Is you all a white man, or is you a black man?"

"I'm black, blacker than you are," said the caller.

The eyes of the old blind Negro,—eyes like two murkey brown marbles—actually twinkled. Then he laughed:

"No, you ain't. I knowed you was white man when you comes up the path and speaks. I jus' always asks that question for fun. It makes white men a little insulted when you dont know they is white, and it makes niggers all conceited up when you think maybe they is white."

And there was the key note to the old Negro's character and temperament. He was making a sort of privileged game with a sportive twist out of his handicap of blindness.

As the interviewer scribbled down a note, the door to the little shanty on Arabella Alley opened and a backless chair was carried out on the porch by a vigorous old colored woman. She was Mrs. Ella Thompson, Felix' youngest sister, who had known only seven years of slavery. After a timid "How-do-you-do," and a comment on the great heat of the June day, she went back in the house. Then the old Negro began searching his 92 years of reminiscences, intermixing his findings with philosophy, poetry and prognostications.

"It's a funny thing how folks always want to know about the War. The war weren't so great as folks suppose. Sometimes you didn't knowed it was goin' on. It was the endin' of it that made the difference. That's when we all wakes up that somethin' had happened. Oh, we knowed what was goin' on in it all the time, 'cause old man Gudlow went to the post office every day and we knowed. We had papers in them days jus' like now.

"But the War didn't change nothin'. We saw guns and we saw soldiers, and one member of master's family, Colmin Gudlow, was gone fightin'—somewhere. But he didn't get shot no place but one—that was in the big toe. Then there was neighbors went off to fight. Some of 'em didn't want to go. They was took away (conscription). I'm thinkin' lots of 'em pretended to want to go as soon as they had to go.

"The ranch went on jus' like it always had before the war. Church went on. Old Mew Johnson, the preacher, seen to it church went on. The kids didn't know War was happenin'. They played marbles, see-saw and rode. I had old Buster, a ox, and he took me about plenty good as a horse. Nothin' was different. We got layed-onto(whipped) time on time, but gen'rally life was good—just as good as a sweet potato. The only misery I had was when a black spider bit me on the ear. It swelled up my head and stuff came out. I was plenty sick and Dr. Brennen, he took good care of me. The whites always took good care of people when they was sick. Hospitals couldn't do no better for you today.... Yes, maybe it was a black widow spider, but we called it the 'devil biter'.

"Sometimes someone would come 'long and try to get us to run up North and be free. We used to laugh at that. There wasn't no reason to run up North. All we had to do was to walk, but walk South, and we'd be free as soon as we crossed the Rio Grande. In Mexico you could be free. They didn't care what color you was, black, white, yellow or blue. Hundreds of slaves did go to Mexico and got on all right. We would hear about 'em and how they was goin' to be Mexicans. They brought up their children to speak only Mexican.

"Me and my father and five brothers and sisters weren't goin' to Mexico. I went there after the war for a while and then I looked 'round and decided to get back. So I come back to San Antonio and I got a job through Colonel Breckenridge with the waterworks. I was handling pipes. My foreman was Tom Flanigan—he must have been a full-blooded Frenchman!

"But what I want to say is, we didn't have no idea of runnin' and escapin'. We was happy. We got our lickings, but just the same we got our fill of biscuits every time the white folks had 'em. Nobody knew how it was to lack food. I tell my chillen we didn't know no more about pants than a hawg knows about heaven; but I tells 'em that to make 'em laugh. We had all the clothes we wanted and if you wanted shoes bad enough you got 'em—shoes with a brass square toe. And shirts! Mister, them was shirts that was shirts! If someone gets caught by his shirt on a limb of a tree, he had to die there if he weren't cut down. Them shirts wouldn't rip no more'n buckskin.

"The end of the war, it come jus' like that—like you snap your fingers."

"How did you know the end of the war had come?" asked the interviewer.

"How did we know it! Hallelujah broke out—

> "'Abe Lincoln freed the nigger
> With the gun and the trigger;
> And I ain't goin' to get whipped any more.
> I got my ticket,
> Leavin' the thicket,
> And I'm a-headin' for the Golden Shore!'

"Soldiers, all of a sudden, was everywhere—comin' in bunches, crossin' and walkin' and ridin'. Everyone was a-singin'. We was all walkin' on golden clouds. Hallelujah!

> "'Union forever,
> Hurrah, boys, hurrah!
> Although I may be poor,
> I'll never be a slave—
> Shoutin' the battle cry of freedom.'

"Everybody went wild. We all felt like heroes and nobody had made us that way but ourselves. We was free. Just like that, we was free. It didn't seem to make the whites mad, either. They went right on giving us food just the same. Nobody took our homes away, but right off colored folks started on the move. They seemed to want to get closer to freedom, so they'd know what it was—like it was a place or a city. Me and my father stuck, stuck close as a lean tick to a sick kitten. The Gudlows started us out on a ranch. My father, he'd round up cattle, unbranded cattle, for the whites. They was cattle that they belonged to, all right; they had gone to find water 'long the San Antonio River and the Guadalupe. Then the whites gave me and my father some cattle for our own. My father had his own brand, 7 B), and we had a herd to start out with of seventy.

"We knowed freedom was on us, but we didn't know what was to come with it. We thought we was goin' to get rich like the white folks. We thought we was goin' to be richer than the white folks, 'cause we was stronger and knowed how to work, and the whites didn't and they didn't have us to work for them anymore. But it didn't turn out that way. We soon found out that freedom could make folks proud but it didn't make 'em rich.

"Did you ever stop to think that thinking don't do any good when you do it too late? Well, that's how it was with us. If every mother's son of a black had thrown 'way his hoe and took up a gun to fight for his own freedom along with the Yankees, the war'd been over before it began. But we didn't do it. We couldn't help stick to our masters. We couldn't no more shoot 'em than we could fly. My father and me used to talk 'bout it. We decided we was too soft and freedom wasn't goin' to be much to our good even if we had a education."

The old Negro was growing very tired, but, at a request, he instantly got up and tapped his way out into the scorching sunshine to have his photograph taken. Even as he did so, he seemed to smile with those blurred, dead eyes of his. Then he chuckled to himself and said:

> "'Warmth of the wind
> And heat of the South,
> And ripe red cherries
> For a ripe, red mouth.'"

"Land sakes, Felix!" came through the window from sister Ella. "How you carries on! Don't you be a-mindin' him, mister."

PHOEBE HENDERSON

PHOEBE HENDERSON, a 105 year old Negro of Harrison Co., was born a slave of the Bradley family at Macon, Georgia. After the death of her mistress, Phoebe belonged to one of the daughters, Mrs. Wiley Hill, who moved to Panola County, Texas in 1859, where Phoebe lived until after the Civil War. For the past 22 years she has lived with Mary Ann Butler, a daughter, about five miles east of Marshall, in Enterprise Friendship Community. She draws a pension of $16.00 a month.

"I was bo'n a slave of the Bradley family in Macon, Georgia. My father's name was Anthony Hubbard and he belonged to the Hubbard's in Georgia. He was a young man when I lef' Georgia and I never heard from him since. I 'member my mother; she had a gang of boys. Marster Hill brought her to Texas with us.

"My ole missus name was Bradley and she died in Tennessee. My lil' missus was her daughter. After dey brought us to Texas in 1859 I worked in the field many a day, plowin' and hoein', but the children didn't do much work 'cept carry water. When dey git tired, dey'd say dey was sick and the overseer let 'em lie down in de shade. He was a good and kindly man and when we do wrong and go tell him he forgave us and he didn't whip the boys 'cause he was afraid they'd run away.

"I worked in de house, too. I spinned seven curts a day and every night we run two looms, makin' large curts for plow lines. We made all our clothes. We didn't wear shoes in Georgia but in this place the land was rough and strong, so we couldn't go barefooted. A black man that worked in the shop measured our feet and made us two pairs a year. We had good houses and dey was purty good to us. Sometimes missus give us money and each family had their garden and some chickens. When a couple marry, the master give them a house and we had a good time and plenty to wear and to eat. They cared for us when we was sick.

"Master Wiley Hill had a big plantation and plenty of stock and hawgs, and a big turnip patch. He had yellow and red oxen. We never went to school any, except Sunday school. We'd go fishin' often down on the creek and on Saturday night we'd have parties in the woods and play ring plays and dance.

"My husband's name was David Henderson and we lived on the same place and belonged to the same man. No, suh, Master Hill didn't have nothin' to do with bringin' us together. I guess God done it. We fell in love, and David asked Master Hill for me. We had a weddin' in the house and was married by a colored Baptist preacher. I wore a white cotton dress and Missus Hill give me a pan of flour for a weddin' present. He give us a house of our own. My husband was good to me. He was a careful man and not rowdy. When we'd go anywhere we'd ride horseback and I'd ride behin' him.

"I's scared to talk 'bout when I was freed. I 'member the soldiers and that warrin' and fightin'. Toby, one of the colored boys, joined the North and was a mail messenger boy and he had his horse shot out from under him. But I guess its a good thing we was freed, after all.

ALBERT HILL

ALBERT HILL, 81, was born a slave of Carter Hill, who owned a plantation and about 50 slaves, in Walton Co., Georgia. Albert remained on the Hill place until he was 21, when he went to Robinson Co., Texas. He now lives at 1305 E. 12th St., Fort Worth, Texas, in a well-kept five-room house, on a slope above the Trinity River.

"I was born on Massa Carter Hill's plantation, in Georgia, and my name am Albert Hill. My papa's name was Dillion, 'cause he taken dat name from he owner, Massa Tom Dillion. He owned de plantation next to Massa Hill's, and he owned my mammy and us 13 chillen. I don't know how old I is, but I 'members de start of de war, and I was a sizeable chile den.

"De plantation wasn't so big and wasn't so small, jus' fair size, but it am fixed first class and everything am good. We has good quarters made out of logs and lots of tables and benches, what was made of split logs. We has de rations and massa give plenty of de cornmeal and beans and 'lasses and honey. Sometimes we has tea, and once in a while we gits coffee. And does we have de tasty and tender hawg meat! I'd like to see some of dat hawg meat now.

"Massa am good but he don't 'low de parties. But we kin go to Massa Dillion's place next to us and dey has lots of parties and de dances. We dances near all night Saturday night, but we has to stay way in de back where de white folks can't hear us. Sometimes we has de fiddle and de banjo and does we cut dat chicken wing and de shuffle! We sho' does.

"I druv de ox, and drivin' dat ox am agitation work in de summer time when it am hot, 'cause dey runs for water every time. But de worst trouble I ever has is with one hoss. I fotches de dinner to de workers out in de field and I use dat hoss, hitched to de two-wheel cart. One day him am halfway and dat hoss stop. He look back at me, a-rollin' de eye, and I knows what dat mean—'Here I stays, nigger.' But I heered to tie de rope on de balky hosses tail and run it 'twixt he legs and tie to de shaft. I done dat and puts some cuckleburrs on de rope, too. Den I tech him with de whip and he gives de rear back'ards. Dat he best rear. When he do dat it pull de rope and de rope pull de tail and de burrs gits busy. Dat hoss moves for'ard faster and harder den what he ever done 'fore, and he keep on gwine. You see, he am trying git 'way from he tail, but de tail am too fast. Course, it stay right behin' him. Den I's in de picklement. Dat hoss am runnin' away and I can't stop him. De workers lines up to stop him but de cart give de shove and dat pull he tail and, lawdy whoo, dat hose jump for'ard like de jackrabbit and go through dat line of workers. So I steers him into de fence row, and dere's no more runnin', but an awful mix-up with de hoss and de cart and de rations. Dat hoss so sceered him have de quavers. Massa say, 'What you doin'?' I says, 'Break de balk.' He say, 'Well, yous got everything else broke. We'll see 'bout de balk later.'

Massa has de daughter, Mary, and she want to marry Bud Jackson, but massa am 'gainst it. Bud am gwine to de army and dat give dis boy work, 'cause I de messenger boy for him and Missy Mary. Dey keeps company unbeknownst and I carry de notes. I puts de paper in de hollow stump. Once I's sho' I's kotched. Dere am de massa and he say, 'Where you been, nigger?' I's sho' skeert and I says, 'I's lookin' for de squirrels.' So massa goes 'way and when I tells you I's left, it ain't de proper word for to 'splain, 'cause I's flew from here.' I tells Missy Mary and she say, 'You sho' am de Lawd's chosen nigger.'

"De 'federate soldiers comes and dey takes de rations, but de massa has dug de pit in de pasture and buried lots of de rations, so de soldiers don't find so much. De clostest battle was Atlanta, more dan 25 mile 'way.

"When de war come over, Bud Jackson he come home. De massa welcome him, to de sprise of everybody, and when Bud say he want to marry Missy Mary, massa say, 'I guesses you has earnt her.'

"When freedom am here, massa call all us together and tells us 'bout de difference 'tween freedom and hustlin' for ourselves and dependin' on someone else. Most of de slaves stays, and massa pays them for de work, and I stays till I's 21 year old, and I gits $7.00 de month and de clothes and de house and all I kin eat. De massa have died 'fore dat, and dere am powerful sorrow. Missy Mary and Massa Bud has de plantation den, and dey don't want me to go to Texas. But dey goes on de visit and while dey gone I takes de train for Robinson County, what am in Texas.

"I works at de pavin' work and at de hostlin' work and I works on de hosses. Den I works for de Santa Fe railroad, handlin' freight, and I works till 'bout three year ago, when I gits too old for to work no more.

"But I tells you 'bout de visit back to de old plantation. I been gone near 40 year and I 'cides to go back, so I reaches de house and dere am Missy Mary peelin' apples on de back gallery. She looks at me, and she say, 'I got whippin' waiting for yous, 'cause you run off without tellin' us.' Dere wasn't no more peelin' dat day, 'cause we sits and talks 'bout de old times and de old massa. Dere sho' am de tears in dis nigger's eyes. Den we talks 'bout de nigger messenger I was, and we laughs a little. All day long we talks a little, and laughs and cries and talks. I stays 'bout two weeks and seed lots of de folks I knowed when I was young, de white folks and de niggers, too.

"I's too old to make any more visits, but I would like to go back to Old Georgia once more. If Missy Mary was 'live, I'd try, but she am dead, so I tries to wait for old Gabriel blow he horn. When he blow he horn, dis nigger say, 'Louder, Gabriel, louder!'

ROSINA HOARD

ROSINA HOARD does not know just where she was born. The first thing she remembers is that she and her parents were purchased by Col. Pratt Washington, who owned a plantation near Garfield, in Travis County, Texas. Rosina, who is a very pleasant and sincere person, says she has had a tough life since she was free. She receives a monthly pension of fourteen dollars, for which she expresses gratitude. Her address is 1301 Chestnut St., Austin, Tex.

"When I's a gal, I's Rosina Slaughter, but folks call me Zina. Yes, sar. It am Zina dat and Zina dis. I says I's born April 9, 1859, but I 'lieve I's older. It was somewhere in Williamson County, but I don't know the massa's name. My mammy was Lusanne Slaughter and she was stout but in her last days she got to be a li'l bit of a woman. She died only last spring and she was a hunerd eleven years old.

"Papa was a Baptist preacher to de day of he death. He had asthma all his days. I 'member how he had de sorrel hoss and would ride off and preach under some arbor bush. I rid with him on he hoss.

"First thing I 'member is us was bought by Massa Col. Pratt Washington from Massa Lank Miner. Massa Washington was purty good man. He boys, George and John Henry, was de only overseers. Dem boys treat us nice. Massa allus rid up on he hoss after dinner time. He hoss was a bay, call Sank. De fields was in de bottoms of de Colorado River. De big house was on de hill and us could see him comin'. He weared a tall, beaver hat allus.

"De reason us allus watch for him am dat he boy, George, try larn us our A B C's in de field. De workers watch for massa and when dey seed him a-ridin' down de hill dey starts singin' out, 'Ole hawg 'round de bench—Ole hawg 'round de bench.'

"Dat de signal and den everybody starts workin' like dey have something after dem. But I's too young to larn much in de field and I can't read today and have to make de cross when I signs for my name.

"Each chile have he own wood tray. Dere was old Aunt Alice and she done all de cookin' for de chillen in de depot. Dat what dey calls de place all de chillen stays till dere mammies come home from de field. Aunt Alice have de big pot to cook in, out in de yard. Some days we had beans and some day peas. She put great hunks of salt bacon in de pot, and bake plenty cornbread, and give us plenty milk.

"Some big chillen have to pick cotton. Old Junus was de cullud overseer for de chillen and he sure mean to dem. He carry a stick and use it, too.

"One day de blue-bellies come to de fields. Dey Yankee sojers, and tell de slaves dey free. Some stayed and some left. Papa took us and move to de Craft plantation, not far 'way, and farm dere.

"I been married three time. First to Peter Collinsworth. I quit him. Second to George Hoard. We stayed togedder till he die, and have five chillen. Den I marries he brother, Jim Hoard. I tells you de truth, Jim never did work much. He'd go fishin' and chop wood by de days, but not many days. He suffered with de piles. I done de housework and look after de chillen and den go out and pick two hunerd pound cotton a day. I was a cripple since one of my boys birthed. I git de rheumatis' and my knees hurt so much sometime I rub wed sand and mud on dem to ease de pain.

"We had a house at Barton Springs with two rooms, one log and one box. I never did like it up dere and I told Jim I's gwine. I did, but he come and got me.

"Since freedom I's been through de toughs. I had to do de man's work, chop down trees and plow de fields and pick cotton. I want to tell you how glad I is to git my pension. It is sure nice of de folks to take care of me in my old age. Befo' I got de pension I had a hard time. You can sho' say I's been through de toughs.

TOM HOLLAND

TOM HOLLAND was born in Walker County, Texas, and thinks he is about 97 years old. His master, Frank Holland, traded Tom to William Green just before the Civil War. After Tom was freed, he farmed both for himself and for others in the vicinity of his old home. He now lives in Madisonville, Texas.

"My owner was Massa Frank Holland, and I's born on his place in Walker County. I had one sister named Gena and three brothers, named George and Will and Joe, but they's all dead now. Mammy's name was Gena and my father's named Abraham Holland and they's brung from North Carolina to Texas by Massa Holland when they's real young.

"I chopped cotton and plowed and split rails, then was a horse rider. In them days I could ride the wildest horse what ever made tracks in Texas, but I's never valued very high 'cause I had a glass eye. I don't 'member how I done got it, but there it am. I'd make a dollar or fifty cents to ride wild horses in slavery time and massa let me keep it. I buyed tobacco and candy and if massa cotch me with tobacco I'd git a whippin', but I allus slipped and bought chewin' tobacco.

"We allus had plenty to eat, sich as it was them days, and it was good, plenty wild meat and cornbread cooked in ashes. We toasted the meat on a open fire, and had plenty possum and rabbit and fish.

"We wore them loyal shirts open all way down the front, but I never seed shoes till long time after freedom. In cold weather massa tanned lots of hides and we'd make warm clothes. My weddin' clothes was a white loyal shirt, never had no shoes, married barefooted.

"Massa Frank, he one real good white man. He was awful good to his Negroes. Missis Sally, she a plumb angel. Their three chillen stayed with me nearly all the time, askin' this Negro lots of questions. They didn't have so fine a house, neither, two rooms with a big hall through and no windows and deer skins tacked over the door to keep out rain and cold. It was covered with boards I helped cut after I got big 'nough.

"Massa Frank had cotton and corn and everything to live on, 'bout three hundred acres, and overseed it himself, and seven growed slaves and five little slaves. He allus waked us real early to be in the field when daylight come and worked us till slap dark, but let us have a hour and a half at noon to eat and rest up. Sometimes when slaves got stubborn he'd whip them and make good Negroes out of them, 'cause he was real good to them.

"I seed slaves sold and auctioned off, 'cause I's put up to the highest bidder myself. Massa traded me to William Green jus' 'fore the war, for a hundred acres land at $1.00

a acre. He thought I'd never be much 'count, 'cause I had the glass eye, but I'm still livin' and a purty fair Negro to my age. All the hollerin' and bawlin' took place and when he sold me it took me most a year to git over it, but there I was, 'longin' to 'nother man.

"If we went off without a pass we allus went two at a time. We slipped off when we got a chance to see young folks on some other place. The patterrollers cotched me one night and, Lawd have mercy on me, they stretches me over a log and hits thirty-nine licks with a rawhide loaded with rock, and every time they hit me the blood and hide done fly. They drove me home to massa and told him and he called a old mammy to doctor my back, and I couldn't work for four days. That never kep' me from slippin' off 'gain, but I's more careful the next time.

"We'd go and fall right in at the door of the quarters at night, so massa and the patterrollers thinks we's real tired and let us alone and not watch us. That very night we'd be plannin' to slip off somewheres to see a Negro gal or our wife, or to have a big time, 'specially when the moon shine all night so we could see. It wouldn't do to have torch lights. They was 'bout all the kind of lights we had them days and if we made light, massa come to see what we're doin', and it be jus' too bad then for the stray Negro!

"That there war brung suffrin' to lots of people and made a widow out of my missis. Massa William, he go and let one them Yankees git him in one of them battles and they never brung him home. Missis, she gits the letter from his captain, braggin' on his bravery, but that never helped him after he was kilt in the war. She gits 'nother letter that us Negroes is free and she tells us. We had no place to go, so we starts to cry and asks her what we gwine do. She said we could stay and farm with her and work her teams and use her tools and land and pay her half of what we made, 'sides our supplies. That's a happy bunch of Negroes when she told us this.

"Late in that evenin' the Negroes in Huntsville starts hollerin' and shoutin' and one gal was hollerin' loud and a white man come ridin' on a hoss and leans over and cut that gal nearly half in two and a covered wagon come along and picks her up and we never heared nothin' more.

"I married Imogene, a homely weddin' 'fore the war. We didn't have much to-do at our weddin'. I asks missis if I could have Imogene and she says yes and that's all they was to our weddin'. We had three boys and three gals, and Imogene died 'bout twenty years ago and I been livin' with one child and 'nother. I gits a little pension from the gov'ment and does small jobs round for the white people.

"I 'lieve they ought to have gived us somethin' when we was freed, but they turned us out to graze or starve. Most of the white people turned the Negroes slam loose. We stayed a year with missis and then she married and her husband had his own workers and told us to git out. We worked for twenty and thirty cents a day then, and I fin'ly got a place with Dr. L.J. Conroe. But after the war the Negro had a hard struggle, 'cause he was turned loose jus' like he came into the world and no education or 'sperience.

"If the Negro wanted to vote the Klu Kluxes was right there to keep him from votin'. Negroes was 'fraid to git out and try to 'xert they freedom. They'd ride up by a Negro and shoot him jus' like a wild hawg and never a word said or done 'bout it.

"I's farmed and makin' a livin' is 'bout all. I come over here in Madison County and rents from B.F. Young, clost to Midway and gits me a few cows. I been right round here ever since. I lives round with my chillen now, 'cause I's gittin' too old to work.

"This young bunch of Negroes is all right some ways, but they won't tell the truth. They isn't raised like the white folks raised us. If we didn't tell the truth our massa'd tear us all to pieces. Of course, they is educated now and can get 'most any kind of work, some of them, what we couldn't.

ELIZA HOLMAN

ELIZA HOLMAN, 82, was born a slave of the Rev. John Applewhite, near Clinton, Mississippi. In 1861 they came to Texas, settling near Decatur. Eliza now lives at 2507 Clinton Ave., Fort Worth, Texas.

"Talk 'bout de past from de time I 'members till now, slave days and all? Dat not so hard. I knows what de past am, but what to come, dat am different. Dey says, 'Let de past be de guide for de future,' but if you don't know de future road, hows you gwine guide? I's sho' glad to tell you all I 'members, but dat am a long 'memberance.

"I know I's past 80, for sho', and maybe more, 'cause I's old 'nough to 'member befo' de war starts. I 'members when de massa move to Texas by de ox team and dat am some trip! Dey loads de wagon till dere ain't no more room and den sticks we'uns in, and we walks some of de time, too.

"My massa am a preacherman and have jus' three slaves, me and pappy and mammy. She am cook and housekeeper and I helps her. Pappy am de field hand and de coachman and everything else what am needed. We have a nice, two-room log house to live in and it am better den what mos' slaves have, with de wood floor and real windows with glass in dem.

"Massa am good but he am strict. He don't have to say much when he wants you to do somethin'. Dere am no honey words round de house from him, but when him am preachin' in de church, him am different. He am honey man den. Massa could tell de right way in de church but it am hard for him to act it at home. He makes us go to church every Sunday.

"But I's tellin' you how we'uns come to Texas. De meals am cook by de campfire and after breakfast we starts and it am bump, bump, bump all day long. It am rocks and holes and mudholes, and it am streams and rivers to cross. We'uns cross one river, musta been de Mississippi, and drives on a big bridge and dey floats dat bridge right 'cross dat river.

"Massa and missus argues all de way to Texas. She am skeert mos' de time and he allus say de Lawd take care of us. He say, 'De Lawd am a-guidin' us.' She say, 'It am fools guidin' and a fool move for to start.' Dat de way dey talks all de way. And when we gits in de mudhole 'twas a argument 'gain. She say, 'Dis am some more of your Lawd's calls.' He say, 'Hush, hush, woman. Yous gittin' sac'ligious.' So we has to walk two mile for a man to git his yoke of oxen to pull us out dat mudhole, and when we out, massa say, 'Thank de Lawd.' And missus say, 'Thank de mens and de oxen.'

"Den one day we'uns camps under a big tree and when we'uns woke in de mornin' dere am worms and worms and worms. Millions of dem come off dat tree. Man, man, dat am a mess. Massa say dey army worms and missus say, 'Why for dey not in de army den?'

"After we been in Texas 'bout a year, missy Mary gits married to John Olham. Missy Mary am massa's daughter. After dat I lives with her and Massa John and den hell start poppin' for dis nigger. Missy Mary am good but Massa John am de devil. Dat man sho' am cruel, he works me to death and whups me for de leas' thing. My pappy say to me, 'You should 'come a runaway nigger.' He runs 'way hisself and dat de las' time we hears of him.

"When surrender come I has to stay on with Massa Olham, 'cause I has no place to go and I's too young to know how to do for myself. I stays 'bout till I's 16 year old and den I hunts some place to work and gits it in Jacksboro and stays dere sev'ral years. I quits when I gits married and dat 'bout nine year after de war end.

"I marries Dick Hines at Silver Creek and he am a farmer and a contrary man. He worked jus' as hard at his contrariness as him did at his farmin'. Mercy, how distressin' and worryment am life with dat nigger! I couldn't stand it no longer dan five year till I tooks my getaway. De nex' year I marries Sam Walker what worked for cattlement here in Fort Worth and he died 'bout 20 year ago. Den 'twas 'bout 13 year ago I marries Jack Holman and he died in 1930. I's sho' try dis marrin' business but I ain't gwine try it no more, no, suh.

"'Twixt all dem husbands and workin' for de white folks I gits 'long, but I's old and de last few years I can't work. Dey pays me $12.00 de month from de State and dat's what I lives on. Shucks, I's not worth nothin' no more. I jus' sets and sets and thinks of de old days and my mammy. All dat make me sad. I'll tell you one dem songs what 'spresses my feelin's 'zactly.

"I's am climbin' Jacob's ladder, ladder,
I's am climbin' Jacob's ladder, ladder,
Soldier of de cross; O-h-h-h! Rise and shine,
Give Gawd de glory, glory, glory,
In de year of Jubilee.
I wants to climb up Jacob's ladder, ladder,
Jacob's ladder, till I gits in de new Jerusalem.

"Dat jus' how I feels."

United States. Work Projects Administration

LARNCE HOLT

LARNCE HOLT, 79, was born near Woodville, in Tyler County, Texas, a slave of William Holt. He now lives in Beaumont, Texas.

"I's jus' small fry when freedom come, 'cause I's born in 1858. Bill Holt was my massa's name, dat why dey calls me Larnce Holt. My massa, he come from Alabama but my mammy and daddy born in Texas. Mammy named Hannah and daddy Elbert. Mammy cooked for de white folks but daddy, he de shoemaker. Dat consider' a fine job on de plantation, 'cause he make all de shoes de white folks uses for everyday and all de cullud people shoes. Every time dey kill de beef dey save de hide for leather and dey put it in de trough call de tan vat, with de oak bark and other things, and leave 'em dere long time. Dat change de raw hide to leather. When de shoe done us black dem with soot, 'cause us have to do dat or wear 'em red. I's de little tike what help my daddy put on de soot.

"Massa have de big plantation and I 'member de big log house. It have de gallery on both sides and dey's de long hall down de center. De dogs and sometimes a possum used to run through de hall at night. De hall was big 'nough to dance in and I plays de fiddle.

"My mammy have four boys, call Eb and Ander and Tobe. My big brother Eb he tote so many buckets of water to de hands in de field he wore all de hair offen de top he head.

"I be so glad when Christmas come, when I's li'l. Down in de quarter us hang up stocking and us have plenty homemake ginger cake and candy make out of sugar and maybe a apple. One Christmas I real small and my mammy buy me a suit of clothes in de store. I so proud of it I 'fraid to sit down in it. 'Terials in dem day was strong and last a long time. One time I git de first pair shoes from a store. I thought dey's gold. My daddy bought dem for me and dey have a brace in de toe and was nat'ral black.

"When freedom come us family breaks up. Old missy can't bear see my mammy go, so us stay. Dey give my daddy a place on credick and he start farm and dey even 'low him hosses and mule and other things he need. My massa good to de niggers. I stays with my mammy till she die when I ten year old and den my brother Eb he take me and raise me till I sixteen. Den I go off for myself.

"Dem young year us have good time. I fiddle to de dance, play 'Git up in de Cool,' and 'Hopus Creek and de Water.' Us sho' dress up for de dance. I have black calico pants with red ribbon up de sides and a hickory shirt. De gals all wears ribbons 'round de waist and one like it 'round de head.

"Us have more hard time after freedom come dan in all de other time together. Us livin' in trouble time. 'Bout 15 year ago I lost a leg, a big log fall 'cross it when I makin' ties. I had plenty den but it go for de hospital.

United States. Work Projects Administration

BILL HOMER

BILL HOMER, 87, was born a slave on June 17, 1850, to Mr. Jack Homer, who owned a large plantation near Shreveport, La. In 1860 Bill was given to Mr. Homer's daughter, who moved to Caldwell, Texas. Bill now lives at 3215 McKinley Ave., Fort Worth, Texas.

"I is 87 years old, 'cause I is born on June 17th, in 1850, and that's 'cording to de statement my missy give me. I was born on Massa Jack Homer's plantation, close to Shreveport. Him owned my mammy and my pappy and 'bout 100 other slaves. Him's plantation was a big un. I don't know how many acres him have, but it was miles long. Dere was so many buildings and sheds on dat place it was a small town. De massa's house was a big two-story building and dere was de spinnin' house, de smokehouse, de blacksmith shop and a nursery for de cullud chillens and a lot of sheds and sich. In de nigger quarters dere was 50 one-room cabins and dey was ten in a row and dere was five rows.

"De cabins was built of logs and had dirt floors and a hole whar a window should be and a stone fireplace for de cookin' and de heat. Dere was a cookhouse for de big house and all de cookin' for de white folks was 'tended to by four cooks. We has lots of food, too—cornmeal and vegetables and milk and 'lassas and meat. For mos' de meat dey kotched hawgs in de Miss'sippi River bottoms. Once a week, we have white flour biscuit.

"Some work was hard and some easy, but massa don' 'lieve in overworkin' his slaves. Sat'day afternoon and Sunday, dere was no work. Some whippin' done, but mos' reasonable. If de nigger stubborn, deys whips 'nough for to change his mind. If de nigger runs on, dat calls de good whippin's. If any of de cullud folks has de misery, dey lets him res' in bed and if de misery bad de massa call de doctor.

"I larnt to be coachman and drive for massa's family. But in de year of 1860, Missy Mary gits married to Bill Johnson and at dat weddin' massa Homer gives me and 49 other niggers to her for de weddin' present. Massa Johnson's father gives him 50 niggers too. Dey has a gran' weddin'. I helps take care of de hosses and dey jus' kep' a-comin'. I 'spect dere was more'n 100 peoples dere and dey have lots of music and dancin' and eats and, I 'spects, drinks, 'cause we'uns made peach brandy. You see, de massa had his own still.

"After de weddin' was over, dey gives de couple de infare. Dere's whar dis nigger comes in. I and de other niggers was lined up, all with de clean clothes on and den de massa say, 'For to give my lovin' daughter de start, I gives you dese 50 niggers. Massa Bill's father done de same for his son, and dere we'uns was, 100 niggers with a new massa.

"Dey loads 15 or 20 wagons and starts for Texas. We travels from daylight to dark, with mos' de niggers walkin'. Of course, it was hard, but we enjoys de trip. Dere was one nigger called Monk and him knows a song and larned it to us, like this:

>"'Walk, walk, you nigger, walk!
>De road am dusty, de road am tough,

Dust in de eye, dust in de tuft;
Dust in de mouth, yous can't talk—
Walk, you niggers, don't you balk.

"'Walk, walk, you nigger walk!
De road am dusty, de road am rough.
Walk 'til we reach dere, walk or bust—
De road am long, we be dere by and by.'

Now, we'uns was a-follerin' behin' de wagons and we'uns sings it to de slow steps of de ox. We'uns don't sing it many times 'til de missy come and sit in de back of de wagon, facin' we'uns and she begin to beat de slow time and sing wid we'uns. Dat please Missy Mary to sing with us and she laugh and laugh.

"After 'bout two weeks we comes to de place near Caldwell, in Texas, and dere was buildin's and land cleared, so we's soon settled. Massa plants mostly cotton and corn and clears more land. I larned to be a coachman, but on dat place I de ox driver or uses de hoe.

"Yous never drive de ox, did yous? De mule ain't stubborn side of de ox, de ox am stubborn and den some more. One time I's haulin' fence rails and de oxen starts to turn gee when I wants dem to go ahead. I calls for haw, but dey pays dis nigger no mind and keeps agwine gee. Den dey starts to run and de overseer hollers and asks me, 'Whar you gwine?' I hollers back, 'I's not gwine, I's bein' took.'

Dem oxen takes me to de well for de water, 'cause if dey gits dry and is near water, dey goes in spite of de devil.

"De treatment from new massa am good, 'cause of Missy Mary. She say to Massa Bill, 'if you mus' 'buse de nigger, 'buse yous own.' We has music and parties. We plays de quill, make from willow stick when de sap am up. Yous takes de stick and pounds de bark loose and slips it off, den slit de wood in one end and down one side, puts holes in de bark and put it back on de stick. De quill plays like de flute.

"I never goes out without de pass, so I never has trouble with de patter rollers. Nigger Monk, him have de 'sperience with 'em. Dey kotched him twice and dey sho' makes him hump and holler. After dat he gits pass or stays to home.

"De War make no diff'runce with us, 'cept de soldiers comes and takes de rations. But we'uns never goes hungry, 'cause de massa puts some niggers hustlin' for wil' hawgs. After surrender, missy reads de paper and tells dat we'uns is free, but dat we'uns kin stay 'til we is 'justed to de change.

"De second year after de War, de massa sells de plantation and goes back to Louisiana and den we'uns all lef'. I goes to Laredo for seven year and works on a stock ranch, den I goes to farmin'. I gits married in 1879 to Mary Robinson and we'uns has 14 chilluns. Four of dem lives here.

"I works hard all my life 'til 1935 and den I's too old. My wife and I lives on de pensions we gits.

SCOTT HOOPER

SCOTT HOOPER, 81, was born a slave of the Rev. Robert Turner, a Baptist minister who owned seven slave families. They lived on a small farm near Tenaha, then called Bucksnort, in Shelby County, Texas. Scott's father was owned by Jack Hooper, a neighboring farmer. Scott married Steve Hooper when she was thirteen and they had eight children, whose whereabouts are now unknown to her. She receives an $8.00 monthly pension.

"Well, I'll do de best I can to tell yous 'bout my life. I used to have de good 'collection, but worryment 'bout ups and downs has 'fected my 'membance. I knows how old I is, 'cause mammy have it in de Bible, and I's born in de year 1856, right in Shelby County, and near by Bucksnort, what am call Tenaha now.

"Massa Turner am de bestest man he could be and taken good care of us, for sho'. He treat us like humans. There am no whuppin's like some other places has. Gosh. What some dem old slaves tell 'bout de whup and de short rations and lots of hard work am awful, so us am lucky.

"Massa don't have de big place, but jus' seven families what was five to ten in de family. My mammy had nine chillen, but my pappy didn't live on us place, but on Jack Hooper's farm, what am four mile off. He comes Wednesday and Saturday night to see us. His massa am good, too, and lets him work a acre of land and all what he raises he can sell. Pappy plants cotton and mostest de time he raises better'n half de bale to he acre. Dat-a-way, he have money and he own pony and saddle, and he brung us chillen candy and toys and coffee and tea for mammy. He done save 'bout $500 when surrender come, but it am all 'Federate money and it ain't worth nothin'. He give it to us chillen to play with.

"Massa Turner am de Baptist preacherman and he have de church at Bucksnort. He run de store, too, and folks laughs 'cause 'sides being a preacherman he sells whiskey in dat store. He makes it medicine for us, with de cherry bark and de rust from iron nails in it. He call it, 'Bitters,' and it a good name. It sho' taste bitter as gall. When us feels de misery it am bitters us gits. Castor oil am candy 'side dem bitters!

"My grandmammy am de cook and all us eats in de shed. It am plenty food and meat and 'lasses and brown sugar and milk and butter, and even some white flour. Course, peas and beans am allus on dat table.

"When surrender come massa calls all us in de yard and makes de talk. He tells us we's free and am awful sorry and show great worryment. He say he hate to part with us and us been good to him, but it am de law. He say us can stay and work de land on shares, but mostest left. Course, mammy go to Massa Hooper's place to pappy and he rents land from Massa Hooper, and us live there seven years and might yet, but dem Klu Klux causes so much troublement. All us niggers 'fraid to sleep in de house and goes to de woods at night. Pappy gits 'fraid something happen to us and come to Fort Worth. Dat in 1872 and he farms over in de bottom.

"I's married to Steve Hooper den, 'cause us marry when I's thirteen years old. He goes in teamin' in Fort Worth and hauls sand and gravel twenty-nine years. He doin' sich when he dies in 1900. Den I does laundry work till I's too old. I tries to buy dis house and does fair till age catches me and now I can't pay for it. All I has is $8.00 de month and I's glad to git dat, but it won't even buy food. On sich 'mount, there am no way to stinch myself and pinch off de payments on de house. Dat am de worryment.

ALICE HOUSTON

ALICE HOUSTON, pioneer nurse and midwife on whom many San Angeloans have relied for years, was born October 22, 1859. She was a slave of Judge Jim Watkins on his small plantation in Hays County, near San Marcos, Texas and served as house girl to her mistress, Mrs. Lillie Watkins for many years after the Civil

War. At Mrs. Watkins' death she came with her husband, Jim Houston, to San Angelo, Texas where she has continued her services as nurse to white families to the present time.

Alice relates her slave day experiences as follows:

"I was jes' a little chile when dat Civil War broke out and I's had de bes' white folks in de world. My ole mistress she train me for her house girl and nurse maid. Dat's whar I's gits so many good ideas fer nursin'.

"My mother's name was Mariah Watkins an' my father was named Henry Watkins. He would go out in de woods on Sat'day nights and ketch 'possums and bring dem home and bake 'em wid taters. Dat was de best eatin' we had. Course we had good food all de time but we jes' like dat 'possum best.

"My marster, he only have four families and he had a big garden fer all of us. We had our huts at de back of de farm. Dey was made out of logs and de cracks daubbed up wid mud. Dey was clean and comfortable though, and we had good beds.

"When we was jes' little kids ole marster he ketch us a stealin' watermelons and he say, 'Git! Git! Git! And when we runs and stoops over to crawl through de crack of de fence he sho' give us a big spank. Den we runs off cryin' and lookin' back like.

"Ole marster, he had lots of hogs and cows and chickens and I can jes' taste dat clabber milk now. Ole miss, she have a big dishpan full of clabber and she tells de girl to set dat down out in de yard and she say, 'Give all dem chillun a spoon now and let dem eat dat.' When we all git 'round dat pan we sho' would lick dat clabber up.

"We had straight slips made out of white lowell what was wove on dat ole spinnin' wheel. Den dey make jeans for de men's breeches and dye it wid copperas and some of de cloth dey dye wid sumac berries and hit was sho' purty too.

"Ole miss, she make soda out of a certain kind of weed and dey makes coffee out of dried sweet taters.

"My marster he didn' have no over-seer. He say his slaves had to be treated right. He never 'lowed none of his slaves to be sold 'way from their folks. I's nev'r, nev'r seen any slaves in chains but I's hear talk of dem chains.

"My white folks, dey tries to teach us to read and spell and write some and after ole marster move into town he lets us go to a real school. That's how come I can read so many docto' books you see.

"We goes to church wid our white folks at dem camp meetin's and oh Lawdy! Yes, mam, we all sho' did shout. Sometimes we jined de church too.

"We washed our clothes on Sat'day and danced dat night.

"On Christmas and New Year we would have all de good things old marster and ole missus had and when any of de white folks marry or die dey sho' carry on big. Weddin's and funerals, dem was de biggest times.

"When we gits sick, ole marster he have de docto' right now. He sho' was good 'bout dat. Ole miss she make us wear a piece of lead 'round our necks fer de malaria and to keeps our nose from bleedin' and all of us wore some asafoetida 'round our necks to keep off contagion.

"When de war close ole marster calls up all de slaves and he say, 'You's all free people now, jes' same as I is, and you can go or stay,' and we all wants to stay 'cause wasn't nothin' we knowed how to do only what ole marster tells us. He say he let us work de land and give us half of what we make, and we all stayed on several years until he died. We stayed with Miss Watkins, and here I is an ole nigga, still adoin' good in dis world, a-tellin' de white folks how to take care of de chilluns."

JOSEPHINE HOWARD

JOSEPHINE HOWARD was born in slavery on the Walton plantation near Tuscaloosa, Alabama. She does not know her age, but when Mr. Walton moved to Texas, before the Civil War, she was old enough to work in the fields. Josephine is blind and very feeble. She lives with a daughter at 1520 Arthur St., Houston, Texas.

"Lawd have mercy, I been here a thousand year, seems like. 'Course I ain't been here so long, but it seems like it when I gits to thinkin' back. It was long time since I was born, long 'fore de war. Mammy's name was Leonora and she was cook for Marse Tim Walton what had de plantation at Tuscaloosa. Dat am in Alabamy. Papa's name was Joe Tatum and he lived on de place 'jinin' ourn. Course, papa and mamy wasn't married like folks now, 'cause dem times de white folks jes' put slave men and women together like hosses or cattle.

"Dey allus done tell us it am wrong to lie and steal, but why did de white folks steal my mammy and her mammy? Dey lives clost to some water, somewheres over in Africy, and de man come in a little boat to de sho' and tell dem he got presents on de big boat. Most de men am out huntin' and my mammy and her mammy gits took out to dat big boat and dey locks dem in a black hole what mammy say so black you can't see nothin'. Dat de sinfulles' stealin' dey is.

"De captain keep dem locked in dat black hole till dat boat gits to Mobile and dey is put on de block and sold. Mammy is 'bout twelve year old and dey am sold to Marse Tim, but grandma dies in a month and dey puts her in de slave graveyard.

"Mammy am nuss gal till she git older and den cook, and den old Marse Tim puts her and papa together and she has eight chillen. I reckon Marse Tim warn't no wor'ser dan other white folks. De nigger driver sho' whip us, with de reason and without de reason. You never knowed. If dey done took de notion dey jes' lays it on you and you can't do nothin'.

"One mornin' we is all herded up and mammy am cryin' and say dey gwine to Texas, but can't take papa. He don't 'long to dem. Dat de lastes' time we ever seed papa. Us and de women am put in wagons but de men slaves am chained together and has to walk.

"Marse Tim done git a big farm up by Marshall but only live a year dere and his boys run de place. Dey jes' like dey papa, work us and work us. Lawd have mercy, I hear dat call in de mornin' like it jes' jesterday, 'All right, everybody out, and you better git out iffen you don't want to feel dat bullwhip 'cross you back.'

"My gal I lives with don't like me to talk 'bout dem times. She say it ain't no more and it ain't good to think 'bout it. But when you has live in slave times you ain't gwine forgit dem, no, suh! I's old and blind and no 'count, but I's alive, but in slave times I'd be dead long time ago, 'cause white folks didn't have no use for old niggers and git shet of dem one way or t'other.

"It ain't till de sojers comes we is free. Dey wants us to git in de pickin', so my folks and some more stays. Dey didn't know no place to go to. Mammy done took sick and die and I hires out to cook for Missy Howard, and marries her coachman, what am Woodson Howard. We farms and comes to Houston nigh sixty year ago. Dey has mule cars den. Woodson gits a job drayin' and 'fore he dies we raises three boys and seven gals, but all 'cept two gals am dead now. Dey takes care of me, and dat all I know 'bout myself.

LIZZIE HUGHES

LIZZIE HUGHES, blind Negress of Harrison County, Texas, was born on Christmas Day, 1848, a slave of Dr. Newton Fall, near Nacogdoches. Lizzie married when she was eighteen and has lived near Marshall since that time. She is cared for by a married daughter, who lives on Lizzie's farm.

"My name am Lizzie Fall Hughes. I was borned on Christmas at Chireno, 'tween old Nacogdoches town and San Augustine. Dat eighty-nine year ago in slavery time. My young master give me my age on a piece of paper when I married but the rats cut it up.

"I 'longed to Dr. Fall and old Miss Nancy, his wife. They come from Georgia. Papa was named Ed Wilson Fall and mammy was June. Dr. Newton Fall had a big place at Chireno and a hundred slaves. They lived in li'l houses round the edge of the field. We had everything we needed. Dr. Newton run a store and was a big printer. He had a printin' house at Chireno and 'nother in California.

"The land was red and they worked them big Missouri mules and sho' raised somethin'. Master had fifty head of cows, too, and they was plenty wild game. When master was gone he had a overseer, but tell him not to whip.

He didn't 'lieve in rushin' his niggers. All the white folks at Chireno was good to they niggers. On Saturday night master give all the men a jug of syrup and a sack of flour and a ham or middlin' and the smokehouse was allus full of beef and pork. We had a good time on that place and the niggers was happy. I 'member the men go out in the mornin', singin':

> "'I went to the barn with a shinin', bright moon,
> I went to the wood a-huntin' a coon.
> The coon spied me from a sugar maple tree,
> Down went my gun and up the tree went me.
> Nigger and coon come tumblin' down,
> Give the hide to master to take off to town,
> That coon was full of good old fat,
> And master brung me a new beaver hat.'

"Part of 'nother song go like this:
> "'Master say, you breath smell of brandy,
> Nigger say, no, I's lick 'lasses candy.'

"When old master come to the lot and hear the men singin' like that, he say, 'Them boys is lively this mornin', I's gwine git a big day's plowin' done. They did, too, 'cause them big Missouri mules sho' tore up that red land. Sometime they sing:

> "'This ain't Christmas mornin', just a long
> summer day,

> Hurry up, yellow boy and don't run 'way,
> Grass in the cotton and weeds in the corn,
> Get in the field, 'cause it soon be morn.'

"At night when the hands come in they didn't do nothin' but eat and cut up round the quarters. They'd have a big ball in a big barn there on the place and sixty and seventy on the floor at once, singin':

> "'Juba this and Juba that,
> Juba killed a yaller cat.
> Juba this and Juba that,
> Hold you partner where you at.'

"The whites preached to the niggers and the niggers preached to theyselves. Gen'man sho' could preach good them times; everybody cried, they preached so good. I's a mourner when I git free.

"I's big 'nough to work round the house when war starts, but not big 'nough to be studyin' 'bout marryin'. I's sho' sorry when we's sot free. Old master didn't tell his niggers they free. He didn't want them to go. On a day he's gone, two white men come and showed us a piece of paper and say we's free now. One them men was a big mill man and told mama he'll give her $12.00 a month and feed her seven li'l niggers if she go cook for his millhands. Papa done die in slavery, so mama goes with the man. I run off and hid under the house. I wouldn't leave till I seed master. When he come home he say, 'Lizzie, why didn't you go?' I say, 'I don't want to leave my preserves and light bread.' He let me stay.

"Then I gits me a li'l man. He works for master in the store and I works round the house. Master give me two dresses and a pair of shoes when I married. We lived with him a year or two and then come to Marshall. My husband worked on public work and I kept house for white folks and we saved our money and buyed this li'l farm. My man's dead fourteen years now and my gal and her husband keeps the farm goin'.

"Me and my man didn't have nothin' when we left Nacogdoches, but we works hard and saves our money and buyed this farm. It 'pear like these young niggers don't try to 'cumulate nothin'.

MOSES HURSEY

MOSE HURSEY believes he is about eighty-two years old. He was born in slavery on a plantation in Louisiana, and was brought to Texas by his parents after they were freed. Mose has been a preacher most of his life, and now believes he is appointed by God to be "Head Prophet of the World." He lives with his daughter at 1120 Tenth St., Dallas, Texas.

"I was born somewhere in Louisiana, but can't rec'lect the place exact, 'cause I was such a little chap when we left there. But I heared my mother and father say they belonged to Marse Morris, a fine gentleman, with everything fine. He sold them to Marse Jim Boling, of Red River County, in Texas. So they changes their name from Morris to Boling, Liza Boling and Charlie Boling, they was. Marse Boling didn't buy my brother and sister, so that made me the olderest child and the onliest one.

"The Bolings had a 'normous big house and a 'normous big piece of land. The house was the finest I ever seen, white and two-story. He had about sixty slaves, and he thought a powerful lot of my folks, 'cause they was good workers. My mother, special, was a powerful 'ligious woman.

"We lived right well, considerin'. We had a little log house like the rest of the niggers and I played round the place. Eatin' time come, my mother brung a pot of peas or beans and cornbread or side meat. I had 'nother brother and sister comin' 'long then, and we had tin plates and cups and knives and spoons, and allus sot to our food.

"We had 'nough of clothes, sich as they was. I wore shirttails out of duckings till I was a big boy. All the little niggers wore shirttails. My mother had fair to middlin' cotton dresses.

"All week the niggers worked plantin' and hoein' and carin' for the livestock. They raised cotton and corn and veg'tables, and mules and horses and hawgs and sheep. On Sundays they had meetin', sometimes at our house, sometimes at 'nother house. Right fine meetin's, too. They'd preach and pray and sing—shout, too. I heared them git up with a powerful force of the spirit, clappin' they hands and walkin' round the place. They'd shout, 'I got the glory. I got that old time 'ligion in my heart.' I seen some powerful 'figurations of the spirit in them days. Uncle Billy preached to us and he was right good at preachin' and nat'rally a good man, anyways. We'd sing:

> "'Sisters, won't you help me bear my cross,
> Help me bear my cross,
> I been done wear my cross.
> I been done with all things here,
> 'Cause I reach over Zion's Hill.
> Sisters, won't you please help bear my cross,
> Up over Zion's hill?'

"I seed a smart number of wagons and mules a-passin' along and some camp along the woods by our place. I heared they was a war and folks was goin' with 'visions and livestock. I wasn't much bigger'n a minute and I was scared clean to my wits.

"Then they's a time when paw says we'll be a-searchin' a place to stay and work on a pay way. They was a consider'ble many niggers left the Bolings. The day we went away, which was 'cause 'twas the breakin' up of slavery, we went in the wagon, out the carriage gate in front the Boling's place. As we was leavin', Mr. Boling called me and give me a cup sweet coffee. He thought consid'ble plenty of me.

"We went to a place called Mantua, or somethin' like that. My paw says he'll make a man of me, and he puts me to breakin' ground and choppin' wood. Them was bad times. Money was scarce and our feedin' was pore.

"My paw died and maw and me and the children, Nancy and Margina and Jessie and George, moves to a little place right outside Sherman. Maw took in washin' and ironin'. I went one week to school and the teacher said I learned fastest of any boy she ever see. She was a nice, white lady. Maw took me out of school 'cause she needed me at home to tend the other children, so's she could work. I had a powerful yearnin' to read and write, and I studied out'n my books by myself and my friends helped me with the cipherin'.

"I did whatever work I could find to do, but my maw said I was a different mood to the other children. I was allus of a 'ligious and serious turn of mind. I was baptised when I was fifteen and then when I was about twenty-five I heared a clear call to preach the Gospel-word. I went to preachin' the word of Gawd. I got married and raised a family of children, and I farmed and preached.

"I was just a preacher till about thirty years ago, and then Gawd started makin' a prophet out of me. Today I am Mose Hursey, Head Prophet to the World. They is lesser prophets, but I is the main one. I became a great prophet by fastin' and prayin'. I fast Mondays and Wednesdays and Fridays. I know Gawd is feedin' the people through me. I see him in visions and he speaks to me. In 1936 I saw him at Commerce and Jefferson Streets (Dallas) and he had a great banner, sayin', 'All needs a pension.' In August this year I had a great vision of war in the eastern corner of the world. I seen miles of men marchin' and big guns and trenches filled with dead men. Gawd tells me to tell the people to be prepared, 'cause the tides of war is rollin' this way, and all the thousands of millions of dollars they spend agin it ain't goin' to stop it. I live to tell people the word Gawd speaks through me.

CHARLEY HURT

CHARLEY HURT, 85, was born a slave of John Hurt, who owned a large plantation and over a hundred slaves, in Oglethorpe County, Georgia. Charley stayed with his master for five years after the Civil War. In 1899 Charley moved to Fort Worth, and now lives at 308 S. Harding St.

"Yes, suh, I'm borned in slavery and not 'shamed of it, 'cause I can't help how I'm borned. Dere am folks what wont say dey borned in slavery.

"Us plantation am near Maxie, over in Oglethorpe County, in Georgia, and massa am John Hurt and he have near a hunerd slaves. Us live in de li'l cabin make from logs chink with mud and straw and twigs am mix with dat mud to make it hold. De big chimley am outside de cabin mostly, and am logs and mud, too. De cabin am 'bout ten by twenty feet and jus' one room.

"Would I like some dem rations we used to git, now? 'Deed I would. Dem was good, dat meat and cornmeal and 'lasses and plenty milk and sometimes butter. De meat am mostest pork, with some beef, 'cause massa raise plenty hawgs and tendin' meat curin' am my first work. I puts dat meat in de brine and den smokes de hams and shoulders. When hawg-killin' time come I'm busy watchin' de smokehouse, what am big, and hams and sich hung on racks 'bout six feet high from de fireplace. Den it my duty to keep dat fire smoulderin' and jus' smokin'. De more smoke, de better. Den I packs dat meat in hawgs heads and puts salt over each layer. Dat am some meat!

"I mus' tell you 'bout dat whiskey and brandy. Massa have he own still and allus have three barrels or more whiskey and brandy on hand. Den on Christmas Day, him puts a tub of whiskey or brandy in de yard and hangs tin cups 'round de tub. Us helps ourselves. At first us start jokin' with each other, den starts to sing and everybody am happy. Massa watches us and if one us gittin' too much, massa sends him to he cabin and he sleep it off. Anyway, dat one day on massa's place all am happy and forgits dey am slaves.

"De last Christmas 'fore surrender I gits too much and am sick. Gosh a-mighty! Dat de sickest I ever be and dat de last time I gits drunk. Yes, suh, dat spoil dis nigger's taste for whiskey.

"Now, 'bout whuppin's, dere am only one whuppin' what am give. Jerry gits dat, 'cause he wont do what massa say. He tie Jerry on de log and have de rawhide whip.

"Dere am system on dat plantation. Everybody do he own work, sich as field hands, stock hands, de blacksmith and de shoemaker and de weavers and clothes makers. I'm all 'round worker and goes after de mail, jus' runnin' 'round de place.

"When de war start, all massa's sons jines de army. He have three. John am de captain and James carry de flag and I guesses August am jus' de plain sojer. Dey all comes home 'fore de war am finish. August git run over by de wheel of de cannon truck and it cripple he legs so he can't walk good. James gits sick with some kind fever misery and he am sent home. Den John am shot in de shoulder and it stay sore and won't heal. One day Jerry say to massa he want to look at dat sore. Him see somethin' stickin' out and he pull it. It a piece of young massa's coat and de bullet have carry it into de flesh and it am dere a whole year. De sore gits all right after dat out.

"'Fore de boys goes to fightin' dey trains near de place where am de big field for to train hunerds of sojer boys. I likes dat, 'cause de drums goes, 'ter-ump, ter-ump, ter-ump, tump, tump,' and de fifes goes, 'te, te, ta, te, tat' and plays Dixie. One day Young massa trainin' dem sojers and he am walkin' backwards and facin' dem sojers, and jus' as him say, 'Halt,' down he go, flat on he back. Right away quick, him say, ''Bout face,' 'cause him don't want dem sojers to laugh in he face, so he turn dem 'round.

"When surrender come, all dem what not kilt comes home and dey have a big 'ception in Maxie. Dey have lots of long tables and de food am put on 'fore de train come in. Dere was two coaches full of de boys and dey doesn't wait for dat train to stop. No, suh, dey crawls out de windows. Well, dere am huggin' and kissin' of de homefolks, and dey all laughin' and cryin' at de same time, 'cause of de joy dey's feelin'. Den dey all sets down to de feast. Massa make de welcome talk. I done hide in de wagon full of hams and cakes and pies and dere a canvas over dat stuff, and dat how I gits to dat welcome home.

"I crawls out 'fore dey unloads de wagon and 'fore long massa see me and him say, 'Gosh for hemlock! Boy, how comes you here?' I lets my face slip a li'l, 'bout half a laugh. I says, 'I rides under dat canvas.' Dat start him laughin' and he tells de people dat I'm a pat'otic nigger. After dey all eats us niggers gits to eat. For once, I gits plenty pie and cake.

"Us never have much joyments in slave time. Only when de corn ready for huskin' all de neighbors comes dere and a whole big crowd am a-huskin' and singin'. I can't 'member dem songs, 'cause I'm not much for singin'. One go like dis:

> "'Pull de husk, break de ear;
> Whoa, I's got de red ear here.'

"When you finds de red ear, dat 'titles you to de prize, like kissin' de gal or de drink of brandy or somethin'. Dey not 'nough red ears to suit us.

"I'm thirteen year when surrender come. Massa don't call us to him like other massas done. Him jus' go 'mongst de folks and say, 'Well, folks, yous am free now and no longer my prop'ty, and yous 'titled to pay for work. I 'member old Jerry sings, 'Free, free as de jaybird, free to flew like de jaybird. Whew!'

"Some de cullud folks stays and some goes. Mostest dem stays and works de land on shares. I stays till I'm eighteen year and den I works for a farmer den for a blacksmith den some carpenter work and some railroadin'. De fact am, I works at anything I could find to does. I does dat most my life.

"It good for me to stay with Massa Hurt after freedom, 'cause den day plenty trouble in every place. Dere am fightin' 'twixt white and cullud folks over votin' and sich. Dey try 'lect my brudder to Congress one time, but he not 'lect, 'cause de white man what am runnin' 'gainst him gits a cullud preacher to run 'gainst dem both. Dat split de cullud votes and de white man am 'lect. I votes like de white man say, couple times, but after dat I stops votin'. It ain't right for me to vote 'less I knows how and why. I larns to read and den starts votin' 'gain.

"After de war de Ku Klux am org'nize and dey makes de niggers plenty trouble. Sometimes de niggers has it comin' to 'em and lots of times dey am 'posed on. Dere a old, cullud man name George and he don't trouble nobody, but one night de white caps—dat what dey called—comes to George's place. Now, George know of some folks what am whupped for no-cause, so he prepare for dem white caps. When dey gits to he house George am in de loft. He tell dem he done nothin' wrong and for dem to go 'way, or he kill dem. Dey say he gwine have a free sample of what he git if he do wrong and one dem white caps starts up de ladder to git George and George shoot him dead. 'Nother white cap starts shootin' through de ceilin'. He can't see George but through de cracks George can see and he shoots de second feller. So dey leaves and say dey come back. George runs to he old massa and he takes George to de law men. Never nothin' am done 'bout him killin' de white caps, 'cause dem white caps goes 'round 'busing niggers.

"I comes to Texas 'bout 40 year since and gits by purty good till de depression comes, den it hard for me. My age am 'gainst me, too, and many de time I's wish for some dat old ham and bacon on de old plantation.

"First I marries Ann Arrant, in 1898 dat was, and us have three chillen but dey all dead. Us git sep'rate in 1917 and I marries Mary Durham in 1921, and us still livin' together. Us have no chillen. Mammy have ten chillen but I'm de only one what am livin' now, 'cause I'm de youngest.

United States. Work Projects Administration

WASH INGRAM

WASH INGRAM, A 93 year old Negro, was born a slave of Capt. Jim Wall, of Richmond, Va. His father, Charley Wall Ingram, ran away and secured work in a gold mine. Later, his mother died and Capt. Wall sold Wash and his two brothers to Jim Ingram, of Carthage, Texas. When Wash's father learned this, he overtook his sons before they reached Texas and put himself back in bondage, so he could be with his children. Wash served as water carrier for the Confederate soldiers at the battle of Mansfield, La. He now lives with friends on the Elysian Fields Road, seven miles southeast of Marshall, Texas.

"I don' know just how ole I is. I was 'bout 18 when de War was over. I was bo'n on Captain Wall's place in Richmond, Virgini'. Pappy's name was Charlie and mammy's name was Ca'line. I had six sisters and two brothers and all de sisters is dead. I haven't heard from my brothers since Master turn us loose, a year after de war.

"Pappy say dat he and mammy was sold and traded lots of times in Virgini'. We always went by de name of whoever we belonged to. I first worked as a roustabout boy dere on Capt. Wall's place in Virgini'. He was sho' a big man, weighed more'n 200 pounds. He owned lots of niggers and worked lots of land. The white folks was good to us, but Pappy was a fightin' man and he run off and got a job in a gold mine in Virgini'.

"After pappy run away, mammy died and den one day de overseer herded up a big bunch of us niggers and driv us to Barnum's Tradin' Ya'd down in Mississippi. Dat's a place where dey sold and traded Niggers jus' lak stock. I cried when Capt. Wall sold me, 'cause dat was one man dat sho' was good to his niggers. But he had too many slaves.

"Cotton was a good price den and dem slave buyers had plenty of money. We was sold to Jim Ingram, of Carthage. He bought a big gang of slaves and refugeed part of 'em to Louisiana and part to Texas. We come to Texas in ox wagons. While we was on the way, camped at Keachie, Louisiana, a man come ridin' into camp and someone say to me, 'Wash, dar's your pappy.' I didn' believe it 'cause pappy was workin' in a gold mine in Virgini'. Some of de men told pappy his chillen is in camp and he come and fin' me and my brothers. Den he jine Master Ingram's slaves so he can be with his chillen.

"Master Ingram had a big plantation down near Carthage and lots of niggers. He also buyed land, cleared it and sol' it. I plowed with oxen. We had a overseer and sev'ral taskmasters. Dey whip de niggers for not workin' right, or for runnin' 'way or pilferin' roun' master's house. We woke up at four o'clock and worked from sunup to sundown. Dey give us an hour for dinner. Dem dat work roun' de house et at tables with plates. Dem dat work in de field was drove in from work and fed jus' like hosses at a big, long wooden trough. Dey had to eat with a wooden spoon. De trough and de food was clean and always plenty of it, and we stood up to eat. We went to bed soon after supper durin' de week for dat's 'bout all we feel like doin' after workin' twelve hours. We slep' in wooden beds what had corded rope mattresses.

"We had to learn de best way we could, 'cause dere was no schools. We had church out in de woods. I didn' see no money till after de surrender. Guess we didn' need any, 'cause dey give us food and clothes and tobacco. We didn' have to buy nothin'. I had broadcloth clothes, a blue jean overcoat and good shoes and boots.

"De niggers had heap better times dan now. Now we work all time and can't git nothin'. Sat'day night we would have parties and dance and play ring plays. We had de parties dere in a big double log house. Dey would give us whiskey and wine and cherry brandy, but dere wasn' no shootin' or gamblin'. Dey didn' 'low it. De men and women didn' do like dey do now. If dey had such carryin's on as dey do now, de white folks would have whipped 'em good.

"I 'member dat war and I sees dem cannons and hears 'em. I toted water for de soldiers what fought at de Battle of Mansfield. Master Ingram had 350 slaves when de war was over but he didn' turn us loose till a year after surrender. He telled us dat de gov'ment goin' to give us 40 acres of land and a pair of mules, but we didn' git nothin'. After Master Ingram turn us loose, pappy bought a place at De Berry, Texas, and I live with him till after I was grown. Den I marry and move to Louisiana. I come back to Texas two years ago and lived with my friends here ever since. My wife died 18 years ago and I had a hard time 'cause I don' have no folks, but I's managed to git someone to let me work for somethin' to eat, a few clothes and a place to sleep.

CARTER J. JACKSON

CARTER J. JACKSON, 85, was born in Montgomery, Alabama, a slave of Parson Dick Rogers. In 1863 the Rogers family brought Carter to Texas and he worked for them as a slave until four years after emancipation. Carter was with his master's son, Dick, when he was killed at Pittsburg, Pa. Carter married and moved to Tatum in 1871.

"If you's wants to know 'bout slavery time, it was Hell. I's born in Montgomery, over yonder in Alabama. My pappy named Charles and come from Florida and mammy named Charlotte and her from Tennessee. They was sold to Parson Rogers and brung to Alabama by him. I had seven brothers call Frank and Benjamin and Richardson and Anderson and Miles, Emanuel and Gill, and three sisters call Milanda, Evaline and Sallie, but I don't know if any of 'em are livin' now.

"Parson Rogers come to Texas in '63 and brung 'bout 42 slaves and my first work was to tote water in the field. Parson lived in a good, big frame house, and the niggers lived in log houses what had dirt floors and chimneys, and our bunks had rope slats and grass mattress. I sho' wish I could have cotch myself sleepin' on a feather bed them days. I wouldn't woke up till Kingdom Come.

"We et vegetables and meat and ash cake. You could knock you mammy in the head, eatin' that ash cake bread. I ain't been fit since. We had hominy cooked in the fireplace in big pots that ain't bad to talk 'bout. Deer was thick them days and we sot up sharp stobs inside the pea field and them young bucks jumps over the fence and stabs themselves. That the only way to cotch them, 'cause they so wild you couldn't git a fair shot with a rifle.

"Massa Rogers had a 300 acre plantation and 200 in cultivation and he had a overseer and Steve O'Neal was the nigger driver. The horn to git up blowed 'bout four o'clock and if we didn't fall out right now, the overseer was in after us. He tied us up every which way and whip us, and at night he walk the quarters to keep us from runnin' 'round. On Sunday mornin' the overseer come 'round to each nigger cabin with a big sack of shorts and give us 'nough to make bread for one day.

"I used to steal some chickens, 'cause we didn't have 'nough to eat, and I don' think I done wrong, 'cause the place was full of 'em. We sho' earned what we et. I'd go up to the big house to make fires and lots of times I seed the mantel board lined with greenbacks, 'tween mantel and wall and I's snitched many a $50.00 bill, but it 'federate money.

"Me and four of her chillen standin' by when mammy's sold for $500.00. Cryin' didn't stop 'em from sellin' our mammy 'way from us.

"I 'member the war was tough and I went 'long with young massa Dick when he went to the war, to wait on him. I's standin' clost by when he was kilt under a big tree in Pittsburg, and 'fore he die he ask Wes Tatum, one the neighbor boys from home, to take care of me and return me to Massa George.

"I worked on for Massa Rogers four year after that, jus' like in slavery time, and one day he call us and say we can go or stay. So I goes with my pappy and lives with him till 1871. Then I marries and works on the railroad when it's built from Longview to Big Sandy, 'bout 1872. I works there sev'ral years and I raises seven chillen. After I quits the railroad I works wherever I can, on farms or in town.

JAMES JACKSON

JAMES JACKSON, 87, was born a slave to the Alexander family, in Caddo Parish, La. When he was about two, his master moved to Travis County, Texas. A short time later he and his two brothers were stolen and sold to Dr. Duvall, in Bastrop Co., Texas. He worked around Austin till he married, when he moved to Taylor and then to

Kaufman. In 1929 he went to Fort Worth where he has lived ever since.

"I was bo'n at Caddo Parish, dats in Louisiana, on de Doc Alexander plantation. My mother says I was bo'n on de 18th day of December, in de year of 1850. I guess dat's right, 'cause I's 87 years ole dis comin' December.

"Jus' 'bout dat time dey started shippin' de darkies to Texas. My marster moved to Travis County, Texas, and tuk all his slaves wid him. I was too young to 'member, but my mother, she told me 'bout it.

"It wasn' long after we was on Marster Alexander's new place in Travis County, till one night a man rode up on a hoss and stole me and my two brothers and rode away wid us. He tuk us to Bastrop County and sold us to Doc Duvall. Marster Duvall sold my brother right after he bought us, but me and John, we stayed wid him till de slaves was freed.

"On Marster Duvall's plantation de slaves all lived in log cabins back of de big house. Dey was one room, two rooms and three room cabins, dependin' on de size of de family. Most had dirt floors, but some of 'em had log slabs. We had dese ole wooden beds wid a rope stretch 'cross de bottom and a mattress of straw or cotton dat de niggers got in de fiel'. We had lots to eat, like biscuit, cornbread, meat and sich stuff. Most times dey made coffee outta parch cornmeal. We had gardens and raised most of de stuff to eat.

"I herds sheep and is houseboy most of de time. When I was ole enough, I picks cotton. I was jus' learnin' when de slaves was freed. Marster Duvall had over 500 acres in cotton and he kep' us in de fiel' all de time, 'cept Saturday afternoon and Sunday.

"Dey had meetin' and dances Saturday nights. I was too young to 'member jus' what de songs was, but dey had a fiddle and played all night long. On ever' Sunday de niggers went to Church in de evenin'. Dey had a white preacher in de mornin' and a cullud preacher in de evenin'.

"Marster Duvall would whip de niggers who was disobedience and he jus' call dem up and ask dem what was de trouble, den he would whip dem wid a cowhide or a rope whip. We could go anywhere iffen we had a pass, but if we didn' de paddlerollers would ketch us. They was kinda like policemen we got today.

"In slavery, dey traded and sold niggers like dey do hosses and mules. Dey carry dem to de court house and put dem on de block and auction 'em off. Some sold for roun' $3,000. It was hard to sell one wid scars on him, 'cause nobody wanted him. I seen 'em come by in droves, all chained together.

"When de slaves was free dey was sho' happy. Dey all got together and had a kin' of cel'bration. Marster told dem if dey wanted to stay and help make de crop, he'd give 'em 50 cents a day and a place to stay. Some tuk him up on dat and stayed, but a lot of dem left dere. Me and my brother, we started walkin' to Austin. In Austin we finds our mother, she was working for Judge Paschal. She hires us out to one place and den another.

"Since freedom I done most everything anybody could do. I been porter and waiter in hotels and rest'rants. I been factory hand, and worked for carpenters and in de roun' house. I picked cotton and worked on de farm.

"I been married 61 years. I gits married at home, like civilize folks do. I raised a big family, 12 chillen, but only five is alive today. I moved here in 1929 and looks like I's here till I die.

MAGGIE JACKSON

MAGGIE JACKSON was born a slave of the Sam Oliver family, in Cass Co., Texas, near Douglasville. She is about 80 years old and her memory is not very good, so her story gives few details. She lives with her daughter near Douglasville, on highway #8.

"I am about 80 years old and was a chile during slavery times. My papa's name was Tom Spencer Hall and my mama's name was Margaret Hall. My brothers and sisters was Maria and Barbara and Alice and Octavia and Andrew and Thomas and Hillary and Eugenia and Silas and Thomas. We was a big fam'ly.

"My mama was Sam Oliver's slave, but my papa lived a mile away with Masta Sam Carlow. We lived in box houses and slep' on wood beds and we et co'nbread and peas and grits and lots of rabbits and 'possums. Mama cooked it on the fireplace.

"Masta Sam's house was big and had six big rooms with a hall through the middle and the kitchen sot way off in the ya'd and had a big cellar under it. Masta Sam had a big orchard and put apples and pears in the cellar for the winter. My brothers use' to slip under there and steal them and mama'd whip 'em.

"The big house set 'mong big oak trees and the slaves houses was scattered roun' the back. Masta Sam had a ole cowhorn he use' to blow for the niggers to come outta the fiel'.

"Mos' all us chillen wen' fishin' on Saturday and we'd fish with pins. One day I slipped off and caught a whole string of fish.

"We learned to read and write and we wen' to church with the white folks. Masta Sam was good to us and gave us plenty food and clothes.

"I never was 'fraid of haints and I never see none, but I know some seen 'em.

"I married John Jackson in a white muslin dress and we was married by Dan Sherman, a cullud preacher from Jefferson. I married John 'cause I loved him and we didn' fuss and fight. I has five chillen and five grandchillen.

MARTIN JACKSON

MARTIN JACKSON, who calls himself a "black Texan", well deserves to select a title of more distinction, for it is quite possible that he is the only living former slave who served in both the Civil War and the World War. He was born in bondage in Victoria Co., Texas, in 1847, the property of Alvy Fitzpatrick. This self-respecting Negro is totally blind, and when a person touches him on the arm to guide him he becomes bewildered and asks his helper to give verbal directions, up, down, right or left. It may be he has been on his own so long that he cannot, at this late date, readjust himself to the touch of a helping hand. His mind is uncommonly clear and he speaks with no Negro colloquialisms and almost no dialect.

Following directions as to where to find Martin Jackson, "the most remarkable Negro in San Antonio," a researcher made his way to an old frame house at 419 Center St., walked up the steps and through the house to an open door of a rear room. There, on an iron bed, lay a long, thin Negro, smoking a cigarette. He was dressed in a woolen undershirt and black trousers and his beard and mustache were trimmed much after the fashion of white gallants of the Gay Nineties. His head was remarkably well-shaped, with striking eminences in his forehead over his brows.

After a moment the intruder spoke and announced his mission. The old Negro, who is stone blind, quickly admitted that he was Martin Jackson, but before making any further comment he carried on an efficient interview himself; he wanted to know who the caller was, who had directed the visit, and just what branch of the Federal service happened to be interested in the days of slavery. These questions satisfactorily answered, he went into his adventures and experiences, embellishing the highlights with uncommon discernment and very little prodding by the researcher.

"I have about 85 years of good memory to call on. I'm ninety, and so I'm not counting my first five years of life. I'll try to give you as clear a picture as I can. If you want to give me a copy of what you are going to write, I'll appreciate it. Maybe some of my children would like to have it.

"I was here in Texas when the Civil War was first talked about. I was here when the War started and followed my young master into it with the First Texas Cavalry. I was here during reconstruction, after the War. I was here during the European World War and the second week after the United States declared war on Germany I enlisted as cook at Camp Leon Springs.

"This sounds as if I liked the war racket. But, as a matter of fact, I never wore a uniform—grey coat or khaki coat—or carried a gun, unless it happened to be one worth saving after some Confederate soldier got shot. I was official lugger-in of men that got wounded, and might have been called a Red Cross worker if we had had such a corps connected with our company. My father was head cook for the battalion and between times I helped him out with the mess. There was some difference in the food served to soldiers in 1861 and 1917!

"Just what my feelings was about the War, I have never been able to figure out myself. I knew the Yanks were going to win, from the beginning. I wanted them to win and lick us Southerners, but I hoped they was going to do it without wiping out our company. I'll come back to that in a minute. As I said, our company was the First Texas Cavalry. Col. Buchell was our commander. He was a full-blooded German and as fine a man and a soldier as you ever saw. He was killed at the Battle of Marshall and died in my arms. You may also be interested to know that my old master, Alvy Fitzpatrick, was the grandfather of Governor Jim Ferguson.

"Lots of old slaves closes the door before they tell the truth about their days of slavery. When the door is open, they tell how kind their masters was and how rosy it all was. You can't blame them for this, because they had plenty of early discipline, making them cautious about saying anything uncomplimentary about their masters. I, myself, was in a little different position than most slaves and, as a consequence, have no grudges or resentment. However, I can tell you the life of the average slave was not rosy. They were dealt out plenty of cruel suffering.

"Even with my good treatment, I spent most of my time planning and thinking of running away. I could have done it easy, but my old father used to say, 'No use running from bad to worse, hunting better.' Lots of colored boys did escape and joined the Union army, and there are plenty of them drawing a pension today. My father was always counseling me. He said, 'Every man has to serve God under his own vine and fig tree.' He kept pointing out that the War wasn't going to last forever, but that our forever was going to be spent living among the Southeners, after they got licked. He'd cite examples of how the whites would stand flatfooted and fight for the blacks the same as for members of their own family. I knew that all was true, but still I rebelled, from inside of me. I think I really was afraid to run away, because I thought my conscience would haunt me. My father knew I felt this way and he'd rub my fears in deeper. One of his remarks still rings in my ears: 'A clear conscience opens bowels, and when you have a guilty soul it ties you up and death will not for long desert you.'

"No, sir, I haven't had any education. I should have had one, though. My old missus was sorry, after the War, that she didn't teach me. Her name, before she married my old master, was Mrs. Long. She lived in New York City and had three sons. When my old master's wife died, he wrote up to a friend of his in New York, a very prominent merchant named C.C. Stewart. He told this friend he wanted a wife and gave him specifications for one. Well, Mrs. Long, whose husband had died, fitted the bill and she was sent down to Texas. She became Mrs. Fitzpatrick. She wasn't the grandmother of Governor Ferguson. Old Fitzpatrick had two wives that preceded Mrs. Long. One of the wives had a daughter named Fanny Fitzpatrick and it was her that was the Texas' governor's mother. I seem to have the complicated family tree of my old master more clear than I've got my own, although mine can be put in a nutshell: I married only once and was blessed in it with 45 years of devotion. I had 13 children and a big crop of grandchildren.

"My earliest recollection is the day my old boss presented me to his son, Joe, as his property. I was about five years old and my new master was only two.

"It was in the Battle of Marshall, in Louisiana, that Col. Buchell got shot. I was about three miles from the front, where I had pitched up a kind of first-aid station. I was all alone there. I watched the whole thing. I could hear the shooting and see the firing. I remember standing there and thinking the South didn't have a chance. All of a sudden I heard someone call. It was a soldier, who was half carrying Col. Buchell in. I didn't do nothing for the Colonel. He was too far gone. I just held him comfortable, and that was the position he was in when he stopped breathing. That was the worst hurt I got when anybody died. He was a friend of mine. He had had a lot of soldiering before and fought in the Indian War.

"Well, the Battle of Marshall broke the back of the Texas Cavalry. We began straggling back towards New Orleans, and by that time the War was over. The soldiers began to scatter. They was a sorry-lookin' bunch of lost sheep. They didn't know where to go, but most of 'em ended up pretty close to the towns they started from. They was like homing pigeons, with only the instinct to go home and, yet, most of them had no homes to go to.

"No, sir, I never went into books. I used to handle a big dictionary three times a day, but it was only to put it on a chair so my young master could sit up higher at the table. I never went to school. I learned to talk pretty good by associating with my masters in their big house.

"We lived on a ranch of about 1,000 acres close to the Jackson County line in Victoria County, about 125 miles from San Antonio. Just before the war ended they sold the ranch, slaves and all, and the family, not away fighting, moved to Galveston. Of course, my father and me wasn't sold with the other blacks, because we was away at war. My mother was drowned years before when I was a little boy. I only remember her after she was dead. I can take you to the spot in the river today where she was drowned. She drowned herself. I never knew the reason behind it, but it was said she started to lose her mind and preferred death to that."

At this point in the old Negro's narrative the sound of someone singing was heard. A moment later the door to the house slammed shut and in accompaniment to the tread of feet in the kitchen came this song:

> "I sing because I'm happy,
> And I sing because I'm free—
> His eyes is on the sparrow
> And I know He watches me."

The singer glanced in the bedroom and the song ended with both embarrassment and anger:

"Father! Why didn't you say you had callers?"

It was not long, however, before the singer, Mrs. Maggie Jackson, daughter-in-law of old Martin Jackson, joined in the conversation.

"The master's name was usually adopted by a slave after he was set free. This was done more because it was the logical thing to do and the easiest way to be identified than it was through affection for the master. Also, the government seemed to be in a almighty hurry to have us get names. We had to register as someone, so we could be citizens. Well, I got to thinking about all us slaves that was going to take the name Fitzpatrick. I made up my mind I'd find me a different one. One of my grandfathers in Africa was called Jeaceo, and so I decided to be Jackson."

After this clear-headed Negro had posed for his photograph, the researcher took his leave and the old blind man bade him a gracious "good-bye." He stood as if watching his new friend walking away, and then lighted a cigarette.

"How long have you been smoking, Martin?" called back the researcher.

"I picked up the deadly habit," answered Martin, "over seventy-five years ago."

NANCY JACKSON

NANCY JACKSON, about 105 years old, was born in Madison Co., Tennessee, a slave of the Griff Lacy family. She was married during slavery and was the mother of three children when she was freed. In 1835, Nancy claims, she was brought to Texas by her owner, and has lived in Panola Co. all her life. She has no proof of her age and, of course, may be in the late nineties instead of over one hundred, as she thinks. She lives with her daughter about five miles west of Tatum, Tex.

"I's live in Panola County now going on 102 year and that a mighty long time for to 'member back, but I'll try to rec'lect. I's born in Tennessee and I think it's in 1830 or 1832. I lives with my baby chile what am now 57 year old and she's born when I's 'bout 'bout 33. But I ain't sho' 'bout my age, noways.

"Massa Griff fetches us to Texas when I a baby and my brudders what am Redic and Anthony and Essex and Allen and Brick and my sisters what am Ann and Matty and Charlotte, we all come to Texas. Mammy come with us but pappy was sold off the Lacy place and stays in Tennessee.

"Massa had the bigges' house in them parts and a passel of slaves. Mammy's name was Letha, and we have a purty good place to live and massa not bad to us. We was treated fair, I guesses, but they allus whipped us niggers for somethin'. But when we got sick they'd git the doctor, 'cause losin' a nigger like losin' a pile of money in them days.

"Massa sometimes outlines the Bible to us and we had a song what we'd sing sometimes:

> "'Stand your storm, Stand your storm,
> Till the wind blows over,
> Stand your storm, Stand your storm,
> I's a sojer of the Cross,
> A follower of the Lamb.'

"We was woke by a bell and called to eat by a bell and put to bed by that bell and if that bell ring outta time you'd see the niggers jumpin' rail fences and cotton rows like deers or something, gettin' to that house, 'cause that mean something bad wrong at massa's house.

"I marries right here in Panola County while slavery still here and my brother-in-law marries me and Lewis Blakely, and I's 'bout nineteen. My husban' 'longed to the Blakely's and after the weddin' he had to go back to them and they 'lowed him come to see me once a week on Saturday and he could stay till Sunday. I works on for the Lacy's more'n a year after slavery till Lewis come got me and we moved to ourselves.

"I 'member one big time we done have in slavery. Massa gone and he wasn't gone. He left the house 'tendin' go on a visit and missy and her chillen gone and us niggers give a big ball the night they all gone. The leader of that ball had on massa's boots and he sing a song he make up:

> "'Ole massa's gone to Philiman York
> And won't be back till July 4th to come;
> Fac' is, I don't know he'll be back at all,
> Come on all you niggers and jine this ball.'

"That night they done give that big ball, massa had blacked up and slip back in the house and while they singin' and dancin', he sittin' by the fireplace all the time. 'Rectly he spit, and the nigger who had on he boots recernizes him and tries climb up the chimmey."

United States. Work Projects Administration

RICHARD JACKSON

RICHARD JACKSON, Harrison County farmer, was born in 1859, a slave of Watt Rosborough. Richard's family left the Rosboroughs when the Negroes were freed, and moved to a farm near Woodlawn. Richard married when he was twenty-five and moved to an adjoining farm, which he now owns.

"I was born on the Rosborough plantation in 1859 and 'longed to old man Watt Rosborough. He brung my mammy out of North Carolina, but my pappy died when I was a baby, and mammy married Will Jackson. Besides me they was six brothers, Jack and Nathan, Josh and Bill and Ben and Mose. I had three sisters named Matilda and Charity and Anna.

"I 'members my mammy's father, Jack, but don't know where he come from. I heared him tell of fightin' the Indians on the frontier, and one mammy's brothers was shot with a Indian arrow.

"The plantation jined the Sabine river and old man Watt owned many a slave. The old home is still standin' cross the road from Rosborough Springs, nine miles south of Marshall.

"They was a white overseer on the place and mammy's stepdaddy, Kit, was niggerdriver and done all the whippin', 'cept of mammy. She was bad 'bout fightin' and the overseer allus tended to her. One day he come to the quarters to whip her and she up and throwed a shovel full of live coals from the fireplace in his bosom and run out the door. He run her all over the place 'fore he cotched her. I seed the overseer tie her down and whip her. The niggers wasn't whipped much 'cept for fightin' 'mongst themselves.

"I 'members mammy allus sayin' the darkies had to pray out in the woods, 'cause they ain't 'lowed to make no fuss round the house. She say they was fed and clothed well 'nough, but the overseer worked the lights out of the darkies. I wasn't big 'nough to do field work, but 'member goin' to the field to take mammy's pipe to her. They wasn't no matches in them days, and I allus took fire from the house and sot a stump afire in the field, so mammy could light her pipe.

"None of our folks larnt to read and write till after slavery. My oldes' brother was larnin' to read on the sly, but the overseer found out 'bout it and stopped him. He found some letters writ on the wall of the quarter with charcoal and made the darkies tell him who writ it. My brother Jack done it. The overseer didn't whip him, but told him he darns't do it 'gain.

"After surrender my folks left the Rosboroughs right straight and moved clost to Woodlawn. My oldes' hired out in Shreveport. When they asks him what he's worth, he told them he didn't know, but he was allus worth a heap of money when anyone wanted to buy him from the Rosboroughs.

"The Ku Kluxers come to our house in Woodlawn, and I got scart and crawled under the bed. They told mammy they wasn't gwine hurt her, but jus' wanted water to drink. They didn't call each other by names. When the head man spoke to any of them he'd say, Number 1, or Number 2, and like that.

"I thunk I heared ghosts on the Driscoll place once, up in the loft of the house. I heared them plain as day. My step-pa done die there and might of been his ghost. We moved away right straight, and old man Driscoll had to burn that house down after that, 'cause wouldn't none the darkies live in it.

"The only time I voted was when they put whiskey out. I heared a white man one time in Marshall, makin' a speech on the square. He said he was gwine tell us darkies why they didn't low us to vote. He didn't tell us, 'cause the law come out and made him git out the wagon and leave.

"This young race is sho' livin' fast, but I guess they's all right. Things is jes' different now to when I was a boy. When I was a boy, folks didn't mind helpin' one 'nother, but now they is in too big a hurry to pay you any mind.

JOHN JAMES

JOHN JAMES, 78, was born a slave to John Chapman, on a large plantation in East Baton Rouge Parish, Louisiana. John took the name of his father, who was owned by John James. John and his mother stayed with Mr. Chapman for six years after they were freed, then John went to Missouri, where he worked for the M. K. & T.

Railroad for twenty years. He then came to Texas, and now lives at 315 S. Jennings Ave., in Fort Worth.

"I doesn't have so much mind for slavery days, 'cause I's too young then, but I 'members when surrender come and some befo' dat. I 'members my mammy lef' me in de nursery with all de other cullud babies when she go work in de field. De old nurse, Jane, tooks care of us.

"Dat were de big place what Massa John have and dere 'bout fifty cullud families on de place, so it am more'n a hunerd slaves what he own. I's runnin' round, like kids am allus doin', first one place, den t'other, watchin' everything. De big bell ring in de mornin' and you'd see all de cullud folks comin' from dey cabins, gwineter de kitchen to breakfast. Dat allus befo' daybreak, and dey have to eat by de light of de pine torch. It am de pineknot torch. De meals am all cooked dere and dey eat at long tables. De young'uns from six to ten year eats at de second table and little'r den dat, in de nursery.

"I sho' 'members 'bout dat nursery feedin'. I never forgits how dat cornmeal mush and milk am served in de big pans. Dey gives we uns de wooden spoon and we'uns crowds round de pans like little pigs. I can see it now. Us push and shove and de nurse walk here and dere, tryin' to make us eat like humans. She have to cuff one of us once in a while. If she don't, dem kids be in de pans with both feet. When dey done eatin', dey faces am all smear with mush and milk.

"Massa allus feed plenty rations, only after war starts de old folks say dey am short of dis and dat, 'cause dem sojers done took it for de army.

"After breakfast I'd see a crew go here and a crew go dere. Some of 'em spin and weave and make clothes, and some tan de leather or do de blacksmith work, and mos' of 'em go out in de field to work. Dey works till dark and den come home and work round de quarters.

"Dem quarters was 'bout ten by fifteen feet, each one, with a hole for de window dat am not dere and de floor am de ground, and de straw bunks for to sleep on. In us cabin am mammy and us three chillen and our aunt. My pappy done die befo' I 'member him. Some kind stomach mis'ry kilt him.

"One day Massa Chapman call all us to de front gallery. Us didn't know what gwine to happen, 'cause it not ord'nary to git called from de work. Him ring de bell and dat am sho' 'nough de liberty bell, 'cause him read from de long paper and say, 'You is slaves no more. You is free, jus' like I is, and have to 'pend on yourselves for de livin'. All what wants to stay I'll pay money to work, and a share of de crop, iffen you don't want money.' Mostest of dem stays, and some what goes gits into troublement, 'cause den dere's trouble 'twixt de white folks and de cullud folks. Some de niggers thinks they am bigger dan de white folks, 'cause dey free, and de Klu Klux, what us call white caps, puts dem in de place dey 'longs.

"I gits chased by dem white caps once, jus' befo' us leave massa. Dat am when I's 'bout thirteen year old. I's 'bout a mile off de place without de pass and it am de rule them days, all cullud folks must have de pass to show where dey 'longs and where dey gwine. I has no business to be off de place without de pass. 'Twas a gal.. Sho', day am it. Us walks down de road 'bout a mile and am settin' 'hind some bushes, off de plantation. Us see dem white caps comin' down de road on hossback and us ain't much scart, 'cause us think dey can't see us 'hind dem bushes. But dat leader say, 'Whoa,' and dey could look down on us, 'cause dey on hossback. Well, gosh for 'mighty! Dere us am and can't move den us so scart. One dem white caps says, 'What you doin', nigger?' 'Jus' settin' here,' I telt him. 'Yous better start runnin', 'cause us gwine try cotch you,' dey says.

"Us two niggers am down dat road befo' dem words am outten he mouth. Dey lets de hosses canter 'hind we'uns and us try to run faster. Fin'ly us gits home and dat de last time I goes off without de pass.

"Mammy moves to Baton Rouge soon after dat and works as de housemaid. Us stay dere two year and I gits some little jobs and den I goes to work for de railroad in Sedalia, up in Missouri, and dere I works as section hand for de Katy railroad for twenty year. Den I gits through and comes to Texas.

"I works at anything till eight year ago and den I's no count for work so I's livin' on de pension, what am $15.00 de month.

"I's never married. I jus' couldn't make de hitch. Dem what I wants, don't want me. Dem what wants me, I don't want, so dere am never no agreement.

"No, I's never voted, 'cause I done heared 'bout de trouble dey has over in Baton Rouge 'bout niggers votin'. I jus' don't like trouble, and for de few years what am left, I's gwine keep de record of stayin' 'way from it.

THOMAS JOHNS

THOMAS JOHNS, 508 Knopp St., Cleburne, Texas, was born April 18, 1847, in Chambers Co., Alabama. He belonged to Col. Robert Johns, who had come to Alabama from Virginia. After Johns was freed he stayed with his old owner's family until 1874, when he moved to Texas.

"My father's name was George and my mother's name was Nellie. My father was born in Africa. Him and two of his brothers and one sister was stole and brought to Savannah, Georgia, and sold. Dey was de chillen of a chief of de Kiochi tribe. De way dey was stole, dey was asked to a dance on a ship which some white man had, and my aunt said it was early in de mornin' when dey foun' dey was away from de land, and all dey could see was de water all 'round. She said they was members of de file-tooth tribe of niggers. My father's teeth was so dat only de front ones met together when he closed his mouth. De back ones didn' set together. W'en his front teeth was together, de back ones was apart, sorta like a V on its side.

"My mother was born a slave in Virginia. She married there and had a little girl, and they was sold away from the husband and brought to Alabama. She said her mother was part Indian and part nigger. Her father was part white and part nigger, but he look about as white as a white man.

"My brother's names was John, Jake and Dave. My sister's names was Ann, Katie, Judie and Easter.

"I belonged to Col. Robert Johns. He owned 30 or 35 slaves. We was well treated and had the same food the white folks did, and didn' none of us go hongry. Col. Johns didn' have his niggers whipped, neither.

"Marster's place had 500 acres in it. We raised cotton, corn and rice, vegetables and every sort of fruit that would grow there, a lot of it growin' wild. We et mostly hog meat, but we had some beef and mutton, too. When we'd kill a beef, we'd send some to all the neighbors.

"We done a good day's work, but didn' have to work after night 'less it was necessary. We was allowed to stop at 12 o'clock and have time for rest 'fore goin' back to work. Other slave owners roun' our place wasn't as good to dere slaves, would work 'em hard and half starve 'em. And some marsters or overseers would whip dere niggers pretty hard, sometimes whip 'em to death. Marster Johns didn' have no overseer. He seed to the work and my father was foreman. For awhile after old Marster died, in 1862 or 1863, I forget which now, we had a overseer, John Sewell. He was mean. He whipped the chillen and my mother told Miss Lucy, old marster's oldest girl.

"We was allus well treated by old marster. We was called, 'John's free niggers,' not dat we was free, but 'cause we was well treated. Jesse Todd, his place joined ours, had 500 slaves, and he treated 'em mighty bad. He whipped some of 'em to death. A man sold him two big niggers which was brothers and they was so near white you couldn' hardly tell 'em from a white man. Some people thought the man what sold 'em was their daddy. The two niggers worked good and dey hadn' never been whipped and dey wouldn' stand for bein' whipped. One mornin' Todd come up to 'em and told de oldest to take his shirt off. He say, 'Marster, what you wan' me to take my shirt off for?' Todd say, 'I told you to take your shirt off.' De nigger say, 'Marster, I ain' never took my shirt off for no man.' Todd run in de house and got his gun and come back and shot de nigger dead. His brother fell down by him where he lay on de groun'. Todd run back to load his gun again, it bein' a single shot. Todd's wife and son grabbed him and dey had all dey coul' do to keep him from comin' out and killin' de other nigger.

"Marse Johns had 12 chillen. De house dey lived in was Colonyal style and had 12 rooms. I was bo'n in dat house.

"De slaves had log cabins. We wore some cotton clothes in de summer but in de winter we wore wool clothes. We allus had shoes. A shoemaker would come 'round once a year and stay maybe 30 days, makin' shoes for everybody on de place; den in about 6 months he would come back and half-sole and make other repairs to de shoes. We made all our clothes on de place. We wove light wool cloth for summer and heavy for winter.

"I could take raw cotton and card and spin it on a spinnin' wheel into thread, fine enough to be sewed with a needle. We woun' de thread on a broche, make like and 'bout de size of a ice pick. De thread was den woun' on a reel 'bout de size of a forewheel of a wagon, and de reel would turn 48 times and den 'cluck'. Dat was for dem to be able to tell we was workin'.

"Dere was plenty wild game, possums, rabbits, turkey and so on. Dere was fish, too, in de creek. I was de leader of de bunch. We would ketch little fish in de creek. We'd cook a lot of fish and den we'd put a rag rug in de yard under a big mulberry tree and pour de fish out on dat and den eat 'em.

"Old marster never beat his slaves and he didn' sell 'em. But some of de owners did. If a owner had a big woman slave and she had a little man for her husban' and de owner had a big man slave, dey would make de little husban' leave, and make de woman let de big man be her husban', so's dere be big chillen, which dey could sell well. If de man and woman refused, dey'd get whipped.

"Course whippin' made a slave hard to sell, maybe couldn' be sold, 'cause when a man went to buy a slave he would make him strip naked and look him over for whip marks and other blemish, jus' like dey would a horse. But even if it done damage to de sale to whip him, dey done it, 'cause dey figgered, kill a nigger, breed another—kill a mule, buy another.

"I'll never forget de rice patch. It shore got me some whippin's, 'cause my daddy tell me to watch de birds 'way from dat rice, and sometimes dey'd get to it. It jus' seem like de blackbirds jus' set 'round and watched for dat rice to grow up where dey could get it. We would cut a block off a pine tree and build a fire on it and burn it out. Den we would cut down into it and scrape out all de char, and den put de rice in dere and beat and poun' it with a pestle till we had all de grain beat out de heads. Den we'd pour de rice out on a cloth and de chaff and trash would blow away.

"Our marster he drilled men for de army. De drill groun' was 'bout a mile from our place. He was a dead shot with a rifle and had a rifle with an extry long barrel.

"De Yankees told us niggers when dey freed us after de war dat dey would give each one of us 40 acres of land and a mule. De nearest I'se ever come to dat is de pension of 'leven dollars I gets now. But I'se jus' as thankful for dat as I can be. In fac', I don't see how I could be any more thankful it 'twas a hun'erd and 'leven dollars.

"A man told me a nigger woman told his wife she would ruther be slave than free. Well, I think, but I might be wrong, anybody which says that is tellin a lie. Dere is sumpin' 'bout bein' free and dat makes up for all de hardships. I'se been both slave and free and I knows. Course, while I was slave I didn' have no 'sponsibility, didn' have to worry 'bout where sumpin' to eat and wear and a place to sleep was comin' from, but dat don't make up for bein' free.

AUNTIE THOMAS JOHNS

AUNTIE THOMAS JOHNS, 508 Knopp St., Cleburne, Texas, was born in Burleson Co., Texas, in 1864. She was only two when her mother was freed, so knows nothing of slavery except stories her mother told her, or that she heard her husband, Thomas Johns, tell.

"I was two years old when my mama was set free. Her owner was Major Odom. He was good to his niggers, my mama said. She tol' me 'bout slavery times. She said other white folks roun' there called Major Odom's niggers, 'Odom's damn free niggers,' 'cause he was so easy on 'em.

"He was never married, but he had a nigger woman, Aunt Phyllis she was called, that he had some children by. She was half white. I remember her and him and five of their sons. The ones I knowed was nearly all white, but Aunt Phyllis had one boy that was nigger black. His daddy was a nigger man. When she was drunk or mad she'd say she thought more of her black chile than all the others. Major Odom treated their children jus' like he treated the other niggers. He never whipped none of his niggers. When his and Aunt Phyllis'es sons was grown they went to live in the quarters, which was what the place the niggers lived was called.

"One of Major Odom's niggers was whipped by a man named Steve Owens. He got to goin' to see a nigger woman Owens owned, and one night they beat him up bad. Major Odom put on his gun for Owens, and they carried guns for each other till they died, but they never did have a shootin'.

"Colonel Sims had a farm joinin' Major Odom's farm, and his niggers was treated mean. He had a overseer, J.B. Mullinax, I 'member him, and he was big and tough. He whipped a nigger man to death. He would come out of a mornin' and give a long, keen yell, and say, 'I'm J.B. Mullinax, just back from a week in Hell, where I got two new eyes, one named Snap and Jack, and t'other Take Hold. I'm goin' to whip two or three niggers to death today.' He lived a long time, but long 'fore he died his eyes turned backward in his head. I seen 'em thataway. He wouldn' give his niggers much to eat and he'd make 'em work all day, and just give 'em boiled peas with just water and no salt and cornbread. They'd eat their lunch right out in the hot sun and then go right back to work. Mama said she could hear them niggers bein' whipped at night and yellin', 'Pray, marster, pray,' beggin' him not to beat 'em.

"Other niggers would run away and come to Major Odom's place and ask his niggers for sumpin' to eat. My mama would get word to bring 'em food and she'd start out to where they was hidin' and she'd hear the hounds, and the runaway niggers would have to go on without gettin' nothin' to eat.

"My husban's tol' me about slavery times in Alabama. He said they would make the niggers work hard all day pickin' cotton and then take it to the gin and gin away into the night, maybe all night. They'd give a nigger on Sunday a peck of meal and three pounds of meat and no salt nor nothin' else, and if you et that up 'fore the week was out, you jus' done without anything to eat till the end of the week.

"My husban' said a family named Gullendin was mighty hard on their niggers. He said ole Missus Gullendin, she'd take a needle and stick it through one of the nigger women's lower lips and pin it to the bosom of her dress, and the woman would go 'round all day with her head drew down thataway and slobberin'. There was knots on the nigger's lip where the needle had been stuck in it.

United States. Work Projects Administration

GUS JOHNSON

GUS JOHNSON, 90 years or more, was born a slave of Mrs. Betty Glover, in Marengo Co., Alabama. Most of his memories are of his later boyhood in Sunnyside, Texas. He lives in an unkempt, little lean-to house, in the north end of Beaumont, Texas. There is no furniture but a broken-down bed and an equally dilapidated trunk and stove. Gus spends most of his time in the yard, working in his vegetable garden.

"Dey brung thirty-six of us here in a box car from Alabama. Yes, suh, dat's where I come from—Marengo County, not so far from 'Mopolis. Us belong to old missy Betty Glover and my daddy name August Glover and my mammy Lucinda. Old missy, she sho' treat us good and I never git whip for anything 'cept lyin'. Old missy, she do de whippin'.

"Old missy she sho' a good woman and all her white folks, dey used to go to church at White Chapel at 'leven in de mornin'. Us cullud folks goes in de evenin'. Us never do no work on Sunday, and on Saturday after twelve o'clock us can go fishin' or huntin'.

"Dey give de rations on Saturday and dat's 'bout five pound salt bacon and a peck of meal and some sorghum syrup. Dey make dat syrup on de plantation. Dey's ten or twelve big clay kettles in a row, sot in de furnace.

"We have lots to eat, and if de rations run short we goes huntin' or fishin'. Some de old men kills rattlesnake and cook 'em like fish and say dey fish. I eat dat many a time and never knowed it. 'Twas good, too.

"Dey used to have a big house where dey kep' de chillen, 'cause de wolves and panthers was bad. Some de mammies what suckle de chillen takes care of all de chillen durin' de daytime and at night dey own mammies come in from de field and take dem. Sometime old missy she help nuss and all de li'l niggers well care for. When dey gits sick dey makes de med'cine of herbs and well 'em dat way.

"When us left Alabama us come through Meridian to Houston and den to Hockley and den to Sunnyside, 'bout 18 mile west of Houston. Dat a country with lots of woods and us sot in to clean up de ground and clean up 150 acres to farm on. Dere 'bout forty-seven hands and more 'cumulates. Dey go back to Meridian for more and brung 'em in a ox cart.

"My brother, Bonzane Johnson, was one dey brung on dat trip. I had 'nother brother, Keen, what die when he 102 year old. Us was all long-life people, 'cause I have a gran' uncle what die when he 136 year old. He and my grandma and grandpa come from South Carolina and dey was all Africa people. I heered dem tell how dey brung from Africa in de ship. My daddy he die at 99 and 'nother brother at 104.

"Us see lots of sojers when us come through from Meridian and dey de cavalry. Dey come ridin' up with high hats like beavers on dey head and us 'fraid of 'em, 'cause dey told us dey gwine take us to Cuba and sell us dere.

"When us first git to Texas it was cold—not sort a cold, but I mean cold. I shovel de snow many a day. Dey have de big, common house and de white folks live upstairs and de niggers sleep on de first floor. Dat to 'tect de white folks at night, but us have our own houses for to live in in de daytime, builded out of logs and daubed with mud and nail rive out boards over dat mud. Dey make de chimney out of sticks and mud, too but us have no windows, and in summer us kind of live out in de bresh arbor, what was cool.

"Us have all kind of crops and more'n 100 acres in fruit, 'cause dey brung all kind trees and seeds from Alabama. Dey was undergroun' springs and de water was sho' good to drink, 'cause in Mobile de water wasn't fitten to drink. It taste like it have de lump of salt melted in it. Us keep de butter and milk in de spring house in dem days, 'cause us ain't have no ice in dem time.

"Old massa, he name Adam and he brother name John, and dey was way up yonder tall people. Old massa die soon and us have missy to say what we do. All her overseers have to be good. She punish de slaves iffen day bad, but not whip 'em. She have de jail builded undergroun' like de stormcave and it have a drop door with de weight on it, so dey couldn't git up from de bottom. It sho' was dark in dat place.

"In slavery time us better be in by eight o'clock, better be in dat house, better stick to dat rule. I 'member after freedom, missy have de big celebration on Juneteenth every year. [Handwritten Note: '?']

"When war come to Texas every plantation was conscrip' for de war and my daddy was 'pinted to selec' de able body men offen us place for to be sojers. My brother Keen was one of dem. He come back all right, though.

"When freedom come missy give all de men niggers $500 each, but dat 'federate money and have pictures of hosses on it. Dat de onlies' money missy have den. Old missy Betty, she die in Sunnyside, Texas, when she 115 year old.

"When I's 18 year old I marry a gal by name Lucy Johnson. She dead now long ago. I got five livin' chillen somewhere, but I done lost track of 'em. One of dem boys serve in de last war.

"I used to hear somethin' 'bout rabbit foot. De old folks used to say dat iffen de rabbit have time to stop and lick he foot de dog can't track him no more and I allus wears de rabbit foot for good luck. I don't know if it brung me dat luck, though.

"I been here 36 year and I work mos' de time as house mover, what I work at 26 year. I'll be honnes' with you, I don't know how old I is, but it mus' be plenty, 'cause I 'members lots 'bout de war. I didn't see no fightin' but I knowed what was goin' on den.

"I belong to de U. B. F. Lodge, what I pays into in case I gits sick. But I never can git sick and I ain't have no ailment 'cept my feets jus' swoll up, and I can't git nothin' for that.

HARRY JOHNSON

HARRY JOHNSON, 86, whose real name was Jim, was born in Missouri, where he was stolen by Harry Fugot, when about twelve years old, and taken to Arkansas. He was given the name of Harry and remained with Fugot until near the close of the Civil War. Fugot then sold him to Graham for 1,200 acres and he was brought to Coryell Co., Texas, and later to Caldwell Co. He worked in Texas two years before finding out the slaves were free. He later went to McMullen Co. to work cattle, but eventually spent most of his time rearing ten white children. He now lives in Pearsall, where he married at the age of 59.

"I come from Missouri to Arkansas and then to Texas, and I was owned by Massa Louis Barker and my name was Jim Johnson. But a white man name Harry Fugot stoled me and run me out to Arkansas and changed my name to Harry. He stoled me from Mississippi County in de southern part of Missouri, down close to de Arkansas line, and I was 'bout 12 year old then.

"My mama's name was Judie and her husban' name Miller. When I wasn't big 'nough to pack a chip, old Massa Louis Barker wouldn't take $400 for me, 'cause he say he wants to make a overseer out of me. My daddy went off durin' de war. He carried off by sojers and he never did come back.

"Dey 'bout 30, 40 acres in Massa Barker's plantation in Missouri. He used to hire me out from place to place and de men what hires me puts me to doin' what he wanted. I was stole from my mammy when I's 'bout 10 or 12 and she never did know what become of me.

"O, my stars! I seed hun'erds and hun'erds of sojers 'fore I stole from Missouri. Dey what us call Yankees. I seed 'em strung out a half-mile long, goin' battle two and three deep. Dey never did destroy any homes. Dey took up a little stuff. I had five sacks of meal one day and was goin' to de mill and de sojers come along and taken me, meal and all. De maddes' woman I ever saw was dat day. De sojers come and druv off her cows. She told 'em not to, dat her husban' fightin' and she have to make de livin' off dem cows, but dey druv de cows to camp and kilt 'bout three of 'em. Dey done dat, I knows, 'cause I's with 'em.

"But down in Arkansas I seed de southern sojers and I's plowin' for a old lady call Williams, and some sojers come and goes in de house. I heered say dey was Green's men, and dey taken everything dat old woman have what dey wants, and dey robs lots of houses.

"It don't look reas'able to say it, but it's a fac'—durin' slavery iffen you lived one place and your mammy lived 'cross de street you couldn't go to see her without a pass.

De paddlerollers would whip you if you did. Dere was one woman owns some slaves and one of 'em asks her for a pass and she give him de piece of paper sposed to be de pass, but she writes on it:

> "'His shirt am rough and his back am tough,
> Do, pray, Mr. Paddleroller, give 'im 'nough.'

"De paddlerollers beat him nearly to death, 'cause that's what's wrote on de paper he give 'em.

"I 'member a whippin' one slave got. It were 100 lashes. Dey's a big overseer right here on de San Marcos river, Clem Polk, him and he massa kilt 16 niggers in one day. Dat massa couldn't keep a overseer, 'cause de niggers wouldn't let 'em whip 'em, and dis Clem, he say, 'I'll stay dere,' and he finds he couldn't whip dem niggers either, so he jus' kilt 'em. One nigger nearly got him and would have kilt him. Dat nigger raise de ax to come down on Polk's head and de massa stopped him jus' in time, and den Polk shoots dat nigger in de breast with a shotgun.

"Dey had court days and when court met, dey passed a bill what say, 'Keep de niggers at home.' Some of 'em could go to church and some of 'em couldn't. Dey'd let de cullud people be baptized, but dey didn't many want it, dey didn't understan' it 'nough.

"After de war ends, Massa Fugot sells me to Massa Graham for 1,200 acres of land, and I lives in Caldwell County. He was purty good to he slaves and we live in a li'l old frame house, facin' west. I sleeps in de same house as massa and missus, to guard 'em. One night some men came and wake me up and tells me to put my clothes on. Missus was in de bed and she 'gin cryin' and tell 'em not to take me, but dey taken me anyway. We called 'em Guerrillas and dey thieves. Dey white men and one of 'em I had knowed a long time. I's with dem thives and hears 'em talk 'bout killin' Yankees. Dey kep' me in de south part of Missouri a long time. I didn't do anything but sit 'round de house with dem.

"When I's sold to Massa Graham I didn't have to come to Texas, 'cause I's free, but I didn't know dat, and I's out here two years 'fore I knowed I's free. Down in Caldwell County is where de bondage was lifted offen me and I found out I's free. I jus' stays on and works and my massa give me he promise I's git a hoss and saddle and $100 in money when I's 21 year old, but he didn't do it. He give me a li'l pony and a saddle what I sold for $3.00 and 'bout eight or nine dollars in money. He had me blindfolded and I thought I gwine git a good hoss and saddle and more money.

"I looks back sometimes and thinks times was better for eatin' in slavery dan what dey is now. My mammy was a reg'lar cook and she made me peach cobblers and apple dumplin's. In dem days, we'd take cornmeal and mix it with water and call 'em corn dodgers and dey awful nice with plenty butter. We had lots of hawg meat and when dey kilt a beef a man told all de neighbors to come git some of de meat.

"Right after de war, times is pretty hard and I's taken beans and parched 'em and got 'em right brown, and meal bran to make coffee out of. Times was purty hard, but I allus could find somethin' to work at in dem days.

"I lived all my life 'mong white folks and jus' worked in first one place and then 'nother. I raised ten white chillen, nine of de Lowe chillen, and dey'd mind me quicker dan dey own pappy and mammy. Dat in McMullin County.

"De day I's married I's 59 year old and my wife is 'bout 60 year old now. De last 20 years I's jus' piddled 'round and done no reg'lar work. I married right here in de church house. I nussed my wife when she a baby and used to court her mammy when she's a girl. We's been real happy together.

JAMES D. JOHNSON

JAMES D. JOHNSON, born Oct. 1st, 1860, at Lexington, Mississippi, was a slave of Judge Drennon. He now lives with his daughter at 4527 Baltimore St., Dallas, Texas. His memory is poor and his conversation is vague and wandering. His daughter says, "He ain't at himself these days." James attended Tuckaloo University, near Jackson, Mississippi, and uses very little dialect.

"My first clear recollection is about a day when I was five years old. I was playing in the sand by the side of the house in Lexington with some other children and some Yankee soldiers came by. They came on horseback and they drew rein by the side of the house and I ran under the house and hid. My mother called to me to come out and told me they were Federal soldiers and I could tell it by their blue uniforms. One of the soldiers reached into his haversack and pulled out a uniform and gave it to me. 'Have your mammy make a suit out of it,' he said. Another soldier gave me a uniform and my mother was a seamstress in the home of the Drennons and she made me two suits out of those uniforms.

"Judge Drennon had married the daughter of Colonel Terry and he had given my parents to his daughter when she married the judge. My father and mother both came from Virginia. Colonel Terry had bought them at separate times from a slave trader who brought them from Virginia to Mississippi. They had a likeness for each other when they learned both came from Virginia. Both of them had white fathers, were light complected and had been brought up in the big house.

"When they told the Colonel they wished to marry he only said, 'Julia, do you take William,' and 'William, do you take Julia?' Then they were man and wife. He gave them the name of Johnson, which was the family name of my father's mother and the name of his father.

"When my parents lived with Judge Drennon they had a house in the yard quarters. The Drennon home was the most beautiful house I ever have seen. It was a big, brick mansion with tall, white pillars reaching up to the second story. The yards and grounds were so beautiful the white folks used to come from long ways off to see them.

"After the surrendering we lived with the Drennons four or five years. They paid my parents for their work and I had an easy time of it. I was youngest of eight children and there was ten years or more between me and the next older child. My mother wanted to make something special out of me.

"I went to three different schools down in the woods before I was nine. White people would come and put up schools for the colored children but the white people in Mississippi said they were not good people and would criticize them. Sometimes the schools would get busted up. We studied out of the Blue Back speller and an arithmetic and a dictionary. I could spell and give the meaning of most nigh every word in that dictionary.

"When I was thirteen they held an examination at Lexington for colored children to see who'd get a scholarship at Tuckaloo University, eight miles from Jackson. I was greatly surprised when I won from my county and I went but didn't finish there. Then I went a little while to a small university near Lexington, called Allcorn University. I loved to go to school and was considered bookish. But my people died and I had to earn a living for myself and I couldn't find any way to use so much what I learned out of books, as far as making money was concerned. So I came to Texas, doing any kind of labor work I could find. Finally I married and went to farming 35 or 40 years and raised five children.

"I'm the only one left now of my brothers and sisters and it won't be long until I'm gone, too, but I don't mind that. We lived a long time. Some of it was hard and some of it was good. I tried all the time to live according to my lights and that is as far as I know how to do. I don't feel resentful of anything, anymore.

"When there is sun, I just sit in the sun."

MARY JOHNSON

MARY JOHNSON does not know her age but is evidently very old. Paralytic strokes have affected mind and body. Her speech, though impaired, is a swift flow of words, often profane. A bitter attitude toward everything is apparent. Mary is homeless and owes the necessities of life to the kindness of a middle aged Negress who takes care of several old women in her home in Pear Orchard, in Beaumont, Texas.

"Now, wait, white folks, I got to scratch my head so's I kin 'member. I's been paralyze so I can't git my tongue to speak good. It git all twist up.

"I don't know how old I is. My daddy he have my age in the big Bible but he done move 'round so much it git lost long ago. He used to 'long to them Guinea men. Them was real small men and they sho' walk fast. He wasn't so tall as my mommer and he name John Allen and he a pore man, all bone. He sold out from the old country, that Mississippi. My mama name Sarah and she come from Choctaw country, 'round in Georgia. I have grandma Rebecca, a reg'lar old Indian woman and she have two long black braid longer'n her waist and she allus wore a big bonnet with splits in it. You know de Indian people totes they chillens on they back and my mommer have me wrop up in a blanket and strop on her back.

"I's the firstborn chile and my mommer have two gal chillen, me and Hannah, and she have seven boy. Where I's born was old wild country and old Virginny run down thataway. Everything was plenty good to eat and I seed strawberries what would push you to git 'em in your mouth.

"Clost to where I's born they's a place where they brung the Africy people to tame 'em and they have big pens where they puts 'em after they takes 'em outta they gun ships. They sho' was wild and they have hair all over jus' like a dog and big hammer rings in they noses. They didn't wore no clothes and sometime they git 'way and run to them swamps in Floridy and git all wild and hairy 'gain. They brung preachers to help tame 'em, but didn't 'low no preacher in them pens by hisself, 'cause they say them preacher won't come back, 'cause some them wild Africy people done kill 'em and eat 'em. They done worship them snake bit as a rake handle, 'cause they ain't knowed no better. When they gits 'em all tame they sells 'em for field hands, but they allus wild and iffen anybody come they duck and hide down.

"My old missy she name Florence Walker and she reg'lar tough. I helps nuss her chile, Mary, and Mary make her mommer be good to me. Us wore li'l brass toe shoes and I call mine gold toe shoes. Them shoes hard 'nough to knock a mule out. After young missy and me git growed us run off to dances and old missy beat us behind good. She say us jes' chillen yet and keep us in short, short dress and we pull out the stitchin' in them hems so us dresses drags and she sho' wore us out for that.

"Did us love to dance? Jesus help me! Them country niggers swing me so hard us land in the corner with a wham.

"My brudder Robert he a pow'ful big boy and he wasn't 'lowed to have no pants till he 21 year old, but that didn't 'scourage him from courtin' the gals. I try tease him 'bout go see the gals with dat split shirt. That not all, that boy nuss he mommer breast till he 21 year old. He have to have that nussin' real reg'lar. But one time he pesterin' mommer and she tryin' milk the cow and the cow git nervous and kick over the bucket and mommer fall off the stool and she so mad she wean him right there and then.

"Old massa he never clean hisself up or dress up. He look like a vagrant thing and he and missy mean, too. My pore daddy he back allus done cut up from the whip and bit by the dogs. Sometime when a woman big they make a hollow out place for her stomach and make her lay down 'cross that hole and whip her behind. They sho' tear that thing up.

"Us chillen git to play and us sing

"'Old possum in the holler log
Sing high de loo,

> Fatter than a old green frog,
> Sing high de loo,
> Whar possum?

"That church they have a 'markable thing. They a deep tranch what cut all 'round the bottom and clay steps what lead all the way to the top the mountain and when the niggers git to shoutin' that church jes' a-rollin' and rockin'. One the songs I 'member was

> "'Shoo the devil out the corner,
> Shoo, members, shoo,
> Shoo the devil out the corner,
> Shoo, members, shoo.'

"Us li'l gals allus wore cottanade dresses ev'ry day. Them what us call nine-stitch dresses. Mammy make fasten-back dresses and fasten-back drawers and knit sweaters and socks for the mens. She git sheep wool what near ruint by cockle burrs and make us chillen set by the hour and pick out them burrs.

"Us houses like chicken coops but us sho' happy in that li'l cabin house. Nothin' to worry 'bout. Mammy cook them grits, that yaller hominy. She make 'ash cat', cornbread wrop in cabbage leaf and put ashes 'round it.

"The old plantation 'bout on the line 'tween Virginny and Mis'sippi and us live near the Madstone. That a big stone, all smooth and when a dog bite you you go run 'round the

Madstone and wash yourself in the hot springs and the bites don't hurt you.

"I seed lots of sojers and my daddy fit with the Yankees and they have a big fight close there and have a while lots of dead bodies layin' 'round like so many logs and they jus' stack 'em up and sot fire to 'em. You seed 'em burnin' night and day. They lay down and shoot and then jump up and stick 'em and sometimes they drunk the blood outten where they stick 'em, 'cause they can't git no water.

"After freedom us go in ox team to New Orleans and daddy he raise cotton and sell it and mommer sell eggs. My daddy a workin' man and he help build the big custom house in New Orleans and help pull the rope to pull the boats up the canal from the river. That Canal Street now. He put he name on top that custom house and it there to this day. You can go there and see it. He help build the hosp'tal, too.

"One time us live close to the bay and that gran' and us take a stove and cotch catfish and perch and cook 'em on the bank and us go meet oyster boats and daddy git 'em by the tub.

"I git marry in Baton Rouge when I sixteen and my husban' he name Arras Shaw and he lots older'n me and I couldn't keep him. He in Port Arthur now. My husban' and I sawmill 20 year in Grayburg, here in Texas, and then us sep'rate. I been in Beaumont 16 year and I's rice farm cook in the camp on the Fannett Road. They tells me I got uncles in Africy. I goes to Sanctified church and that all I can do now.

MARY ELLEN JOHNSON

MARY ELLEN JOHNSON, owner of a little restaurant at 1301 Marilla St., Dallas, Texas, is 77 years old. She was born in slavery to the Murth family, about ten miles from San Marcos, Texas. She neither reads nor writes but talks with little dialect.

"I don't know so fur back as befo' I was born, 'cept what my mammy told me, and she allus said little black chillen wasn't sposed to ask so many questions. Her name was Missouri Ellison, 'cause she belonged to Miss Micelder Ellison and then when she married with Mr. Murth, her daddy said my mammy was her 'heritance.

"My first mem'ries are us playin' in the backyard with Miss Fannie and Miss Martha and Mr. Sammie. They was the little Murth chillen. We used to make playhouses out there and sweep the ground clean down to the level with brush brooms and dec'rate it all up with little broken glasses and crockery.

"In them days we lived in a little, old log cabin in the backyard and there was just one room, but it was snug and we had a plenty of livin'. My mammy had a nice cotton bed and she weren't no field nigger, but my pappy were.

"Miss Micelder had a fine farm and raised most everything we ate and the food nowadays ain't like what it was then. Miss Micelder had a wood frame house with a big kitchen and they were cookin' goin' on all the time. They cooked on a wood stove with iron pots and skillets, and the roastin' ears and chicken fried right out of your own yard is tastier than what you git now. Grated 'tater puddin' was my dish.

"When I am seven years old I hear talk 'bout a war and the separation but I don't pay much 'tention. It seem far away and I don't bother my kinky head 'bout it. But then they tells eme [typo: me] the war is over and I'm goin' to be raised free and that I don't 'long to anybody but Gawd and my pappy and mammy, but it don't make me feel nothin', 'cause I ain't never know I ain't free.

"After the war we removed to a house on a hill where they is five houses, little log houses all in a row. We had good times, but we had to work in the cotton and corn and wheat in the daylight time, but when the dusk come we used to sing and dance and play into the moonlight.

"But one man called Milton, he's past his yearling boy days and he didn't like to see us spend our time in sin, so he'd preach to us from the Gospel, but I had the hardest time to get 'ligion of anybody I knowed. Fin'ly I got sick when I were fifteen and was in my bed and somethin' happened. Lawd, it was the most 'lievable thing ever happened to me. I was layin' there when sin formed a heavy, white veil just like a blanket over my bed and it just eased down over me till it was mashing the breath out of me. I crys out to the Lawd to save me and, sho' 'nough, He hear the cry of a pore mis'able sinner. I ran to my mammy and pappy a-shoutin'.

"The next year I marries and went on 'nother farm right near by and starts havin' chillen. I has ten and think I done rightly my part, 'cause I lived right by the word and taught my chillen the same. I'm lookin' to the promise to live in Glory after my days here is done.

PAULINE JOHNSON AND FELICE BOUDREAUX

P AULINE JOHNSON and FELICE BOUDREAUX, sisters, were once slaves on the plantation of Dermat Martine, near Opelousas, Louisiana. As their owners were French, they are more inclined to use a Creole patois than English.

"Us was both slaves on de old plantation close to Opelousas," Pauline began. As the elder of the two sisters she carried most of the conversation, although often referring to Felice before making positive statements.

"I was 12 year old when freedom come and Felice was 'bout six. Us belonged to Massa Dermat Martine and the missy's name Mimi. They raise us both in the house and they love us so they spoil us. I never will forget that. The little white chillen was younger than me, 'bout Felice's age. They sho' had pretty li'l curly black hair.

"Us didn't have hard time. Never even knowed hard time. That old massa, he what you call a good man.

"Us daddy was Renee and he work in the field. The old massa give him a mud and log house and a plot of ground for he own. The rain sho' never get in that log house, it so tight. The furniture was homemake, but my daddy make it good and stout.

"Us daddy he work de ground he own on Sunday and sold the things to buy us shoes to put on us feet and clothes. The white folks didn't give us clothes but they let him have all the money he made in his own plot to get them.

"Us mama name Marguerite and she a field hand, too, so us chillen growed up in the white folks house mostly. 'Fore Felice get big enough to leave I stay in the big house and take care of her.

"One day us papa fall sick in the bed, just 'fore freedom, and he kep' callin' for the priest. Old massa call the priest and just 'fore us papa die the priest marry him and my mama. 'fore dat they just married by the massa's word.

"Felice and me, us have two brothers what was born and die in slavery, and one sister still livin' in Bolivar now. Us three uncles, Bruno and Pophrey and Zaphrey, they goes to the war. Them three dies too young. The Yankees stole them and make them boys fight for them.

"I never done much work but wash the dishes. They wasn't poor people and they uses good dishes. The missy real particular 'bout us shinin' them dishes nice, and the silver spoons and knives, too.

"Them white people was good Christian people and they christen us both in the old brick Catholic church in Opelousas. They done torn it down now. Missy give me pretty dress to get christen in. My godmother, she Mileen Nesaseau, but I call her 'Miran'. My godfather called 'Paran.'

"On Sunday mornin' us fix our dress and hair and go up to the missy's looking-glass to see if us pretty enough go to church. Us goes to Mass every Sunday mornin' and church holiday, and when the cullud folks sick massa send for the priest same's for the white folks.

"We wears them things on the strings round the neck for the good of the heart. They's nutmeg.

"The plantation was a big, grand place and they have lots of orange trees. The slaves pick them oranges and pack then down on the barrel with la mosse (Spanish moss) to keep them. They was plenty pecans and figs, too.

"In slavery time most everybody round Opelousas talk Creole. That make the words hard to come sometime. Us both talk that better way than English.

"Durin' the war, it were a sight. Every mornin' Capt. Jenerette Bank and he men go a hoss-back drillin' in the pasture and then have drill on foot. A white lady take all us chillen to the drill ground every mornin'. Us take the lunch food in the basket and stay till they done drill out.

"I can sing for you the song they used to sing:

> "O, de Yankee come to put de nigger free,
> Says I, says I, pas bonne;
> In eighteen-sixty-three,
> De Yankee get out they gun and say,
> Hurrah! Let's put on the ball.

"When war over none the slaves wants leave the plantation. My mama and us chillen stays on till old massa and missy dies, and then goes live on the old Repridim place for a time.

"Both us get marry in that Catholic church in Opelousas. As for me, it most too long ago to talk about. His name Alfred Johnson and he dead 12 years. Our youngest boy,

John, go to the World War. Two my nephews die in that war and one nephew can't walk now from that war.

"Felice marry Joseph Boudreaux and when he die she come here to stay with me. There's more hard time now than in the old day for us, but I hope things get better.

United States. Work Projects Administration

SPENCE JOHNSON

SPENCE JOHNSON was born free, a member of the Choctaw Nation, in the Indian Territory, in the 1850's. He does not know his exact age. He and his mother were stolen and sold at auction in Shreveport to Riley Surratt, who lived near Shreveport, on the Texas-Louisiana line. He has lived in Waco since 1874.

"De nigger stealers done stole me and my mammy out'n de Choctaw Nation, up in de Indian Territory, when I was 'bout three years old. Brudder Knox, Sis Hannah, and my mammy and her two step-chillun was down on de river washin'. De nigger stealers driv up in a big carriage and mammy jus' thought nothin', 'cause the road was near dere and people goin' on de road stopped to water de horses and res' awhile in de shade. By'n by, a man coaxes de two bigges' chillun to de carriage and give dem some kind-a candy. Other chillun sees dis and goes, too. Two other men was walkin' 'round smokin' and gettin' closer to mammy all de time. When he kin, de man in de carriage got de two big step-chillun in with him and me and sis' clumb in too, to see how come. Den de man holler, 'Git de ole one and let's git from here.' With dat de two big men grab mammy and she fought and screeched and bit and cry, but dey hit her on de head with something and drug her in, and throwed her on de floor. De big chilluns begin to fight for mammy, but one of de men hit 'em hard and off dey driv, with de horses under whip.

"Dis was near a place called Boggy Depot. Dey went down de Red Ribber, 'cross de ribber and on down in Louisian to Shreveport. Down in Louisan us was put on what dey call de 'block' and sol' to de highes' bidder. My mammy and her three chillun brung $3,000 flat. De step chillun was sol' to somebody else, but us was bought by Marse Riley

Surratt. He was de daddy of Jedge Marshall Surratt, him who got to be jedge here in Waco.

"Marse Riley Surratt had a big plantation; don't know how many acres, but dere was a factory and gins and big houses and lots of nigger quarters. De house was right on de Tex-Louisan line. Mammy cooked for 'em. When Marse Riley bought her, she couldn' speak nothin' but de Choctaw words. I was a baby when us lef' de Choctaw country. My sister looked like a full blood Choctaw Indian and she could pass for a real full blood Indian. Mammy's folks was all Choctaw Indians. Her sisters was Polly Hogan, and Sookey Hogan and she had a brudder, Nolan Tubby. Dey was all known in de Territory in de ole days.

"Near as Marse Riley's books can come to it, I mus' of been bo'n 'round 1859, up in de Territory.

"Us run de hay press to bale cotton on de plantation and took cotton by ox wagons to Shreveport. Seven or eight wagons in a train, with three or four yoke of steers to each wagon. Us made 'lasses and cloth and shoes and lots of things. Old Marse Riley had a nigger who could make shoes and if he had to go to court in Carthage, he'd leave nigger make shoes for him.

"De quarters was a quarter mile long, all strung out on de creek bank. Our cabin was nex' de big house. De white folks give big balls and had supper goin' all night. Us had lots to eat and dey let us have dances and suppers, too. We never go anywhere. Mammy always cry and 'fraid of bein' stole again.

"Dere was a white man live close to us, but over in Louisan. He had raised him a great big black man what brung fancy price on de block. De black man sho' love dat white man. Dis white man would sell ole John—dat's de black man's name—on de block to some man from Georgia or other place fur off. Den, after 'while de white man would steal ole John back and bring him home and feed him good, den sell him again. After he had sol' ole John some lot of times, he coaxed ole John off in de swamp one day and ole John foun' dead sev'ral days later. De white folks said dat de owner kilt him, 'cause 'a dead nigger won't tell no tales.'

"Durin' de Freedom War, I seed soldiers all over de road. Dey was breakin' hosses what dey stole. Us skeered and didn' let soldiers see us if we could he'p it. Mammy and I stayed on with Marse Riley after Freedom and till I was 'bout sixteen. Den Marse Riley died and I come to Waco in a wagon with Jedge Surratt's brother, Marse Taylor Surratt. I come to Waco de same year dat Dr. Lovelace did, and he says that was 1874. I married and us had six chillun.

"I can't read or write, 'cause I only went to school one day. De white folks tried to larn me, but I's too thickheaded.

HARRIET JONES

HARRIET JONES, 93, was born a slave of Martin Fullbright, who owned a large plantation in North Carolina. When he died his daughter, Ellen, became Harriet's owner, and was so kind to Harriet that she looks back on slave years as the happiest time in her life.

"My daddy and mammy was Henry and Zilphy Guest and Marse Martin Fullbright brung dem from North Carolina to Red River County, in Texas, long 'fore freedom, and settled near Clarksville. I was one of dere eight chillen and borned in 1844 and am 93 years old. My folks stayed with Marse Martin and he daughter, Miss Ellen, till dey went to de reward where dey dies no more.

"De plantation raise corn and oats and wheat and cotton and hawgs and cattle and hosses, and de neares' place to ship to market am at Jefferson, Texas, ninety miles from Clarksville, den up river to Shreveport and den to Memphis or New Orleans. Dey send cotton by wagon train to Jefferson but mostly by boat up de bayou.

"When Marse Martin die he 'vide us slaves to he folks and I falls to he daughter, Miss Ellen. Iffen ever dere was a angel on dis earth she was it. I hopes wherever it is, her spirit am in glory.

"When Miss Ellen marry Marse Johnnie Watson, she have me fix her up. She have de white satin dress and pink sash and tight waist and hoop skirt, so she have to go through de door sideways. De long curls I made hang down her shoulders and a bunch of pink roses in de hand. She look like a angel.

"All de fine folks in Clarksville at dat weddin' and dey dances in de big room after de weddin' supper. It was de grand time but it make me cry, 'cause Miss Ellen done growed up. When she was a li'l gal she wore de sweetes' li'l dresses and panties with de lace ruffles what hung down below her skirt, and de jacket button in de back and shoes from soft leather de shoeman tan jus' for her. When she li'l bigger she wear de tucked petticoats, two, three at a time to take place of hoops, but she still wear de white panties with lace ruffles what hang below de skirt 'bout a foot. Where dey gone now? I ain't seed any for sich a long time!

"When de white ladies go to church in dem hoop skirts, dey has to pull dem up in da back to set down. After freedom dey wears de dresses long with de train and has to hold up de train when dey goes in de church, lessen dey has de li'l nigger to go 'long and hold it up for dem.

"All us house women larned to knit de socks and head mufflers, and many is de time I has went to town and traded socks for groceries. I cooked, too, and helped 'fore old Marse died. For everyday cookin' we has corn pone and potlicker and bacon meat and mustard and turnip greens, and good, old sorghum 'lasses. On Sunday we has chicken or turkey or roast pig and pies and cakes and hot, salt-risin' bread.

"When folks visit dem days dey do it right and stays several days, maybe a week or two. When de quality folks comes for dinner, Missie show me how to wait on table. I has to come in when she ring de bell, and hold de waiter for food jus' right. For de breakfas' we has coffee and hot waffles what my mammy make.

"Dere was a old song we used to sing 'bout de hoecake, when we cookin' dem:

> "'If you wants to bake a hoecake,
> To bake it good and done,
> Slap it on a nigger's heel,
> And hold it to de sun.
>
> "'My mammy baked a hoecake,
> As big as Alabama,
> She throwed it 'gainst a nigger's head,
> It ring jus' like a hammer.
>
> "'De way you bake a hoecake,
> De old Virginny way,
> Wrap it round a nigger's stomach,
> And hold it dere all day.'

"Dat de life we lives with old and young marse and missie, for dey de quality folks of old Texas.

"'Bout time for de field hands to go to work, it gittin' mighty hot down here, so dey go by daylight when it cooler. Old Marse have a horn and 'long 'bout four o'clock it 'gin to blow, and you turn over and try take 'nother nap, den it goes arguin', b l o w, how loud dat old horn do blow, but de sweet smell de air and de early breeze blowin' through de trees, and de sun peepin' over de meadow, make you glad to git up in de early mornin'.

> "'It's a cool and frosty mornin'
> And de niggers goes to work,
> With hoes upon dey shoulders,
> Without a bit of shirt.'

"'When dey hears de horn blow for dinner it am de race, and dey sings:

> "'I goes up on de meatskins,
> I comes down on de pone—
> I hits de corn pone fifty licks,
> And makes dat butter moan.'

"De timber am near de river and de bayou and when dey not workin' de hosses or no other work, we rides down and goes huntin' with de boys, for wild turkeys and prairie chickens, but dey like bes' to hunt for coons and possums.

> "'Possum up de gum stump,
> Raccoon in de hollow—
> Git him down and twist him out,
> And I'll give you a dollar.'

"Come Christmas, Miss Ellen say, 'Harriet, have de Christmas Tree carry in and de holly and evergreens.' Den she puts de candles on de tree and hangs de stockin's up for de white chillen and de black chillen. Nex' mornin', everybody up 'fore day and somethin' for us all, and for de men a keg of cider or wine on de back porch, so dey all have a li'l Christmas spirit.

"De nex' thing am de dinner, serve in de big dinin' room, and dat dinner! De onlies' time what I ever has sich a good dinner am when I gits married and when Miss Ellen marries Mr. Johnnie. After de white folks eats, dey watches de servants have dey dinner.

"Den dey has guitars and banjoes and fiddles and plays old Christmas tunes, den dat night marse and missie brung de chillen to de quarters, to see de niggers have dey dance. 'Fore de dance dey has Christmas supper, on de long table out in de yard in front de cabins, and have wild turkey or chicken and plenty good things to eat. When dey all through eatin', dey has a li'l fire front de main cabins where de dancin' gwine be. Dey moves everything out de cabin 'cept a few chairs. Next come de fiddler and banjo-er and when dey starts, de caller call, 'Heads lead off,' and de first couple gits in middle de floor, and all de couples follow till de cabin full. Next he calls, 'Sashay to de right, and do-si-do.' Round to de right dey go, den he calls, 'Swing you partners, and dey swing dem round twice, and so it go till daylight come, den he sing dis song:

> "'Its gittin' mighty late when de Guinea hen squall,
> And you better dance now if you gwine dance a-tall—
> If you don't watch out, you'll sing 'nother

tune,
   For de sun rise and cotch you, if you don't go soon,
   For de stars gittin' paler and de old gray coon
   Is sittin' in de grapevine a-watchin' de moon.'

"Den de dance break up with de Virginny Reel, and it de end a happy Christmas day. De old marse lets dem frolic all night and have nex' day to git over it, 'cause its Christmas.

"'Fore freedom de soldiers pass by our house and stop ask mammy to cook dem something to eat, and when de Yankees stop us chillen hides. Once two men stays two, three weeks lookin' round, pretends dey gwine buy land. But when de white folks gits 'spicious, dey leaves right sudden, and it turn out dey's Yankee spies.

"I marries Bill Jones de year after freedom. It a bright, moonlight night and all de white folks and niggers come and de preacher stand under de big elm tree, and I come in with two li'l pickininnies for flower gals and holdin' my train. I has on one Miss Ellen's dresses and red stockin's and a pair brand new shoes and a wide brim hat. De preacher say, 'Bill, does you take dis woman to be you lawful wife?' and Bill say he will. Den he say, 'Harriet, will you take dis nigger to be you lawful boss and do jes' what he say?' Den we signs de book and de preacher say, 'I quotes from de scripture:

   "'Dark and stormy may come de weather,

> I jines dis man and woman together.
> Let none but Him what make de thunder,
> Put dis man and woman asunder.'

"Den we goes out in de backyard, where de table sot for supper, a long table made with two planks and de peg legs. Miss Ellen puts on de white tablecloth and some red berries, 'cause it am November and dey is ripe. Den she puts on some red candles, and we has barbecue pig and roast sweet 'taters and dumplin's and pies and cake. Dey all eats dis grand supper till dey full and mammy give me de luck charm for de bride. It am a rabbit toe, and she say:

> "'Here, take dis li'l gift,
> And place it near you heart;
> It keep away dat li'l riff
> What causes folks to part.
>
> "'It only jes' a rabbit toe,
> But plenty luck it brings,
> Its worth a million dimes or more,
> More'n all de weddin' rings.'

"Den we goes to Marse Watson's saddleshop to dance and dances all night, and de bride and groom, dat's us, leads de grand march.

"De Yankees never burned de house or nothin', so Young Marse and Missie jes' kep' right on livin' in de old home after freedom, like old Marse done 'fore freedom. He pay de families by de day for work and let dem work land on de halves and furnish dem teams and grub and dey does de work.

"But bye'n-bye times slow commence to change, and first one and 'nother de old folks goes on to de Great Beyon', one by one dey goes, till all I has left am my great grandchild what I lives with now. My sister was livin' at Greenville six years ago. She was a hundred and four years old den. I don't know if she's livin' now or not. How does we live dat long? Way back yonder 'fore I's born was a blessin' handed down from my great, great, grandfather. It de blessin' of long life, and come with a blessin' of good health from livin' de clean, hones' life. When nighttime come, we goes to bed and to sleep, and dat's our blessin'.

LEWIS JONES

LEWIS JONES, 86, was born a slave to Fred Tate, who owned a large plantation on the Colorado River in Fayette Co., Texas. Lewis' father was born a slave to H. Jones and was sold to Fred Tate, who used him as a breeder to build up his slave stock. Lewis took his father's name after Emancipation, and worked for twenty-three years in a cotton gin at La Grange. He came to Fort Worth in 1896 and worked for Armour & Co. until 1931. Lewis lives at 3304 Loving Ave., Fort Worth, Texas.

"My birth am in de year 1851 on de plantation of Massa Fred Tate, what am on de Colorado River. Yes, suh, dat am in de state of Texas. My mammy am owned by Massa Tate and so am my pappy and all my brudders and sisters. How many brudders and sisters? Lawd A-mighty! I'll tell you 'cause you asks and dis nigger gives de facts as 'tis. Let's see, I can't 'lect de number. My pappy have 12 chillen by my mammy and 12 by anudder nigger name Mary. You keep de count. Den dere am Liza, him have 10 by her, and dere am Mandy, him have 8 by her, and dere am Betty, him have six by her. Now, let me 'lect some more. I can't bring de names to mind, but dere am two or three other what have jus' one or two chillen by my pappy. Dat am right. Close to 50 chillen, 'cause my mammy done told me. It's disaway, my pappy am de breedin' nigger.

"You sees, when I meets a nigger on dat plantation, I's most sho' it am a brudder or sister, so I don't try keep track of 'em.

"Massa Tate didn't give rations to each family like lots of massas, but him have de cookhouse and de cooks, and all de rations cooked by dem and all us niggers sat down to de long tables. Dere am plenty, plenty. I sho' wishes I could have some good rations like dat now. Man, some of dat ham would go fine. Dat was 'Ham, what am.'

"We'uns raise all de food right dere on de place. Hawgs? We'uns have three, four hundred and massa raise de corn and feed dem and cure de meat. We'uns have de cornmeal and de wheat flour and all de milk and butter we wants, 'cause massa have 'bout 30 cows. And dere am de good old 'lasses, too.

"Massa feed powerful good and he am not onreas'ble. He don't whup much and am sho' reas'ble 'bout de pass, and he 'low de parties and have de church on de place. Old Tom am de preacherman and de musician and him play de fiddle and banjo. Sometime dey have jig contest, dat when dey puts de glass of water on de head and see who can jig de hardes' without spillin' de water. Den dere am joyment in de singin'. Preacher Tom set all us niggers in de circle and sing old songs. I jus' can't sing for you, 'cause I's lost my teeth and my voice am raspin', but I'll word some, sich as

> "'In de new Jerusalem,
> In de year of Jubilee.'

"I done forgit de words. Den did you ever hear dis one:

> "'Oh, do, what Sam done, do dat again,
> He went to de hambone, bit off de end.'

"When Old Tom am preacherman, him talks from he heartfelt. Den sometime a white preacherman come and he am de Baptist and baptize we'uns.

"Massa have de fine coach and de seat for de driver am up high in front and I's de coachman and he dresses me nice and de hosses am fine, white team. Dere I's sat up high, all dress good, holdin' a tight line 'cause de team am full of spirit and fast. We'uns goes lickity split and it am a purty sight. Man, 'twarnt anyone bigger dan dis nigger.

"I has de bad luck jus' one time with dat team and it am disaway: massa have jus' change de power for de gin from hoss to steam and dey am ginnin' cotton and I's with dat team 'side de house and de hosses am a-prancin' and waitin' for missy to come out. Massa am in de coach. Den, de fool niggers blows de whistle of dat steam engine and de hosses never heered sich befo' and dey starts to run. Dey have de bit in de teeths and I's lucky dat road am purty straight. I thinks of massa bein' inside de coach and wants to save him. I says to myself, 'Dem hosses skeert and I don't want to skeer 'em no more.' I jus' hold de lines steady and keep sayin', 'Steady, boys, whoa boys.' Fin'ly dey begins to slow down and den stops and massa gits out and de hosses am puffin' hard and all foam. He turns to me and say, 'Boy, you's made a wonnerful drive, like a vet'ran.' Now, does dat make me feel fine! It sho' do.

"When surrender come I's been drivin' 'bout a year and it's 'bout 11 o'clock in de mornin', 'cause massa have me ring de bell and all de niggers runs quick to de house and massa say dey am free niggers. It am time for layin' de crops by and he say if dey do dat he pay 'em. Some stays and some goes off, but mammy and pappy and me stays. Dey never left dat plantation, and I stays 'bout 8 years. I guess it dat coachman job what helt me.

"When I quits I goes to work for Ed Mattson in La Grange and I works in dat cotton gin 18 years. Fin'ly I comes here to Fort Worth. Dat am 1896. I works for Armours 20 years but dey let me off six years ago, 'cause I's too old. Since den I works at any little old job, for to make my livin'.

"Sho', I's been married and it to Jane Owen in La Grange, and we'uns have three chillen and dey all dead. She died in 1931.

"It am hard for dis nigger to git by and sometime I don't know for sho' dat I's gwine git anudder meal, but it allus come some way. Yes, suh, dey allus come some way. Some of de time dey is far apart, but dey comes. De Lawd see to dat, I guess.

LIZA JONES

LIZA JONES, 81, was born a slave of Charley Bryant, near Liberty, Texas. She lives in Beaumont, and her little homestead is reached by a devious path through a cemetery and across a ravine on a plank foot-bridge. Liza sat in a backless chair, smoking a pipe, and her elderly son lay on a blanket nearby. Both were resting after a hot day's work in the field. Within the open door could be seen Henry Jones, Liza's husband for sixty years, a tall, gaunt Negro who is helpless. Blind, deaf and almost speechless, he could tell nothing of slavery days, although he was grown when the war ended.

"When de Yankees come to see iffen dey had done turn us a-loose, I am a nine year old nigger gal. That make me about 81 now. Dey promenade up to de gate and de drum say a-dr-um-m-m-m-m, and de man in de blue uniform he git down to open de gate. Old massa he see dem comin' and he runned in de house and grab up de gun. When he come hustlin' down off de gallery, my daddy come runnin'. He seed old massa too mad to know what he a-doin', so quicker dan a chicken could fly he grab dat gun and wrastle it outten old massa's hands. Den he push old massa in de smokehouse and lock de door. He ain't do dat to be mean, but he want to keep old massa outten trouble. Old massa know dat, but he beat on de door and yell, but it ain't git open till dem Yankees done gone.

"I wisht old massa been a-livin' now, I'd git a piece of bread and meat when I want it. Old man Charley Bryant, he de massa, and Felide Bryant de missus. Dey both have a good age when freedom come.

"My daddy he George Price and he boss nigger on de place. Dey all come from Louisiana, somewhere round New Orleans and all dem li'l extra places.

"Liz'beth she my mama and dey's jus' two us chillen, me and my brudder, John. He lives in Beaumont.

"'Bout all de work I did was 'tend to de rooms and sweep. Nobody ever 'low us to see nobody 'bused. I never seed or heared of nobody gittin' cut to pieces with a whip like some. Course, chillen wasn't 'lowed to go everywhere and see everything like dey does now. Dey jump in every corner now.

"Miss Flora and Miss Molly am de only ones of my white folks what am alive now and dey done say dey take me to San Antonio with dem. Course, I couldn't go now and leave Henry, noway. De old Bryant place am in de lawsuit. Dey say de brudder, Mister Benny, he done sharped it 'way from de others befo' he die, but I 'lieve the gals will win dat lawsuit.

"My daddy am de gold pilot on de old place. Dat mean anything he done was right and proper. Way after freedom, when my daddy die in Beaumont, Cade Bryant and Mister Benny both want to see him befo' he buried. Dey ride in and say, 'Better not you bury him befo' us see him. Dat's us young George.' Dey allus call daddy dat, but he old den.

"My mama was de spring back cook and turkey baker. Dey call her dat, she so neat, and cook so nice. I's de expert cook, too. She larnt me.

"Us chillen used to sing

> "'Don't steal,
> Don't steal my sugar.
> Don't steal,
> Don't steal my candy.
> I's comin' round de mountain.'

"Dey sho' have better church in dem days dan now. Us git happy and shout. Dey too many blind taggers now. Now dey say dey got de key and dey ain't got nothin'. Us used to sing like dis:

> "'Adam's fallen race,
> Good Lawd, hang down my head and cry.
> Help me to trust him,
> Help me to trust him,
> Help me to trust him,
> Gift of Gawd.

"'Help me to trust him,
Help me to trust him,
Help me to trust him,
Eternal Life.

"'Had not been for Adam's race,
I wouldn't been sinnin' today,
Help me to trust him,
Gift of Gawd.'

"Dey 'nother hymn like dis:
"'Heavenly land,
Heavenly land,
I's gwineter beg Gawd,
For dat Heavenly land.

"'Some come cripplin',
Some come lame,
Some come walkin',
In Jesus' name.'

"You know I saw you-all last night in my sleep? I ain't never seed you befo' today, but I seed you last night. Dey's two of you, a man and a woman, and you come crost dat bridge and up here, askin' me iffen I trust in de Lawd. And here you is today.

"Dey had nice parties in slavery time and right afterwards. Dey have candy pullin' and corn shuckin's and de like. Old Massa Day and Massa Bryant, dey used to put dey niggers together and have de prize dances. Massa Day allus lose, 'cause us allus beat he niggers at dancin'. Lawd, when I clean myself up, I sho' could teach dem how to buy a cake-walk in dem days. I could cut de pigeon wing, jes' pull my heels up and clack dem together. Den us do de back step and de banquet, too.

"Us allus have de white tarleton Swiss dress for dances and Sunday. Dem purty good clothes, too and dey make at home. Us knowed how to sew and one de old man's gals, she try teach me readin' and writin'. I didn't have no sense, though, and I cry to go out and play.

"When freedom come old massa he done broke down and cry, so my daddy stay with him. He stay a good many year, till both us chillen was growed. Us have de li'l log house on de place all dat time. Dey 'nother old cullud man what stay, name George Whitehouse. He have de li'l house, too. He stay till he die.

"Dey was tryin' to make a go of it after de war, 'cause times was hard. De white boys, dey go out in de field and work den, and work hard, 'cause dey don't have de slaves no more. I used to see de purty, young white ladies, all dress up, comin' to de front door. I slips out and tell de white boys, and dey workin' in de field, half-naked and dirty, and dey sneak in de back door and clean up to spark dem gals.

"I been marry to dat Henry in dere sixty year, and he was a slave in Little Rock, in Arkansas, for Anderson Jones. Henry knowed de bad, tejous part of de war and he must be 'bout 96 year old. Now he am in pain all de time. Can't see, can't hear and can't talk. Us never has had de squabble. At de weddin' de white folks brung cakes and every li'l thing. I had a white tarleton dress with de white tarleton wig. Dat de hat part what go over de head and drape on de shoulder. Dat de sign you ain't never done no wrong sin and gwinter keep bein' good.

"After us marry I move off de old place, but nothin' must do but I got to keep de house for Mister Benny. I's cleanin' up one time and finds a milk churn of money. I say, 'Mr. Benny, what for you ain't put dat money in de bank?' He say he will. De next time I cleanin' up I finds a pillow sack full of money. I says, 'Mr. Benny, I's gwineter quit. I ain't gwineter be 'sponsible for dis money.' He's sick den and I put de money under he pillow and git ready to go. He say, 'You better stay, or I send Andrew, de sheriff, after you.' I goes and cooks dinner and when I gits back dey has four doctors with Mr. Benny. He wife say to me, 'Liza, you got de sight. Am Benny gwineter git well?' I goes and looks and I knowed he gwine way from dere. I knowed he was gone den. Dey leant on me a heap after dat.

"It some years after dat I leaves dem and Henry and me gits married and us make de livin' farmin'. Us allus stays right round hereabouts and gits dis li'l house. Now my son and me, us work de field and gits 'nough to git through on.

United States. Work Projects Administration

LIZZIE JONES

LIZZIE JONES, an 86 year old ex-slave of the R.H. Hargrove family, was born in 1861, in Harrison County, Texas. She stayed with her owner until four years after the close of the Civil War. She now lives with Talmadge Buchanan, a grandson, two miles east of Karnack, on the Lee road.

"I was bo'n on the ole Henry Hargrove place. My ole missus was named Elizabeth and mammy called me Lizzie for her. But the Hargroves called me 'Wink' since I was a chile, 'cause I was so black and shiny. Massa Hargrove had four girls and four boys and I helped tend them till I was big enough to cook and keep house. I wagged ole Marse Dr. Hargrove, dat lives in Marshall, round when he was a baby.

"I allus lived in de house with the white folks and ate at their table when they was through, and slep' on the floor. We never had no school or church in slavery time. The niggers couldn' even add. None of us knowed how ole we was, but Massa set our ages down in a big book.

"I 'member playin' peep-squirrel and marbles and keepin' house when I was a chile. Massa 'lowed the boys and girls to cou't but they couldn' marry 'fore they was 20 years ole, and they couldn' marry off the plantation. Slaves warn't married by no Good Book or the law, neither. They'd jes' take up with each other and go up to the Big House and ask massa to let them marry. If they was ole enough, he'd say to the boy, 'Take her and go on home.'

"Mammy lived 'cross the field at the quarters and there was so many nigger shacks it look like a town. The slaves slep' on bunks of homemade boards nailed to de wall with poles for legs and they cooked on the fireplace. I didn' know what a stove was till after de War. Sometime they'd bake co'nbread in the ashes and every bit of the grub they ate come from the white folks and the clothes, too. I run them looms many a night, weavin' cloth. In summer we had lots of turnips and greens and garden stuff to eat. Massa allus put up sev'ral barrels of kraut and a smokehouse full of po'k for winter. We didn' have flour or lard, but huntin' was good 'fore de war and on Sat'day de men could go huntin' and fishin' and catch possum and rabbits and squirrels and coons.

"The overseer was named Wade and he woke the han's up at four in the mornin' and kep' them in the field from then till the sun set. Mos' of de women worked in de fields like de men. They'd wash clothes at night and dry them by the fire. The overseer kep' a long coach whip with him and if they didn' work good, he'd thrash them good. Sometime he's pretty hard on them and strip 'em off and whip 'em till they think he was gonna kill 'em. No nigger ever run off as I 'member.

"We never have no parties till after 'mancipation, and we couldn' go off de place. On Sundays we slep' or visited each other. But the white folks was good to us. Massa Hargrove didn' have no doctor but there wasn' much sickness and seldom anybody die.

"I don' 'member much 'bout de War. Massa went to it, but he come home shortly and say he sick with the 'sumption, but he got well real quick after surrender.

"The white folks didn' let the niggers know they was free till 'bout a year after the war. Massa Hargrove took sick sev'ral months after and 'fore he did he tell the folks not to let the niggers loose till they have to. Finally they foun' out and 'gun to leave.

"My pappy died 'fore I was bo'n and mammy married Caesar Peterson and 'bout a year after de war dey moved to a farm close to Lee, but I kep' on workin' for de Hargroves for four years, helpin' missus cook and keep house.

TOBY JONES

TOBY JONES was born in South Carolina, in 1850, a slave of Felix Jones, who owned a large tobacco plantation. Toby has farmed in Madisonville, Texas, since 1869, and still supports himself, though his age makes it hard for him to work.

"My father's name was Eli Jones and mammy's name was Jessie. They was captured in Africa and brought to this country whilst they was still young folks, and my father was purty hard to realize he was a slave, 'cause he done what he wanted back in Africa.

"Our owner was Massa Felix Jones and he had lots of tobacco planted. He was real hard on us slaves and whipped us, but Missie Janie, she was a real good woman to her black folks. I 'members when their li'l curlyheaded Janie was borned. She jus' loved this old, black nigger and I carried her on my back whole days at a time. She was the sweetes' baby ever borned.

"Massa, he lived in a big, rock house with four rooms and lots of shade trees, and had 'bout fifty slaves. Our livin' quarters wasn't bad. They was rock, too, and beds built in the corners, with straw moss to sleep on.

"We had plenty to eat, 'cause the woods was full of possum and rabbits and all the mud holes full of fish. I sho' likes a good, old, fat possum cooked with sweet 'taters round him. We cooked meat in a old-time pot over the fireplace or on a forked stick. We grated corn by hand for cornbread and made waterpone in the ashes.

"I was borned 'bout 1850, so I was plenty old to 'member lots 'bout slave times. I 'members the loyal clothes, a long shirt what come down below our knees, opened all the way down the front. On Sunday we had white loyal shirts, but no shoes and when it was real cold we'd wrap our feet in wool rags so they wouldn't freeze. I married after freedom and had white loyal breeches. I wouldn't marry 'fore that, 'cause massa wouldn't let me have the woman I wanted.

"The overseer was a mean white man and one day he starts to whip a nigger what am hoein' tobacco, and he whipped him so hard that nigger grabs him and made him holler. Missie come out and made them turn loose and massa whipped that nigger and put him in chains for a whole year. Every night he had to be in jail and couldn't see his folks for that whole year.

"I seed slaves sold, and they'd make them clean up good and grease their hands and face, so they'd look real fat, and sell them off. Of course, most the niggers didn't know their parents or what chillen was theirs. The white folks didn't want them to git 'tached to each other.

"Missie read some Bible to us every Sunday mornin' and taught us to do right and tell the truth. But some them niggers would go off without a pass and the patterrollers would beat them up scand'lous.

"The fun was on Saturday night when massa 'lowed us to dance. There was lots of banjo pickin' and tin pan beatin' and dancin', and everybody would talk 'bout when they lived in Africa and done what they wanted.

"I worked for massa 'bout four years after freedom, 'cause he forced me to, said he couldn't 'ford to let me go. His place was near ruint, the fences burnt and the house would have been but it was rock. There was a battle fought near his place and I taken missie to a hideout in the mountains to where her father was, 'cause there was bullets flyin' everywhere. When the war was over, massa come home and says, 'You son of a gun, you's sposed to be free, but you ain't, 'cause I ain't gwine give you freedom.' So, I goes on workin' for him till I gits the chance to steal a hoss from him. The woman I wanted to marry, Govie, she 'cides to come to Texas with me. Me and Govie, we rides that hoss most a hundred miles, then we turned him a-loose and give him a scare back to his house, and come on foot the rest the way to Texas.

"All we had to eat was what we could beg and sometimes we went three days without a bite to eat. Sometimes we'd pick a few berries. When we got cold we'd crawl in a breshpile and hug up close together to keep warm. Once in awhile we'd come to a farmhouse and the man let us sleep on cottonseed in his barn, but they was far and few between, 'cause they wasn't many houses in the country them days like now.

"When we gits to Texas we gits married, but all they was to our weddin' am we jus' 'grees to live together as man and wife. I settled on some land and we cut some trees and split them open and stood them on end with the tops together for our house. Then we deadened some trees and the land was ready to farm. There was some wild cattle and hawgs and that's the way we got our start, caught some of them and tamed them.

"I don't know as I 'spected nothin' from freedom, but they turned us out like a bunch of stray dogs, no homes, no clothin', no nothin', not 'nough food to last us one meal. After we settles on that place, I never seed man or woman, 'cept Govie, for six years, 'cause it was a long ways to anywhere. All we had to farm with was sharp sticks. We'd stick holes and plant corn and when it come up we'd punch up the dirt round it. We didn't plant cotton, 'cause we couldn't eat that. I made bows and arrows to kill wild game with and we never went to a store for nothin'. We made our clothes out of animal skins.

"We used rabbit foots for good luck, tied round our necks. We'd make medicine out of wood herbs. There is a rabbit foot weed that we mixed with sassafras and made good cough syrup. Then there is cami weed for chills and fever.

"All I ever did was to farm and I made a livin'. I still makes one, though I'm purty old now and its hard for me to keep the work up. I has some chickens and hawgs and a yearling or two to sell every year.

United States. Work Projects Administration

AUNT PINKIE KELLY

AUNT PINKIE KELLY, whose age is a matter of conjecture, but who says she was "growed up when sot free," was born on a plantation in Brazoria Co., owned by Greenville McNeel, and still lives on what was a part of the McNeel plantation, in a little cabin which she says is much like the old slave quarters.

"De only place I knows 'bout is right here, what was Marse Greenville McNeel's plantation, 'cause I's born here and Marse Greenville and Missy Amelia, what was his wife, is de only ones I ever belonged to. After de war, Marse Huntington come down from up north and took over de place when Marse Greenville die, but de big house burned up and all de papers, too, and I couldn't tell to save my life how old I is, but I's growed up and worked in de fields befo' I's sot free.

"My mammy's name was Harriet Jackson and she was born on de same plantation. My pappy's name was Dan, but folks called him Good Cheer. He druv oxen and one day they show me him and say he my pappy, and so I guess he was, but I can't tell much about him, 'cause chillen then didn't know their pappys like chillen do now.

"Most I 'members 'bout them times is work, 'cause we's put out in de fields befo' day and come back after night. Then we has to shell a bushel of corn befo' we goes to bed and we was so tired we didn't have time for nothin'.

"Old man Jerry Driver watches us in de fields and iffen we didn't work hard he whip us and whip us hard. Then he die and 'nother man call Archer come. He say, 'You niggers now, you don't work good, I beat you,' and we sho' worked hard then.

"Marse Greenville treated us pretty good but he never give us nothin'. Sometime we'd run away and hide in de woods for a spell, but when they cotch us Marse Greenville tie us down and whip us so we don't do it no more.

"We didn't have no clothes like we do now, jes' cotton lowers and rubber shoes. They used to feed us peas and cornbread and hominy, and sometime they threw beef in a pot and bile it, but we never had hawg meat.

"Iffen we took sick, old Aunt Becky was de doctor. They was a building like what they calls a hospital and she put us in there and give us calomel or turpentine, dependin' on what ailed us. They allus kep' the babies there and let de mammies come in and suckle and dry 'em up.

"I never heered much 'bout no war and Marse Greenville never told us we was free. First I knows was one day we gwine to de fields and a man come ridin' up and say,

'Whar you folks gwine?' We say we gwine to de fields and then he say to Marse Greenville, 'You can't work these people, without no pay, 'cause they's as free as you is.' Law, we sho' shout, young folks and old folks too. But we stay there, no place to go, so we jes' stay, but we gits a little pay.

"After 'while I marries. Allen Kelley was de first husban' what I ever owned and he die. Houston Edmond, he the las' husban' I ever owned and he die, too.

"Law me, they used to be a sayin' that chillen born on de dark of de moon ain't gwineter have no luck, and I guess I sho' was born then!"

SAM KILGORE

SAM KILGORE, 92, was born a slave of John Peacock, of Williams County, Tennessee, who owned one of the largest plantations in the south. When he was eight years old, Sam accompanied his master to England for a three-year stay. Sam was in the Confederate Army and also served in the Spanish-American War. He came to

Fort Worth in 1889 and learned cement work. In 1917 he started a cement contracting business which he still operates. He lives at 1211 E. Cannon St., Fort Worth, Texas.

"You asks me when I's born and was I born a slave. Well, I's born on July 17, 1845, so I's a slave for twenty years, and had three massas. I's born in Williamson County, near Memphis, in Tennessee. Massa John Peacock owned de plantation and am it de big one! Dere am a thousand acres and 'bout a thousand slaves.

"De slave cabins am in rows, twenty in de first row and eighteen in de second and sixteen in de third. Den dere am house servants quarters near de big house. De cabins am logs and not much in dem but homemade tables and benches and bunks 'side de wall. Each family has dere own cabin and sometimes dere am ten or more in de family, so it am kind of crowded. But massa am good and let dem have de family life, and once each week de rations am measure out by a old darky what have charge de com'sary, and dere am allus plenty to eat.

"But dem eats ain't like nowadays. It am home-cured meat and mostly cornmeal, but plenty veg'tables and 'lasses and brown sugar. Massa raised lots of hawgs, what am Berkshires and Razorbacks. Razorback meat am 'sidered de best and sweetest.

"De work stock am eighty head of mules and fifty head of hosses and fifteen yoke of oxen. It took plenty feed for all dem and massa have de big field of corn, far as we could see. De plantation am run on system and everything clean and in order, not like lots of plantations with tools scattered 'round and dirt piles here and there. De chief overseer am white and de second overseers am black. Stien was nigger overseer in de shoemakin' and harness, and Aunty Darkins am overseer of de spinnin' and weavin'.

"Dat place am so well manage dat whippin's am not nec'sary. Massa have he own way of keepin' de niggers in line. If dey bad he say, 'I 'spect dat nigger driver comin' round tomorrow and I's gwine sell you.' Now, when a nigger git in de hands of de nigger driver it am de big chance he'll git sold to de cruel massa, and dat make de niggers powerful skeert, so dey 'haves. On de next plantation we'd hear de niggers pleadin' when dey's whipped, 'Massa, have mercy,' and sich. Our massa allus say, 'Boys, you hears dat mis'ry and we don't want no sich on dis place and it am up to you.' So us all 'haves ourselves.

"When I's four years old I's took to de big house by young Massa Frank, old massa's son. He have me for de errand boy and, I guess, for de plaything. When I gits bigger I's his valet and he like me and I sho' like him. He am kind and smart, too, and am choosed from nineteen other boys to go to England and study at de mil'tary 'cademy. I's 'bout eight when we starts for Liverpool. We goes from Memphis to Newport and takes de boat, Bessie. It am a sailboat and den de fun starts for sho'. It am summer and not much wind and sometimes we jus' stand still day after day in de fog so thick we can't see from one end de boat to de other.

"I'll never forgit dat trip. When we gits far out on de water, I's dead sho' we'll never git back to land again. First I takes de seasick and dat am something. If there am anything worser it can't be stood! It ain't possible to 'splain it, but I wants to die, and if dey's anything worser dan dat seasick mis'ry, I says de Lawd have mercy on dem. I can't 'lieve dere am so much stuff in one person, but plenty come out of me. I mos' raised de ocean! When dat am over I gits homesick and so do Massa Frank. I cries and he tries to 'sole me and den he gits tears in he eyes. We am weeks on dat water, and good old Tennessee am allus on our mind.

"When we gits to England it am all right, but often we goes down to de wharf and looks over de cotton bales for dat Memphis gin mark. Couple times Massa Frank finds some and he say, 'Here a bale from home, Sam,' with he voice full of joy like a kid what find some candy. We stands round dat bale and wonders if it am raised on de plantation.

"But we has de good time after we gits 'quainted and I seed lots and gits to know some West India niggers. But we's ready to come home and when we gits dere it am plenty war. Massa Frank jines de 'Federate Army and course I's his valet and goes with him, right over to Camp Carpenter, at Mobile. He am de lieutenant under General Gordon and befo' long dey pushes him higher. Fin'ly he gits notice he am to be a colonel and dat sep'rates us, 'cause he has to go to Floridy. 'I's gwine with you,' I says, for I thinks I 'longs to him and he 'longs to me and can't nothing part us. But he say, 'You can't go with me this time. Dey's gwine put you in de army.' Den I cries and he cries.

"I's seventeen years old when I puts my hand on de book and am a sojer. I talks to my captain 'bout Massa Frank and wants to go to see him. But it wasn't more'n two weeks after he leaves dat him was kilt. Dat am de awful shock to me and it am a long time befo' I gits over it. I allus feels if I'd been with him maybe I could save his life.

"My company am moved to Birmingham and builds breastworks. Dey say Gen. Lee am comin' for a battle but he didn't ever come and when I been back to see dem breastworks, dey never been used. We marches north to Lexington, in Kentuck' but am gone befo' de battle to Louisville. We comes back to Salem, in Georgia, but I's never in no big battle, only some skirmishes now and den. We allus fixes for de battles and builds bridges and doesn't fight much.

"I goes back after de war to Memphis. My mammy am on de Kilgore place and Massa Kilgore takes her and my pappy and two hundred other slaves and comes to Texas. Dat how I gits here. He settles at de place called Kilgore, and it was named after him, but in 1867 he moves to Cleburne.

"Befo' we moved to Texas de Klu Kluxers done burn my mammy's house and she lost everything. Dey was 'bout $100 in greenbacks in dat house and a three hundred pound hawg in de pen, what die from de heat. We done run to Massa Rodger's house. De riders gits so bad dey come most any time and run de cullud folks off for no cause, jus' to be orn'ry and plunder de home. But one day I seed Massa Rodgers take a dozen guns out his wagon and he and some white men digs a ditch round de cotton field close to de road. Couple nights after dat de riders come and when dey gits near dat ditch a volley am fired and lots of dem draps off dey hosses. Dat ended de Klux trouble in dat section.

"After I been in Texas a year I jines de Fed'ral Army for de Indian war. I's in de transportation division and drives oxen and mules, haulin' supplies to de forts. We goes to Fort Griffin and Dodge City and Laramie, in Wyoming. Dere am allus two or three hundred sojers with us, to watch for Indian attacks. Dey travels on hosses, 'head, 'side and 'hind de wagon. One day de Sent'nel reports Indians am round so we gits hid in de trees and bresh. On a high ledge off to de west we sees de Indians travelin' north, two abreast. De lieutenant say he counted 'bout seven hundred but dey sho' missed us, or maybe I'd not be here today.

"I stays in de service for seven years and den goes back to Johnson County, farmin' on de Rodgers place, and stays till I comes to Fort Worth in 1889. Den I gits into 'nother war, de Spanish 'merican War. But I's in de com'sary work so don't see much fightin'. In all dem wars I sees most no fightin', 'cause I allus works with de supplies.

"After dat war I goes to work laborin' for buildin' contractors. I works for sev'ral den gits with Mr. Bardon and larns de cement work with him. He am awful good man to work for, dat John Bardon. Fin'ly I starts my own cement business and am still runnin' it. My health am good and I's allus on de job, 'cause dis home I owns has to be kept up. It cost sev'ral thousand dollars and I can't 'ford to neglect it.

"I's married twict. I marries Mattie Norman in 1901 and sep'rates in 1904. She could spend more money den two niggers could shovel it in. Den I marries Lottie Young in 1909, but dere am no chillens. I's never dat lucky.

"I's voted ev'ry 'lection and 'lieves it de duty for ev'ry citizen to vote.

"Now, I's told you everything from Genesis to Rev'lations, and it de truth, as I 'members it.

United States. Work Projects Administration

BEN KINCHLOW

BEN KINCHLOW, 91, was the son of Lizaer Moore, a half-white slave owned by Sandy Moore, Wharton Co., and Lad Kinchlow, a white man. When Ben was one year old his mother was freed and given some money. She was sent to Matamoras, Mexico and they lived there and at Brownsville, Texas, during the years before and directly following the Civil War. Ben and his wife, Liza, now live in Uvalde, Texas, in a neat little home. Ben has straight hair, a Roman nose, and his speech is like that of the early white settler. He is affable and enjoys recounting his experiences.

"I was birthed in 1846 in Wharton, Wharton County, in slavery times. My mother's name was Lizaer Moore. I think her master's name was Sandy Moore, and she went by his name. My father's name was Lad Kinchlow. My mother was a half-breed Negro; my father was a white man of that same county. I don't know anything about my father. He was a white man, I know that. After I was borned and was one year old, my mother was set free and sent to Mexico to live. When we left Wharton, we was sent away in an ambulance. It was an old-time ambulance. It was what they called an ambulance—a four-wheeled concern pulled by two mules. That is what they used to traffic in. The big rich white folks would get in it and go to church or on a long journey. We landed safely into Matamoros, Mexico, just me and my mother and older brother. She had the means to live on till she got there and got acquainted. We stayed there about twelve years. Then we moved back to Brownsville and stayed there until after all Negroes were free. She went to washing and she made lots of money at it. She charged by the dozen. Three or four handkerchiefs were considered a piece. She made good because she got $2.50 a dozen for men washing and $5 a dozen for women's clothes.

"I was married in February, 1879, to Christiana Temple, married at Matagorda, Matagorda County. I had six children by my first wife. Three boys and three girls. Two girls died. The other girl is in Gonzales County. Lawrence is here workin' on the Kincaid Ranch and Andrew is workin' for John Monagin's dairy and Henry is seventy miles from Alpine. He's a highway boss. This was my first wife. Now I am married again and have been with this wife forty years. Her name was Eliza Dawson. No children born to this union.

"The way we lived in those days—the country was full of wild game, deer, wild hogs, turkey, duck, rabbits, 'possum, lions, quails, and so forth. You see, in them days they was all thinly settled and they was all neighbors. Most settlements was all Meskins mostly; of course there was a few white people. In them days the country was all open and a man could go in there and settle down wherever he wanted to and wouldn't be molested a-tall. They wasn't molested till they commenced putting these fences and putting up these barbwire fences. You could ride all day and never open a gate. Maybe ride right up to a man's house and then just let down a bar or two.

"Sometime when we wanted fresh meat we went out and killed. We also could kill a calf or goat whenever we cared to because they were plenty and no fence to stop you. We also had plenty milk and butter and home-made cheese. We did not have much coffee. You know the way we made our coffee? We just taken corn and parched it right brown and ground it up. Whenever we would get up furs and hides enough to go into market, a bunch of neighbors would get together and take ten to fifteen deer hides each and take 'em in to Brownsville and sell 'em and get their supplies. They paid twenty-five cents a pound for them. That's when we got our coffee, but we'd got so used to using corn-coffee, we didn't care whether we had that real coffee so much, because we had to be careful with our supplies, anyway. My recollection is that it was fifty cents a pound and it would be green coffee and you would have to roast it and grind it on a mill. We didn't have any sugar, and very rare thing to have flour. The deer was here by the hundreds. There was blue quail—my goodness! You could get a bunch of these blue top-knot quail rounded up in a bunch of pear and, if they was any rocks, you could kill every one of 'em. If you could hit one and get 'im to fluttering the others would bunch around him and you could kill every one of 'em with rocks.

"We lived very neighborly. When any of the neighbors killed fresh meat we always divided with one another. We all had a corn patch, about three or four acres. We did not have plows; we planted with a hoe. We were lucky in raisin' corn every year. Most all the neighbors had a little bunch of goats, cows, mares, and hogs. Our nearest market was forty miles, at old Brownsville. When I was a boy I wo'e what was called shirt-tail. It was a long, loose shirt with no pants. I did not wear pants until I was about ten or twelve. The way we got our supplies, all the neighbors would go in together and send into town in a dump cart drawn by a mule. The main station was at Brownsville. It was thirty-five miles from where they'd change horses. They carried this mail to Edinburg, and it took four days. Sometimes they'd ride a horse or mule. We'd get our mail once a week. We got our mail at Brownsville.

"The country was very thinly settled then and of very few white people; most all Meskins, living on the border. The country was open, no fences. Every neighbor had a little place. We didn't have any plows; we planted with a hoe and went along and raked the dirt over with our toes. We had a grist mill too. I bet I've turned one a million miles. There was no hired work then. When a man was hired he got $10 or $12 per month, and when people wanted to brand or do other work, all the neighbors went together and helped without pay. The most thing that we had to fear was Indians and cattle rustlers and wild animals.

"While I was yet on the border, the plantation owners had to send their cotton to the border to be shipped to other parts, so it was transferred by Negro slaves as drivers. Lots of times, when these Negroes got there and took the cotton from their wagon, they would then be persuaded to go across the border by Meskins, and then they would never return to their master. That is how lots of Negroes got to be free. The way they used to transfer the cotton—these big cotton plantations east of here—they'd take it to

Brownsville and put it on the wharf and ship it from there. I can remember seeing, during the cotton season, fifteen or twenty teams hauling cotton, sometimes five or six, maybe eight bales on a wagon. You see, them steamboats used to run all up and down that river. I think this cotton went out to market at New Orleans and went right out into the Gulf.

"Our house was a log cabin with a log chimney da'bbed with mud. The cabin was covered with grass for a roof. The fireplace was the kind of stove we had. Mother cooked in Dutch ovens. Our main meal was corn bread and milk and grits with milk. That was a little bit coarser than meal. The way we used to cook it and the best flavored is to cook it out-of-doors in a Dutch oven. We called 'em corn dodgers. Now ash cakes, you have your dough pretty stiff and smooth off a place in the ashes and lay it right on the ashes and cover it up with ashes and when it got done, you could wipe every bit of the ashes off, and get you some butter and put on it. M-m-m! I tell you, its fine! There is another way of cookin' flour bread without a skillet or a stove, is to make up your dough stiff and roll it out thin and cut it in strips and roll it on a green stick and just hold it over the coals, and it sure makes good bread. When one side cooks too fast, you can just turn it over, and have your stick long enough to keep it from burnin' your hands. How come me to learn this was: One time we were huntin' horse stock and there was an outfit along and the pack mule that was packed with our provisions and skillets and coffee pots and things—we never did carry much stuff, not even no beddin'—the pack turned on the mule and we lost our skillet and none of us knowed it at the time. All of us was cooks, but that old Meskin that was along was the only one that knew how to cook bread that way. Sometimes we would be out six weeks or two months on a general round-up, workin' horse stock; the country would just be alive with cattle, and horses too. We used to have lots of fun on those drives.

"I tell you, I didn't enjoy that 'court' at night. They got so tough on us you couldn't spit in camp, couldn't use no cuss words—they would sure 'put the leggin's on you' if you did!"

Uncle Ben hitched his chair, and with much chuckling, recalled the "kangaroo court" the cowboys used to hold at night in camp. These impromptu courts were often all the fun the cowboys had during the long weeks of hunting stock in the open range country.

"Oh, it was all in fun. Just catch somebody so we could hold court! They would have two or three as a jury. They would use me as sheriff and appoint a judge. The prisoner was turned over to the judge and whatever he said, it had to be carried out exactly. The penalty? Well, sometimes—it was owing to the crime—but sometimes they would put it up to about twenty licks with the leggin's. If they was any bendin' trees, they would lay you across the log. They got tough, all right, but we sure had fun. We had to salute the boss every mornin', and if we forgot it...! They never forgot it that night; you'd sure get tried in court.

"We camped on the side of a creek one time, and we had a new man, a sort of green fellow. This new man unsaddled his horse by the side of the creek and he lay down there. He had on a big pair of spurs, and I was watchin' him and studyin' up some kind of prank to play on 'im. So I went and got me a string and tied one of his spurs to his saddle and then I told the boss what I'd done and he had one of the fellows put a saddle on and tie tin cups and pots on it and then they commenced shootin' and yellin'. This man with the saddle on went pitchin' right toward that fellow, and that man got up, scared to death, and started to run. He run the length of the string and then fell down, but he didn't take time to get up; he went runnin' on his all-fours as fur as he could, till he drug the saddle to where it hung up. He woulda run right into the creek, but the saddle held 'im back. We didn't hold kangaroo court over that! Nobody knowed who did it. Of course, they all knowed, but they didn't let on. But nobody ever got in a bad humor; it didn't do no good.

"I've stood up of many a bad night, dozin'. It would be two weeks, sometimes, before we got to lay down on our beds. I have stood up between the wagon wheel and the bed (of the wagon) and dozed many a night. Maybe one or two men would come in and doze an hour or two, but if the cattle were restless and ready to run, we had to be ready right now. Sho! Those stormy nights thunderin' and lightnin'! You could just see the lightnin' all over the steers' horns and your horse's ears and mane too. It would dangle all up and down his mane. It never interfered with you a-tall. And you could see it around the steer's horns in the herd, the lightnin' would dangle all over 'em. If the hands (cowboys) or the relief could get to 'em before they got started to runnin', they could handle 'em; but if they got started first, they would be pretty hard to handle.

"The first ranch I worked on after I left McNelly was on the Banqueta on the Agua Dulce Creek for the Miley boys, putting up a pasture fence. I worked there about two months, diggin' post holes. From there to the King Ranch for about four months, breaking horses. I kept travelin' east till I got back to Wharton, where my mother was. She died there in Wharton. I didn't stay with her very long. I went down to Tres Palacios in Matagorda County. I did pasture work there, and cattle work. I worked for Mr. Moore for twelve years. Then he moved to Stockdale and I worked for him there eight years. From there, after I got through with Mr. Moore, I went back to Tres Palacios and I worked there for first one man and then another. I think we have been here at Uvalde for about twenty-three years.

"I've been the luckiest man in the world to have gone through what I have and not get hurt. I have never had but two horses to fall with me. I could ride all day right now and never tire. You never hear me say, 'I'm tired, I'm sleepy, I'm hongry.' And out in camp you never see me lay down when I come in to camp, or set down to eat, and if I do, I set down on my foot. I always get my plate in my hand and eat standin' up, or lean against the wagon, maybe.

"When Cap'n. McNelly taken sick and resigned, I traveled east and picked up jobs of work on ranches. The first work after I left the Rio Grande was on the Banqueta, and then I went to work on the King Ranch about fifty miles southeast (?) of Brownsville. It wasn't fixed up in them days like it is now. But the territory is like it was then. They worked all Meskin hands. They were working about twenty-five or thirty Meskins at the headquarters' ranch. And the main caporal was a Meskin. His wages was top wages and he got twelve dollars a month. And the hands, if you was a real good hand, you got seven or eight dollars a month, and they would give you rations. They would furnish you all the meat you wanted and furnish you corn, but you would have to grind it yourself for bread. You know, like the Meskins make on a metate. You could have all the home-made cheese you want, and milk. In them days, the Meskins didn't have sense enough to make butter. I seen better times them days than I am seein' now. We just had a home livin'. You could go out any time and kill you anything you wanted—turkeys, hogs, javalinas, deer, 'coons, 'possums, quail.

"I'll tell you about a Meskin ranch I worked on. It was a big lake. It covered, I reckin, fifty acres, and these little Meskin huts just surrounded that big lake. And fish! My goodness, you could just go down there and throw your hook in without a bait and catch a fish. That was what you call the Laguna de Chacona. That was out from Brownsville about thirty-five miles. That ranch was owned by the old Meskin named Chacon, where the lake got its name.

"It seems funny the way they handled milk calves—you know, the men-folks didn't milk cows, they wouldn't even fool with 'em. They would have a great big corral and maybe they would have fifteen or twenty cows and they would be four or five families go there to milk. Every calf would have a rawhide strap around his neck about six foot long. Now, instead of them makin' a calf pen—of evenin's the girls would go down there and I used to go help 'em—they would pull the calf up to the fence and stick the strap through a crack and pull the calf's head down nearly to the ground where he couldn't suck. Of course, the old cow would hang around right close to the calf as she could git. When they let the calf suck, they'd leave 'im tied down so he couldn't suck in the night. They always kep' the cows up at night and they'd leave the calves in the pen with 'em, but tied down. But buildin' just what you call a calf pen, they'd set posts in the ground just like these stock pens at the railroad and lay the poles between 'em. Then again, they would dig a trench and set mesquite poles so thick and deep, why, you couldn't push it down!

"Now, in dry times, they would have a banvolete (ban-bo-la-te). Hand me two of them sticks, mama. Now, you see, like here would be the well and you cut a long stick as long as you could get it, with a fork up here in this here pole, and have this here stick in the fork of the pole. They'd bolt the cross piece down in the fork of the pole that was put in the ground right by the well, and have it so it would work up and down. They'd be a weight tied on the end of the other pole and they could sure draw water in a hurry. I made one out here on the Anderson Ranch. Just as fast as you could let your bucket down, then jerk it up, you had the water up. The well had cross pieces of poles laid around it and cut to fit together.

"Now, about the other way we had to draw water. We had a big well, only it was fenced around to keep cattle from gettin' in there. The reason they had to do that, they had a big wheel with footpieces, like steps, to tread, and you would have the wheel over the well and they had about fifteen or twenty rawhide buckets fastened to a rope (that the wheel pulled it went around), and when they went down, they would go down in front of you. You had to sit down right behind the wheel, and you would push with your feet and pull with your hands, and the buckets came up behind you and as they went up, they would empty and go back down. They had some way of fixin' the rawhide. I think they toasted it, or scorched the hide to keep it hard so the water wouldn't soak it up and get it soft. That was on that place, the Chacona Lakes. That old Meskin was a native of the Rio Grande and run cattle and horses. In them days, you could buy an acre of land for fifty cents, river front, all the land you wanted. Now that land in that valley, you couldn't buy it for a hundred dollars an acre.

"Did I tell you about diggin' that pit right in the fence of our corn patch to catch javalines? The way we done, why, we just dug a big pit right on the inside of the field, right against the fence, and whenever they would go through that hole to go in the corn patch, they would drop off in that hole. I think we caught nine, little and big, at one trappin' once. It was already an old trompin' place where they come in and out, and we had put the pit there. But after you use it, they won't come in there again.

"You see, I tell you about them brush fences. The deer had certain places to go to that fence to jump it, and after we found the regular jumpin' place, we would cut three sticks—pretty good size, about like your wrist, about three foot long—and peel 'em and scorch 'em in the fire and sharpen the ends right good and we would go to set our traps. We would put these three sharp sticks right about where the forefeet of the deer would hit. You'd just set the sticks about four inches from where his forefeet would hit the ground, and you'd set the sticks leanin' towards the brush fence, and they would be one in the center and two on the side and about two inches apart. When he jumped, you would sure get 'im right about the point of the brisket. He'd hardly ever miss 'em, and you'd find 'im right there. Oh, sometimes he'd pull up a stick and run a piece with it, but he didn't run very far.

"I been listenin' to the radio about Cap'n McNelly and I tell you it didn't sound right to me. In what way? Why, they never was no cattle on the steamboats down the Rio Grande. I just tell you they was no way of shippin' cattle on a steamboat. They couldn't get 'em down the hatch and they couldn't keep 'em on deck and they wasn't no wharf to load 'em, either. I was there and I seen them boats too long and I know they never shipped no cattle on them steamboats. After they crossed the Rio Grand into Mexico, they might have been shipped from some port down there, but all them cattle they crossed was swum across. They was big boats, but they wasn't no stock boats. They shipped lots of cotton on them steamboats, but they wasn't fixed to ship no cattle. They was up there for freight and passengers. The passengers was going on down the Gulf, maybe to New Orleans. They would get on at Brownsville. The steamboats couldn't go very fur up the river only in high water, but they could come up to Brownsville all the time.

"I was in the Ranger service for about a year with Captain McNelly, or until he died. I was his guide. I was living thirty-five miles above Brownsville. I was working for a man right there on the place by the name of John Cunningham.

It was called Bare Stone. You see, hit was a ranch there. McNelly was stationed there after the government troops moved off. They had 'em (the troops) there for a while, but they never did do no good, never did make a raid on nothin'. I was twenty or twenty-one. How come me to get in with McNelly, they had a big meadow there, a big 'permuda' (Bermuda) grass meadow. Me and another fellow used to go in there, and John Cunningham furnished Cap'n McNelly hay for his horses. That's how come me to get in with 'im. Fin'ly, he found out I knew all about that country and sometimes he would come over there and get me to map off a road, though they wasn't but one main road right there. So, one day I was over in the camp with 'im and I say, 'Cap'n, how would you like to give me a job to work with you?' He said, 'I'd like to have you all right, but you couldn't come here on state pay, and under no responsibility.' I told 'im that was all right. I knew how I was going to get my money, 'cause I gambled. Sometimes I would have a hundred or a hundred, twenty-five dollars. Durin' the month I would win from the soljers dealin' monte or playin' seven-up. They wasn't no craps in them days. We played luck too; we never had no shenanigans, a-stealin' a man's money. If you had a good streak o' luck, you made good; if you didn't, you was out o' luck. Sometimes, I had up as high as twenty-five or thirty dollars.

"One thing about the cap'n, he'd tell his men—well, we had a sutler's shop right across from our camp, all kinds of good drinks—and he would tell his men he didn't care how much they drank but he didn't want any of 'em fighting'. He kep' 'em under good control.

"You see, they was all dependin' on me for guidin'. There was no way for them cow rustlers or bandits to get to the cow ranches after they crossed the river (Rio Grande) excep' to cross that road for there was no other way for 'em to get out there. You see, there was where it would be easy for me, pickin' up a trail. I would just follow that road on if I had a certain distance to go, and if I didn't find no trail I would come back and report, and if I would find a trail he would ask me how many they was and where they was goin', and I would tell 'im which way, 'cause I didn't know exactly where they was goin' to round-up. He would always give 'em about two or three days to make the round-up from the time that trail crossed. And we always went to meet 'em, or catch 'em at the river. We got into two or three real bad combats.

"The worst one was on Palo Alto Prairie, one of Santa Anna's battle grounds. About twelve or fifteen miles east of old Brownsville. They was sixteen of the bandits and they was fifteen of 'em killed—all Meskins excep' one white man. One Meskin escaped. The cap'n just put 'em all up together in a pile and sent a message to Brownsville to the authorities and told 'em where they was at and what shape they was in. They must have had two hundred or two hundred and twenty-five head (of cattle) with 'em. It was open country and they would get anybody's cattle. They just got 'em off the range.

"They mostly would cross that road at night, and by me gettin' out early next mornin' and findin' that trail, I could tell pretty much how old it was. I reckon that place wasn't over thirteen miles from Brownsville and our camp was thirty-five miles, I guess it must have been twenty-five miles from our camp to where we had that battle. We sure went there to get 'em. I trailed them horses and I knowed from the direction they was takin' that they was goin' to those big lakes called Santa Lalla. They was between Point Isabel and Brownsville and that made us about a forty-five mile ride to get to that crossin', to a place called Bagdad, right on the waters of the Rio Grande.

"We got our lunch at Brownsville and started out to go to this crossin'. I knowed right about where this crossin' was and I says to the cap'n, 'Don't you reckon I better go and see if they was any sign?' We stayed there about three hours and didn't hear a thing. And then the cap'n said, 'Boys, we better eat our lunch'. While we was eatin', we heard somebody holler, and he said, 'Boys, there they are.' And he said to me, 'Ben, you want to stay with the horses or be in the fun?' And I said, 'I don't care.' So he said, 'You better stay with the horses; you ain't paid to kill Meskins! I went out to where the horses were. The rangers were afoot in the brush. It was about an hour from the time we heard the fellow holler before the cattle got there. When the rangers placed themselves on the side of the road, the Meskins didn't know what they was goin' to get into!

"The Meskins was all singin' at the top of their voices and they was comin' on in. The cap'n waited till they went to crossin' the herd, he waited till these rustlers all got into the river behind the cattle, and then the cap'n opened fire on the bandits. They didn't have no possible show. They was in the water, and he just floated 'em down the river. They was one man got away. I saw 'im later, and he told me about it. The way he got away, he says he was a good swimmer and he just fell off his horse in the water and the swift water took 'im down and he just kep' his nose out of the water and got away that way. They was fo'teen in that bunch, I know.

"The echo of the shootin' turned the cattle back to the American side. The lead cattle was just gettin' ready to hit the other side of the river when the shootin' taken place and the echo of the shootin' turned 'em and they come back across. Now, in swimmin' a bunch of cattle, if you pop your whip, you are just as liable to turn 'em back, or if you holler the echo might turn 'em back. It'll do that nearly every time.

"After the fight, the cap'n says to the boys, 'Well, boys, the fun is all over now, I guess we'd better start back to camp.' And they all mounted their horses and begun singin':

"O, bury me not on the lone prairie-e-e
Where the wild coyotes will howl o'er me-e-e,
Right where all the Meskins ought to be-e-e!"

United States. Work Projects Administration

MARY KINDRED

MARY KINDRED was a slave on the Luke Hadnot plantation in Jasper, Texas. She does not know her age but thinks she is about 80. She now lives in Beaumont, Texas.

"My mind don't dwell back. The older I gits the lessen I thinks 'bout the old times. I ain't gittin' old. I's done got old. I not been one of them bad, outlawed fellers, so de good Lawd done 'low me live a long time. Some things I knows I heered from my mother and my grandma. They so fresh to them in that time, though, I mostly sure they's truth.

"My mother name was Hannah Hadnot and my daddy was Ruffin Hadnot and he used to carry the mail from Weiss Bluff to Jasper. They waylay him 'long the road in 1881 and kill him and rob the mail.

"Luke Hadnot was our old massa. He good to my grandma and give her license for a doctor woman. Old massa must of thought lots of her, 'cause he give her forty acres of land and a home fer herself. That house still standin' up there in Jasper, yet.

"Grandma used to sing a li'l song to us, like this:

> "'One mornin' in May,
> I spies a beautiful dandy,
> A-rakin' way of de hay.
> I asks her to marry.
> She say, scornful, 'No.'
> But befo' six months roll by
> Her apron strings wouldn't tie
> She wrote me a letter,
> She marry me then,
> I say, no, no, my gal, not I.'

"Grandma git de bark offen de thorn tree and bile it with turpentine for de toothache. She used herbs for de medicine and they's good.

"Old missy was tall and slim, a rawbone sort of woman. Her name was Matilda Hadnot. Massa have as big a still as ever I seed and dey used to make everything there. They has it civered with boards they rive out the woods. There wasn't no revenuers in dem days.

"Us gits de groceries by steamboat and the wagons go down the old Bevilport Road to the steamboat landin'. That the Ang'leen River. One the biggest boats was own by Capt. Bryce Hadnot, the 'Old Grim.'

"I 'member back durin' the war the people couldn't git no coffee. They used to take bran and peanuts and okra seed and sich and parch 'em for coffee. It make right drinkable coffee. They gits sugar from the store or the sugar cane. When they buy it, it's in a big, white lump what they calls 'sugar loaf.' When they has no sugar they uses the syrup to sweeten the coffee and they call syrup 'long sweetenin' and sugar, 'short sweetenin'.

"Us has lots of dances with fiddle and 'corjum player. Us sing, 'Swing you partner, Promenade.' Another li'l song start out:

> "'Dinah got a meat skin lay away,
> Grease dat wooden leg, Dinah.
> Grease dat wooden leg, Dinah.

Shake dat wooden leg, Dinah,
Shake dat wooden leg, Dinah.'

I 'members this song:

"'Down in Shiloh town,
Down in Shiloh town,
De old grey mare come
Tearin' out de wilderness.
Down in Shiloh town,
O, boys, O,
O, boys, O,
Down in Shiloh town.'

"I's seed lots of blue gum niggers and they say iffen they bite you dey pizen you. They hands diff'rent from other niggers. Now, my hand's right smart white in the inside, but blue gum nigger hand is more browner on the inside.

"I used to have a old aunt name Harriett and iffen she tell you anythin' you kin jes' put it down it gwineter come out like she say. She have the big mole on the inside her mouth and when she shake her finger at you it gwine happen to you jes' like she say. That what they call puttin' bad mouth on them and she sho' could do it.

"I's had 12 chillen. My first husban was Anthony Adams and the last Alfred Kindred. I only got three chillen livin' now, though. One of the sons am the outer door guard of the lodge here in Beaumont.

NANCY KING

NANCY KING, 93, was born in Upshur County, Texas, a slave of William Jackson. She and her husband moved to Marshall, Texas, in 1866. Nancy now lives with her daughter, Lucy Staples.

"I was borned and raised on William Jackson's place, jus' twelve miles east of Gilmer. I was growed and had one child at surrender, and my mother told me I was a woman of my own when Old Missie sot us free, jus' after surrender, so you can figurate my age from that.

"My first child was borned the January befo' surrender in June, and I 'members hoeing in the field befo' the war come on. Massa William raised lots of cotton and corn and tobacco and most everything we et. I never worked in the field, 'cept to chase the calves in, till I was most growed. Massa was good to us. Course, I never went to school, but Old Missie sent my brother, Alex, two years after the war, with her own chillen.

"I was married durin' the war and it was at church, with a white preacher. Old Missie give me the cloth and dye for my weddin' dress and my mother spun and dyed the cloth, and I made it. It was homespun but nothin' cheap 'bout it for them days. After the weddin' massa give us a big dinner and we had a time.

"Massa done all the bossin' his own self. He never whipped me, but Old Missie had to switch me a little for piddlin' round, 'stead of doin' what she said. Every Sat'day night we had a candy pullin' and played games, and allus had plenty of clothes and shoes.

"I seed the soldiers comin' and gwine to the war, and 'members when Massa William left to go fight for the South. His boy, Billie, was sixteen, and tended the place while massa's away. Massa done say he'd let the niggers go without fightin'. He didn't think war was right, but he had to go. He 'serts and comes home befo' the war gits goin' good and the soldiers come after him. He run off to the bottoms, but they was on hosses and overtook him. I was there in the room when they brung him back. One of them says, 'Jackson, we ain't gwine take you with us now, but we'll fix you so you can't run off till we git back.' They put red pepper in his eyes and left. Missie cried. They come back for him in a day or two and made my father saddle up Hawk-eye, massa's best hoss. Then they rode away and we never seed massa 'gain. One day my brother, Alex, hollers out, 'Oh, Missie, yonder is the hoss, at the gate, and ain't nobody ridin' him.' Missie throwed up her hands and says, 'O, Lawdy, my husban' am dead!' She knowed somehow when he left he wasn't comin' back.

"Old Missie freed us but said we had a home as long as she did. Me and my husban' stays 'bout a year, but my folks stays till she marries 'gain.

"My brother-in-law, Sam Pitman, tells us how he put one by the Ku Kluxers. Him and some niggers was out one night and the Kluxers chases them on hosses. They run down a narrow road and tied four strands of grapevine 'cross the road, 'bout breast high to a hoss. The Kluxers come gallopin' down that road and when the hosses hit that grapevine, it throwed them every which way and broke some their arms. Sam used to laugh and tell how them Kluxers cussed them niggers.

"Me and my husban' come to Marshall the year after surrender, and I is lived here every since. My man works on farms till he got on the railroad. I's been married four times and raised six chillen. The young people is diff'rent from what we was, but diff'rent times calls for diff'rent ways, I 'spect. My chillen allus done the best they could by me.

SILVIA KING

SILVIA KING, French Negress of Marlin, Texas, does not know her age, but says that she was born in Morocco. She was stolen from her husband and three children, brought to the United States and sold into slavery. Silvia has the appearance of extreme age, and may be close to a hundred years old, as she thinks she is, because of her memories of the children she never saw again and of the slave ship.

"I know I was borned in Morocco, in Africa, and was married and had three chillen befo' I was stoled from my husband. I don't know who it was stole me, but dey took me to France, to a place called Bordeaux, and drugs me with some coffee, and when I knows anything 'bout it, I's in de bottom of a boat with a whole lot of other niggers. It seem like we was in dat boat forever, but we comes to land, and I's put on de block and sold. I finds out afterwards from my white folks it was in New Orleans where dat block was, but I didn't know it den.

"We was all chained and dey strips all our clothes off and de folks what gwine buy us comes round and feels us all over. Iffen any de niggers don't want to take dere clothes off, de man gits a long, black whip and cuts dem up hard. I's sold to a planter what had a big plantation in

Fayette County, right here in Texas, don't know no name 'cept Marse Jones.

"Marse Jones, he am awful good, but de overseer was de meanest man I ever knowed, a white man name Smith, what boasts 'bout how many niggers he done kilt. When Marse Jones seed me on de block, he say, 'Dat's a whale of a woman.' I's scairt and can't say nothin', 'cause I can't speak English. He buys some more slaves and dey chains us together and marches us up near La Grange, in Texas. Marse Jones done gone on ahead and de overseer marches us. Dat was a awful time, 'cause us am all chained up and whatever one does us all has to do. If one drinks out of de stream we all drinks, and when one gits tired or sick, de rest has to drag and carry him. When us git to Texas, Marse Jones raise de debbil with dat white man what had us on da march. He git de doctor man and tell de cook to feed us and lets us rest up.

"After 'while, Marse Jones say to me, 'Silvia, am you married?' I tells him I got a man and three chillen back in de old country, but he don't understand my talk and I has a man give to me. I don't bother with dat nigger's name much, he jes' Bob to me. But I fit him good and plenty till de overseer shakes a blacksnake whip over me.

"Marse Jones and Old Miss finds out 'bout my cookin' and takes me to de big house to cook for dem. De dishes and things was awful queer to me, to what I been brung up to use in France. I mostly cooks after dat, but I's de powerful big woman when I's young and when dey gits in a tight [Handwritten Note: 'place?'] I helps out.

"'Fore long Marse Jones 'cides to move. He allus say he gwine git where he can't hear he neighbor's cowhorn, and he do. Dere ain't nothin' but woods and grass land, no houses, no roads, no bridges, no neighbors, nothin' but woods and wild animals. But he builds a mighty fine house with a stone chimney six foot square at de bottom. The sill was a foot square and de house am made of logs, but dey splits out two inch plank and puts it outside de logs, from de ground clean up to de eaves. Dere wasn't no nails, but dey whittles out pegs. Dere was a well out de back and a well on de back porch by de kitchen door. It had a wheel and a rope. Dere was 'nother well by de barns and one or two round de quarters, but dey am fixed with a long pole sweep. In de kitchen was de big fireplace and de big back logs am haul to de house. De oxen pull dem dat far and some men takes poles and rolls dem in de fireplace. Marse Jones never 'low dat fire go out from October till May, and in de fall Marse or one he sons lights de fire with a flint rock and some powder.

"De stores was a long way off and de white folks loans seed and things to each other. If we has de toothache, de blacksmith pulls it. My husband manages de ox teams. I cooks and works in Old Miss's garden and de orchard. It am big and fine and in fruit time all de women works from light to dark dryin' and 'servin' and de like.

"Old Marse gwine feed you and see you quarters am dry and warm or know de reason why. Most ev'ry night he goes round de quarters to see if dere any sickness or trouble. Everybody work hard but have plenty to eat. Sometimes de preacher tell us how to git to hebben and see de ring lights dere.

"De smokehouse am full of bacon sides and cure hams and barrels lard and 'lasses. When a nigger want to eat, he jes' ask and git he passel. Old Miss allus 'pend on me to spice de ham when it cure. I larnt dat back in de old country, in France.

"Dere was spinnin' and weavin' cabins, long with a chimney in each end. Us women spins all de thread and weaves cloth for everybody, de white folks, too. I's de cook, but times I hit de spinnin' loom and wheel fairly good. Us bleach de cloth and dyes it with barks.

"Dere allus de big woodpile in de yard, and de big, caboose kettle for renderin' hawg fat and beef tallow candles and makin' soap. Marse allus have de niggers take some apples and make cider, and he make beer, too. Most all us had cider and beer when we want it, but nobody git drunk. Marse sho' cut up if we do.

"Old Miss have de floors sanded, dat where you sprinkles fine, white sand over da floor and sweeps it round in all kinds purty figgers. Us make a corn shuck broom.

"Marse sho' a fool 'bout he hounds and have a mighty fine pack. De boys hunts wolves and painters (panthers) and wild game like dat. Dere was lots of wild turkey and droves of wild prairie chickens. Dere was rabbits and squirrels and Indian puddin', make of cornmeal. It am real tasty. I cooks goose and pork and mutton and bear meat and beef and deer meat, den makes de fritters and pies and dumplin's. Sho' wish us had dat food now.

"On de cold winter night I's sot many a time spinnin' with two threads, one in each hand and one my feets on de wheel and de baby sleepin' on my lap. De boys and old men was allus whittlin' and it wasn't jes' foolishment. Dey whittles traps and wooden spoons and needles to make seine nets and checkers and sleds. We all sits workin' and singin' and smokin' pipes. I likes my pipe right now, and has two clay pipes and keeps dem under de pillow. I don't aim for dem pipes to git out my sight. I been smokin' clost to a hunerd years now and it takes two cans tobaccy de week to keep me goin'.

"Dere wasn't many doctors dem days, but allus de closet full of simples (home remedies) and most all de old women could git med'cine out de woods. Ev'ry spring, Old Miss line up all de chillen and give dem a dose of garlic and rum.

"De chillen all played together, black and white. De young ones purty handy trappin' quail and partridges and sech. Dey didn't shoot if dey could cotch it some other way, 'cause powder and lead am scarce. Dey cotch de deer by makin' de salt lick, and uses a spring pole to cotch pigeons and birds.

"De black folks gits off down in de bottom and shouts and sings and prays. Dey gits in de ring dance. It am jes' a kind of shuffle, den it git faster and faster and dey gits warmed up and moans and shouts and claps and dances. Some gits 'xhausted and drops out and de ring gits closer. Sometimes dey sings and shouts all night, but come break of day, de nigger got to git to he cabin. Old Marse got to tell dem de tasks of de day.

"Old black Tom have a li'l bottle and have spell roots and water in it and sulphur. He sho' could find out if a nigger gwine git whipped. He have a string tie round it and say, 'By sum Peter, by sum Paul, by de Gawd dat make us all, Jack don't you tell me no lie, if marse gwine whip Mary, tell me.' Sho's you born, if dat jack turn to de laft, de nigger git de whippin', but if marse ain't makeup he mind to whip, dat jack stand and quiver.

"You white folks jes' go through de woods and don't know nothin'. Iffen you digs out splinters from de north side a old pine tree what been struck by lightnin', and gits dem hot in a iron skillet and burns dem to ashes, den you puts dem in a brown paper sack. Iffen de officers gits you and you gwine have it 'fore de jedge, you gits de sack and goes outdoors at midnight and hold de bag of ashes in you hand and look up at de moon—but don't you open you mouth. Nex' mornin' git up early and go to de courthouse and sprinkle dem ashes in de doorway and dat law trouble, it gwine git tore up jes' like de lightnin' done tore up dat tree.

"De shoestring root am powerful strong. Iffen you chews on it and spits a ring round de person what you wants somethin' from, you gwine git it. You can git more money or a job or most anythin' dat way. I had a black cat bone, too, but it got away from me.

"I's got a big frame and used to weigh a hunerd pounds, but day tells me I only weighs a hunerd now. Dis Louis Southern I lives with, he's de youngest son of my grandson, who was de son of my youngest daughter. My marse, he knowed Gen. Houston and I seed him many a time. I lost what teeth I had a long time ago and in 1920 two more new teeth come through. Dem teeth sho' did worry me and I's glad when dey went, too.

www.ingramcontent.com/pod-product-compliance
Lightning Source LLC
Chambersburg PA
CBHW071645160426
43195CB00012B/1365